Adult Psychological Problems:
An Introduction

lee C

Edited by

Lorna A. Champion and Michael J. Power

 The Falmer Press

(A member of the Taylor & Francis Group)
London • Washington, DC

UK   The Falmer Press, 4 John Street, London, WC1N 2ET
USA   The Falmer Press, Taylor & Francis Inc., 1900 Frost Road, Suite 101, Bristol, PA 19007

First published 1992. Reprinted 1995

A catalogue record for this book is available from the British Library

Library of Congress Cataloging-in-Publication Data are available on request

ISBN 0 750 70 037 8
ISBN 0 750 70 038 6 (pbk)

Jacket design by Benedict Evans

Typeset in 10/11.5pt Garamond
by Graphicraft Typesetters Ltd., Hong Kong.

Printed in Great Britain by Burgess Science Press, Basingstoke on paper which has a specified pH value on final paper manufacture of not less than 7.5 and is therefore 'acid free'.

Contents

Series Editor's Preface

The aim of this book is to introduce the reader to the study of adult psychological problems. Lorna Champion and Mick Power begin with a balanced overview of the main approaches that are currently in use in abnormal psychology and allied disciplines. The historical background to each approach is sketched out in order to provide a sense of the context in which the approach developed. A number of the controversies that surround the area as a whole are also outlined. Champion and Power set the scene in the hope that the reader will feel sufficiently enthused to follow up some of the recommended reading and pursue his or her own study of the area.

All of the contributors to the book are practising clinicians in addition to their academic and research interests. The aim of each chapter is to provide the reader with a sense of the particular disorder described and how it manifests itself, before going on to discuss the ways in which the disorder may be understood and treated.

It is inevitable that contributors have preferences for some approaches rather than others and that the individual chapters should reflect these preferences. For example, the chapter on alcohol and drugs and on obsessive-compulsive disorders are strongest on cognitive and behavioural approaches, whereas the chapter on family problems focuses on systems models. These emphases, however, not only reflect the authors' preferences but also indicate current trends in how these disorders are most commonly treated.

Many students come to psychology because of a desire to understand the nature and origins of psychological problems, and this book provides an ideal introduction to the topic which has been written to be accessible to the beginning student, but also goes into sufficient depth to satisfy the person seriously considering a career in clinical psychology.

Ray Cochrane

List of Figures

Chapter 1

An Overview of Models of Psychological Problems

Michael Power and Lorna Champion

Introduction

Why are you interested in psychology? When asked this question early in their studies, most psychology students do not report a burning interest in visual perception in the frog, or a fascination for vestibular balance mechanisms in the guinea pig. Instead, they say that they may have read something about Freud and found it interesting, or that a friend or relative had psychological problems, or even, in the more honest and insightful cases, that they were aware of personal problems that they hoped psychology would address. Catch the same students a few years later, however, and either they will tell you that Freud is not worth a jot because he is not a scientist and that their heroes are now people with strange names who nobody has ever heard of but who are doing wonderful things with the caudate nucleus (wherever that is!), or, alternatively they will say that psychology had nothing to offer them personally which is why they are now joining a leading advertising firm in The City. Between these extremes, however, we believe that psychology *does* have something to offer on both a personal and a scientific level. The purpose of this book is to demonstrate both of these sides of psychology — the personal and the scientific — and to show how the various theories and therapies can contribute to our understanding of the problems that can beset us all during our adult lives.

Psychology is a very strange subject. Like politics and religion there are as many opposing views as there are psychologists. Unlike politics and religion, no wars have yet been started in the name of psychology. Nevertheless, battles are waged daily throughout the civilized psychological world in books, academic journals, lecture rooms, and conference halls between the supporters of opposing approaches to psychology. As will be evident from the contents of their chapters, some of the contributors to this volume have clearly identified which side they are on, Cavalier or Roundhead, the righteous or the infidel. We believe, however, that each approach has something to offer, has something of value, has good theoretical constructs and bad theoretical constructs, has good practitioners and bad practitioners.

But what is psychology? The student who comes from a scientific background will be shocked, even disturbed, by the lack of incontrovertible fact, by the contradictory nature of the theories, and by the importance of opinion and choice. The student from an arts background will be thrown by numbers and statistics, the use of computers and animals. In order to examine the question therefore of 'What is psychology?', we must first examine the question 'What is science?' in order to understand some of the disagreements. In so doing, we will see that two views of science can be identified: first, the traditional view taught in schools which emphasizes fact, experiment and measurement and which has had a strong influence on behavioural psychology, and, second, a modern view of science which emphasizes subjectivity, unpredictability, and non-deterministic processes. This modern view is more compatible with Cognitive Psychology.

What is Science?

The traditional view of science emphasizes a number of basic principles which have proven of great value in the history and development of science. In fact, nineteenth century scientists thought that they had answered all of the major problems of science and that only the details were left to be filled in: witness the achievements of Newton's mechanics, thermodynamics, Darwin's theory of evolution, and so on. The basic principles on which these developments were considered to depend are outlined in the following points:

1) Observation and Fact

Facts are observable measurable properties of the world: tigers are indigenous to India; the eye is sensitive to light: water freezes at 0 degrees centigrade. A large part of any science therefore is the routine accumulation of facts and observations; thus, the modern computer can store a vast number of facts about weather conditions, star positions, activity in a bubble chamber, or amino acid sequences in proteins. Of course, even traditional science was aware that 'facts' do not always turn out to be what they appear to be. The earth was originally thought to be flat because it looked flat, besides which if it wasn't flat you would fall of the edge; then astronomers discovered that the earth was round. Later on we learned that the earth was not perfectly round but flattened at the poles; finally, science told us that in fact the earth is geoid-shaped (i.e., the fact is the earth turns out to have been 'earth-shaped' all along!).

2) Description and Classification

If science only consisted of observation and fact, it would turn out to be like one long boring gossip session with little meaning or use. 'Have you heard that water consists of hydrogen and oxygen?' 'No, really!' 'Two parts hydrogen, what's more!' 'Get away'. Instead the next step is finding the appropriate level of description which can be meaningfully included in a classification system. For example, Linnaeus' classification of living things provided a magnificient taxonomy that helped to advance biology; the appropriate level of description seems relatively straightforward in that individual plants or animals provide the lowest level of description, which, in turn, can be grouped together at more general levels (species, phyla, etc). Classification systems may nevertheless contain surprises that are counter to common sense: whales are animals, tomatoes are fruit.

A second example of a classification system that had powerful predictive properties was Mendeleev's periodic table which provides a meaningful classification of chemical elements. The original Greek classification of the four 'elements', earth, air, fire and water proved to be an inappropriate one for science in that each of these so-called 'elements' was divisible into more basic elements in the way that salt is divisible into the elements sodium and chlorine. The power of Mendeleev's system which classified elements by atomic weight was that it revealed gaps or missing elements which had not been discovered at that time, but which have subsequently been discovered.

3) Theory and Hypothesis

Theories group together facts and descriptions in a way that provides an overall working model relevant to the domain in question. A good theory in the philosopher Karl Popper's terms is both useful and falsifiable; thus, a good theory should generate hypotheses which may be novel and surprising and which can be tested in man-made or 'natural' experiments. For example, Einstein's theory of relativity predicted that light would bend in a gravitational field, a prediction that was dramatically upheld when the light from a distant source was shown to bend as it passed the sun.

Popper has used his criterion of falsifiability to argue that certain 'theories' such as psychoanalysis are not scientific theories at all because they are not falsifiable. Whatever happens in the rest of science, theories in psychology are rarely if ever rejected because of evidence to the contrary, but rather they go out of fashion. We will return however to Popper's allegations about psychoanalysis later in the chapter.

4) Experiment

Hypotheses derived from scientific theories may be tested in man-made and natural experiments in order to decide whether or not the experimental outcome is that predicted by the hypothesis. Experiments have to be carefully designed in order to be sure that the variable that the experimenter manipulates is truly the one that leads to differences in the variable that is measured. If the experimental outcome is due to some other confounding variable rather than the one that is manipulated, then the experiment is invalid. Psychology experiments on human subjects are notoriously difficult because what the *subject* thinks the experiment is about can be more important that what the *experimenter* thinks the experiment is about.

The modern view of science (see Penrose, 1989) does not reject the role of facts, measurement, observation, hypothesis, classification and experiment, but it does point to some severe limitations which draw modern science and modern psychology closer together. To begin with let us take the building blocks of science, that is, 'facts' or 'observations'. These holy objects have the status of absolute truths in traditional science, but modern science has emphasized their possible subjective nature and the role that inference as well as observation plays in making a fact a fact. For example, our sensory experience tells us the 'fact' that the sun rises in the East and sinks in the West. The fact is, however, that it is not the sun that rises and falls, but the earth that rotates on its axis. Every schoolchild knows about the existence of electrons, protons, and neutrons, but nobody has ever observed these particles directly. Instead, it is both useful and necessary to infer their existence from other observations such as pathways in a bubble chamber.

Traditional science has emphasised prediction and control in deterministic systems, that is, the idea that outcomes are always knowable if all of the initial conditions are known. In contrast, modern science emphasizes unpredictability and non-deterministic systems. Even at the atomic level, Heisenberg's uncertainty principle tells us that we cannot know both the position of an electron and its momentum, because the measurement of one affects the other; at best all we can do is make probabilistic statements about what might or might not happen. In a similar manner in psychology we can study the rules that people use to construct sentences and participate in conversations but we can never determine what any speaker will say on any particular occasion. Meteorologists face similar problems even for short-term weather predictions and may gain public notoriety for the extent of their inaccuracy, as when the British meteorologist Michael Fish's immortal words 'there will not be a hurricane tonight' were followed by the worst storm in two hundred years! The problems faced by the complex systems that meteorologists and psychologists study is that very small differences in initial conditions can make a considerable difference to outcome: the new developments in so-called 'chaos' or 'catastrophe theory' in the physical sciences demonstrate vividly how even simple systems can have unpredictable outcomes (see e.g., Gleick, 1988).

The moral of this tale for psychology is that both the traditional and the modern views of science have their advantages and disadvantages. Behavioural and experimental psychologists have focused on observation and measurement and, as we shall see, have made considerable contributions to our understanding of the laws of learning and the acquisition and treatment of a range of behaviour disorders. However, many psychoanalytic and cognitive psychologists have come to emphasize the importance of subjective factors and how they influence an individual's thoughts and actions. The focus in psychoanalysis on factors that are both subjective and unobservable does not imply that psychoanalysis is unscientific, contrary to what some psychologists and philosophers would have us believe. The aim of this book is to demonstrate how each approach to psychology has something to offer for our understanding of psychological disorders. In the next section, therefore, the basic principles of psychoanalysis, behaviourism, and cognitive psychology will be outlined, and in a subsequent section the relationship between psychology and biological and social models will also be examined.

Outline of Three Approaches to Psychology

In this section three key approaches to psychology will be outlined which have had a general impact on the theory and treatment of adult psychological disorders. These three areas are psychoanalysis, behaviourism, and cognitive psychology. The purpose of the section is to provide the key concepts for each approach without covering too much detail about specific applications. The specific applications of these and other approaches will be provided in subsequent chapters.

Psychoanalysis

The key figure in the development of psychoanalysis was Sigmund Freud (1856–1939). Freud's early career was as a neurologist; he invented the gold chloride method of staining nervous tissue, he was almost the first to discover the use of cocaine as a local anaesthetic, he published a book on aphasia and coined the term 'agnosia' (the inability to name objects), and was one of the world's leading authorities on childhood paralyses, all before the age of forty! The important point is that Freud was very much a scientist working in a scientific tradition and it was this scientific rigour that he brought to psychoanalysis. In fact, one of his early unpublished works called 'Project For a Scientific Psychology' (1895/1950) outlined a set of scientific principles which in many ways provided the basis for the subsequent developments. Unfortunately, he became disillusioned with the Project, left the manuscript with his friend Wilhelm Fliess, and never asked for it back.

In order to understand the basic concepts that underpin psychoanalysis an outline of the following will be provided; the unconscious, psychic energy, repression, developmental stages, transference and countertransference, and the free association technique. Although these are only a few of the basic concepts, they should be sufficient to understand the psychoanalytic accounts presented in later chapters.

The unconscious.   Freud was by no means the first to suggest that the greater part of our psychic life occurs outside of conscious awareness (see Power and Brewin, 1991), but his major contribution was his emphasis on the *dynamic* aspects of the unconscious. That is, Freud did not simply see the unconscious as an inactive storehouse of past memories, but rather as a system of wishes, fantasies, impulses, and memories that actively influenced our thoughts, actions, symptoms, dreams, mistakes, accidents, and emotions. He proposed that the unconscious was derived from innate drives of which we could never become directly conscious, and repressed material which was typically of an unpleasant personal nature. In his earlier writings he saw the unconscious as a system in itself, though later on in 'The Ego and The Id' (1923/1984) he proposed an alternative system that consisted of Id, Ego, and Superego. Different aspects of these three structures were then viewed as unconscious.

One of the key points Freud proposed about the unconscious was that it defied time and logic and was not constrained by reality. For example, painful memories could be recalled from many years past as if they were happening now and had lost none of their emotional impact. In a similar manner, opposite and contradictory thoughts and impulses can be held in the unconscious; the same person can be both loved and hated at the same time.

Psychic energy. Freud believed that the mind was fuelled by psychic energy very much in the way that physical energy is needed to fuel a physical machine. This energy, or 'libido' as it was called, he initially considered to be derived from the life-preserving drives, 'Eros'. However, following the First World War and the loss of his favourite daughter (see Gay, 1988), he added a second set of life-destroying drives, 'Thanatos', which typically manifested themselves as aggression towards the self or towards others. A number of subsequent analysts have disagreed with the concept of destructive drives, though one notable exception is found in the work of Melanie Klein and her followers.

The comparison that Freud made between psychic energy and physical energy led to him adopting the so-called Principle of Constancy; namely, that by analogy with the laws of thermodynamics *psychic* energy can never be created nor destroyed, but can only be changed from one form to another. For example, if sexual energy is blocked from being expressed through the normal channels, then it has to be expressed in other forms. In milder cases these forms could be disguised in dreams, in symptoms such as headaches or spots, in excessive intellectual activity, and so on. However, in more extreme cases Freud suggested that severe psychological disorders including anxiety, depression, and obsessional disorders resulted from the blocking of sexual energy.

Repression. Freud used the terms 'repression' in various ways in his writings in order to refer to either the conscious or the unconscious avoidance of painful or unwanted information, in particular, information about the self or the self in relation to significant others. Freud used repression as a general term therefore to refer to almost any defence mechanism, though his daughter, Anna Freud in 1937 provided a systematic list that, along with repression (in the specific sense of an *unconscious* avoidance of an unacceptable impulse or idea), included a number of other defence mechanisms such as reaction-formation, sublimation, and projection.

In order to illustrate the actions of repression we can consider two different models of anxiety that Freud considered during his lifetime. In the early study in collaboration with his mentor Josef Breuer, 'Studies on Hysteria' (1895/1974), Freud argued that anxiety occurred as a consequence of repressed energy that was directly transformed into anxiety. However, in his later work, 'Inhibitions, Symptoms and Anxiety' (1926/1979) he reversed this equation and proposed that anxiety can be a warning state of the ego that signals the necessity for repression in order to defend the ego against internal danger arising from forbidden wishes and impulses. Freud likened the warning state to immunization, in that immunization works through experiencing a mild dose of the illness in order to protect the individual from a more lethal dose.

Developmental stages. Freud is normally credited with the concept of developmental sexual stages through which the child passes. In fact, the idea for such stages came from colleagues, such as Karl Abraham, based on their clinical observations. The proposal is that the child passes through a series of developmental stages labelled oral, anal, phallic, latency, and genital phases. The main sources of pleasure in the oral, anal and phallic stages are the mouth, the anus and the genitals, respectively.

One of the additional proposals is that fixation can occur at different stages of development which can either be apparent as personality traits, or revealed at times of stress. Typical oral characteristics are talkativeness, greed, gullability, and generosity, whereas anal characteristics include obstinacy, orderliness, and miserliness.

A significant extension of the notion of developmental stages was provided by Erik Erikson (1963), who focused on more general psychosocial development rather than just sexual development, and who also proposed that development does not stop in childhood or adolescence but continues through into adulthood. The adult stages emphasize the interpersonal roles that individuals take on and their productivity within those roles.

Transference. Freud's early collaborator, Josef Breuer, found that one of his hysterical patients, Anna O, developed very strong feelings towards him in the course of his treatment of her. Breuer was unable to cope with the strength of her feelings (and presumably his own) and terminated her treatment. The feelings that the patient has for the therapist are called transference. Originally, therefore, transference was seen as a nuisance that got in the way of therapy, but Freud eventually came to encourage the development of transference, because he believed that transference was a re-enactment in the relationship with the therapist of earlier significant relationships and provided an opportunity to examine their nature via the exploration of fantasies and feelings in the transference relationship. In fact, the exploration of transference is considered to be the key therapeutic tool in psychoanalytic work, because it provides insight into past and present relationships and allows the working through of related conflicts and problems. The intimate situation in which the therapist and patient are placed and the fact that the psychoanalyst sits behind the patient is one way in which transference is encouraged; the technique of free association, whereby the patient is meant to say whatever comes into his or her mind, also allows the patient to dwell on fantasies about the therapist which the more directive therapies such as behaviour therapy and cognitive therapy (to be described later) would typically steer the patient away from.

The fact that patients have strong reactions to their therapists does not preclude the fact that therapists may have strong reactions, both positive and negative, to their patients. Such reactions are called counter-transference and again can either be seen as nuisance phenomena that have no relevance to the treatment process or can be used in the course of therapy as a source of important information about the therapeutic relationship (see Casement, 1985).

Is Psychoanalysis Scientific?

The philosopher Karl Popper and the psychologist Hans Eysenck have been two of the most vehement critics of psychoanalysis, both claiming that psychoanalysis is not scientific. We hope that the discussion so far has highlighted that science must in its modern form address both the 'objective' and the 'subjective', but in so doing changes the very nature of science itself. The accusation of Popper that psychoanalysis is not falsifiable has been rejected by more recent philosophers of science (Grunbaum, 1984). In fact, many of the specific proposals outlined in this section are both testable and falsifiable. Whether or not believers and practitioners choose to ignore such empirical evidence is another matter, but we would note that this problem applies equally to behaviour therapists as to psychoanalytic therapists!

Behaviourism

The American psychologist J.B. Watson was the early champion of the behavioural approach to psychology. Watson reacted against the then domin-ant 'introspectionist' approach to psychology, in which armchair psychologists who were specially trained and selected sat and recorded their own mental processes. Not surprisingly, despite careful selection the occasional disagree-ment arose. Watson's reaction was to dismiss the study of mind as of scientific irrelevance because it is unobservable and, indeed, he subsequently focused solely on the environment. He argued that only behaviour is observable and therefore that a science of psychology must be a science of behaviour. Watson, by the way, was subsequently caught out by his own environment, when, following a scandalous affair with a graduate student, he left psychology and like all the best psychologists went into advertising.

One of the key areas of research that the behaviourists drew on was the work of the Russian physiologist Ivan Pavlov. Pavlov was awarded the Nobel Prize for his work on the physiology of digestion. In the course of subsequent work on salivation in the dog, he noticed that the dogs began to salivate before food was presented to them, if they simply noticed the attendant who normally fed them. A lesser scientist than Pavlov would probably have carried on regardless or told the attendants off, but Pavlov made those observations the basis for his subsequent study of the conditioned reflex (or 'conditional reflex' in Pavlov's own terms). His most famous studies were of bell-ringing and salivation in dogs. Perhaps it is no surprise that the scientist who became famous for studies of bell-ringing was the son of a priest.

Two other significant figures in behavioural psychology were Edward Thorndike and B.F. Skinner. Thorndike became famous for locking cats in puzzle boxes; over a number of trials the cats were found through trial-and-error learning to escape more quickly from the boxes. Thorndike's so-called 'law of effect' stated that responses were either more likely or less likely to occur according to the consequences they produced. B.F. Skinner was, by his own account, a failed novelist, a claim that he eventually proved when, at the height of his fame as a psychologist, he published one of the world's worst Utopian novels, *Walden Two*. His work in psychology however had more impact, and it was in his continuation of Thorndike's study of learning based on the consequences of behaviour that he provided his greatest contribution. Many behaviourists accepted that thoughts and feelings had a causal role to play in our behaviour, but because they were unobservable were not the proper stuff of science. In contrast to these 'methodological behaviourists' Skinner espoused a so-called 'radical behaviourist' philosophy which stated that although such private events existed, they played no causal role in behaviour but were merely by-products of internal physiological processes. Skinner stated that the true determinants of behaviour were the environment and the organism's genetics and learning history which were both represented neurophysiologically.

In parallel to the discussion of psychoanalysis, a number of key concepts that are crucial to the understanding of behaviourism will now be outlined. The concepts to be presented include classical conditioning, operant conditioning and escape/avoidance following which an outline of their application in behaviour therapy will be given.

Classical conditioning. This type of learning is the one originally identified by Pavlov, therefore it is also known as Pavlovian conditioning. The basic paradigm is shown in Figure 1.1.

Figure 1.1: An outline of classical (Pavlovian) conditioning

		UCS (Food)	---->	UCR (Salivation)
CS (Bell)	+	UCS (Food)	---->	UCR (Salivation)
		CS (Bell)	---->	CR (Salivation)

It shows that an unconditioned stimulus (UCS) such as food leads to an unconditioned response (UCR) such as salivation. The pairing of an initially neutral stimulus such as a bell with the UCS eventually leads the bell to become a conditioned stimulus (CS) for the conditioned response (CR) of salivation. Pavlov demonstrated that conditioning occurs optimally if the CS occurs just prior to the UCS, that conditioning will generalize to other stimuli that are similar to the original CS, and that the CR will gradually extinguish over a number of trials if the CS is presented on its own without the UCS. Pavlov originally thought that any stimulus could be paired with any other stimulus, though subsequent research questioned this idea. For example, Seligman (1971) suggested that certain evolutionarily significant stimuli or 'prepared stimuli' may be more conditionable than others in fear reactions; thus, it is far more common for people to develop snake phobias than to develop kitchen sink phobias even though they may never have had any direct experience with a snake, yet have unpleasant experiences with kitchen sinks everyday. However, the evidence for Seligman's proposal is still unclear (Rachman, 1990).

One of the main applications of classical conditioning to adult psychological disorders has been through an analysis of 'conditioned emotional responses'. The idea is that the pairing of a neutral stimulus with an aversive or traumatic UCS which produces an unpleasant emotional response will lead the neutral stimulus to produce conditioned emotional responses. A famous early demonstration of this sequence was carried out by Watson and Rayner (1920) with a one-year-old child named Little Albert. The child was happily playing with a white rat (the CS) when a loud noise (the UCS) behind him produced a startle reaction and considerable distress (the UCR). After a few such pairings of the white rat and the noise, the white rat eventually produced an unpleasant emotional reaction (the CR) on its own. This reaction generalised to other similar objects such as white rabbits. We shall see later that this traumatic conditioning demonstration was taken as the account of the onset of many anxiety disorders.

Operant conditioning. Both Skinner and Thorndike emphasized that classical conditioning was one type of learning that applied in the main to more reflex-like or autonomic nervous system behaviour. In contrast, they argued that voluntary behaviour is dependent on its consequences for whether or not it is likely to be repeated. More formally, Skinner stated that operant (or 'instrumental') conditioning is based on the three-term contingency of *discriminative stimulus, response*, and *outcome*. A discriminative stimulus indicates whether or not a particular contingency applies, for example, a green light might indicate that any pressing of a lever in a Skinner box would lead to a food reward. The notion of a response is defined functionally in the sense that it is not how the rat presses the bar that is important, but, rather the fact that the bar is pressed whether with its paw or its nose, or whatever. The outcome can be positive (e.g., food) and therefore the likelihood of the response increases, that is, it is positively reinforcing or can be negative (e.g., electric shock) in which case the response is punished and is less likely to occur again under those stimulus conditions.

Other key concepts in operant conditioning are *negative reinforcement, schedules of reinforcement*, and *shaping*. In contrast to the punishment procedure described above in which a response is less likely to occur because the outcome is unpleasant, in negative reinforcement the response is *more* likely to occur because it switches off an aversive stimulus such as shock or loud noise. The term 'schedule of reinforcement' refers to the fact that in many situations not every response is reinforced; for example, people are typically rewarded with money for their work once a week or once a month (a 'fixed-interval' schedule), though some individuals on piecework are rewarded for the amount that they produce (normally a 'fixed-ratio' schedule). One of the properties of these partial rather than continuous reinforcement schedules is that the behaviour is more resistant to extinction; thus, if reinforcement is no longer presented, an individual who has been rewarded for every response will normally stop responding sooner than someone who has received partial reinforcement. The term 'shaping' refers to the technique whereby the organism is initially rewarded for responses that only vaguely resemble the desired response, but, gradually the reinforced response approximates closer to the final response. For example, a pigeon is unlikely to pirouette three times and then curtsy straight-off, but through shaping could be trained to do so.

Escape and *avoidance* are two further important types of operant conditioning. In escape learning, the organism receives an aversive stimulus such as an electric shock, which a particular response such as pressing a lever will remove. In avoidance learning, an initial discriminative stimulus signals that if the appropriate response does not occur, then the aversive stimulus will be presented. One well-known variant on escape/avoidance learning is Seligman's (1975) 'learned helplessness'. In learned helplessness tasks, the organism initially receives non-contingent punishment, that is, the aversive stimulus is received whatever response the animal makes. The contingency is then changed such that a response would lead to escape from the aversive stimulus, but the typical finding is that the animal remains helpless and does not find the escape response. Seligman proposed that learned helplessness could provide a model for the acquisition and maintenance of depression in humans, though as will be evident from Chapter Two, the theory has subsequently undergone a number of major revisions.

Behaviour therapy. A classic demonstration of behaviour therapy was carried out by Mary Cover Jones (1924). Following in the Little Albert tradition, she successfully treated a young boy's fear of rabbits by having him eat in the presence of a rabbit, while gradually bringing the rabbit closer to him over a number of occasions. The basic idea of the encouragement of a response such as eating which is incompatible with fear was further elaborated by Joseph Wolpe (1958). Wolpe first taught phobic adults a muscle relaxation technique which they then used while imagining increasingly fearful stimuli; a technique that Wolpe called *systematic desensitization.* Although sometimes still used, where possible, behaviour therapists now prefer actual exposure to the feared object or situation rather than just working in imagination.

One of the classic theories on which behaviour therapy was based was Mowrer's (1939) two-factor theory of the acquisition and maintenance of fear. Mowrer proposed that both classical and operant conditioning were involved. The first step was that an originally neutral stimulus acquired fearful properties by being paired with a frightening or painful event, that is, through a classical conditioning procedure. The second step is that through a process of operant conditioning, the individual learns to reduce the fear by avoidance of the relevant object or situation. Much of the focus of behavioural interventions in anxiety (see Chapter 3) and obsessional disorders (see Chapter 6) has therefore included exposure to the feared objected or situation, a procedure that is repeated until the fear response drops substantially. However, it is now well-recognised that not all fears are acquired in accordance with the two-factor theory (e.g., Rachman, 1990). For example, most people with a fear of flying have never actually flown, so their fear could not have been acquired by classical conditioning in the situation itself. Conversely, not everybody who has experienced a traumatic event while flying (e.g., a hijack or plane crash) develops a phobia. Instead, the observation of someone else (e.g., a parent) being fearful about an object or situation (known as *'vicarious'* or *'observational'* *learning*) is also a common source of fears and phobias.

There have, of course, been a large number of behavioural techniques that have been adopted for use with clinical conditions, but we will leave these for subsequent chapters, which will examine specific adult disorders and the types of theories and therapies that have been developed to deal with them.

Cognitive Psychology

In contrast to the great heroes of psychoanalysis and behaviourism, the recent heroes of cognitive psychology can hardly be described as household names. These lesser deities include individuals such as George Miller, Noam Chomsky, Jerome Bruner, Allan Newell and Herbert Simon. Bruner (1983) suggests that the birth of modern cognitive psychology was on September 11, 1956, with the delivery taking place during a symposium at the Massachusetts Institute of Technology.

The general area of cognitive psychology is a broad one that overlaps with other disciplines such as linguistics, philosophy, artificial intelligence and anthropology and, indeed, a new discipline of 'cognitive science' has emerged from this overlap. Rather than attempt to cover everything, however, the focus will be on those issues that have some bearing on adult psychological problems. There is as yet no one grand theory in cognitive psychology, nor even one that can be said to be more dominant than others. Instead, there is a general agreement that, whatever form they might take, internal mental states play important causal roles in the generation of action. Beyond this, there is agreement that the system must process information from a range of sensory inputs, that this information needs to be transformed in various ways so that, for example, meaningless sequences of sounds can be interpreted meaningfully, and that there must be an overall system that co-ordinates these multiple functions. Most of this information processing of necessity occurs outside of our awareness, and we only become aware of the extent to which it is automatic when we put shaving cream on our toothbrush, or drive home to the flat that we used to live in rather than the one that we've just moved to. In the remainder of this section an outline will be provided of a number of key areas from cognitive psychology that are relevant to adult psychological disorders. Included in this list will be perception and attention, memory, reasoning, and emotion. We will then look at cognitive therapy and how it might relate to cognitive psychology in general.

Perception and attention.   The German physicist and physiologist Hermann von Helmholtz is considered to be the father of perception. Long before Freud had developed his ideas on the dynamic unconscious, Helmholtz, in the 1860s, had argued that perception must be based on 'unconscious inferences'. For example, when we look at an object at different distances it looks the same size, even though the physical size of the object on the retina is very different (known as 'object constancy'); the same object can be looked at from different angles yet appears to preserve its shape ('shape constancy'); and an object can be viewed under different lighting conditions and appear the same colour ('colour constancy'). Although the unconscious perceptual processes which give rise to these constancies have clear advantages, the fact that processing necessarily distorts the incoming information can under other circumstances lead to disadvantages which, at one extreme can be mildly amusing perceptual illusions, and at the other extreme can lead the individual to perceive life-threatening danger where there is none.

One of the central questions in the perception and attention literature has been the extent to which sensory information is analysed prior to conscious awareness. Broadbent (1958) argued that this input is analysed at a superficial physical level and that only input that reaches awareness is analysed for its meaning. Subsequent work however has suggested that the sensory input can be analysed for meaning without the individual having to be aware of the input; in the so-called 'cocktail party phenomenon' an individual can be attending to one conversation, but suddenly become aware of his or her name being taken in vain in another conversation. The phenomenon demonstrates that the unattended information must have been analysed for meaning for this switch of attention to occur. The relevance of the area of perception and attention will become clearer in the section on cognitive therapy and also in the chapters on anxiety (see Chapter 3) and schizophrenia (see Chapter 9).

Memory.   One of the questions that cognitive psychology has addressed is the form that internal representation of the world takes. Do we remember visual scenes as if they were video-recorded sequences? or conversations as if they were tape-recorded? Given the arguments that couples have about who said what to whom and when (see Chapter 7), it might seem unlikely that memory is veridical in the manner of tape and video-recorders. The question then is to what extent is memory a reconstruction, one part truth to nine parts fiction? In his classic book on cognitive psychology Ulric Neisser (1967) took an extreme constructivist view that the process of remembering is like the palaentologist who, on the basis of a couple of small bones, constructs an awesome dinosaur. More recently, Neisser has stepped back from this extreme view in the recognition that, although as every storyteller will verify, it is occasionally necessary to exaggerate, memory can also be surprisingly accurate. We must recognise too that in the development of childhood vulnerability for later adult disorders (e.g., see Chapter 2 on depression) the child may be given conflicting information that is difficult to integrate in memory; for example, a mother may repeatedly insist to the child that she loves him above all else, though her actions may clearly contradict her statements. There is no reason, of course, why there could not be more than one memory (or group of memories) of a particular event or person; a number of current views of memory would be consistent with such a possibility. In such cases some of the aims of therapy may be to help the adult identify such discrepancies, to work through the consequent emotions, and to re-integrate the memories into a more realistic overall representation of the person or the event.

A further question that cognitive psychologists ask about memory is what the basic psychological units are. To this question there have been numerous answers and few if any conclusions. One of the types of internal representation that has played a significant role, from the work of Bartlett earlier this century onwards, is the '*schema*'. Piaget also used the term schema in his studies of child development, and Beck in his account of cognitive therapy. Although there is considerable variation in the use of the term (see Power and Champion, 1986), schemata refer to unitary representations of regularly encountered objects, events and situations, and activation of one part of a schema leads automatically to activation of all other parts. To give a simple example, if subjects are shown a picture of a car which does not show the wheels, they may make the schematic error later in recall and include wheels which were not originally shown, because cars normally have wheels. Schema theory therefore predicts that processes such as memory and perception are prone to schema-congruent errors. It must be noted that in certain clinical conditions these schemata are less than benign and may, for example, lead the depressed individual to perceive or to recall loss (see Chapter 2), or the anxious person to perceive or to recall life-endangering threat (see Chapter 3). It must be remembered that despite their widespread use, schemata are one of a whole panoply of units that have been used for knowledge representation.

Reasoning.   An assumption made by many philosophers and psychologists is that people use formal logical rules in reasoning. Perhaps the clearest account of such a system was provided by Jean Piaget in his studies of child development. However, there is now a considerable body of research that demonstrates the limits of the adult capacity for reasoning, though the debate still continues over whether errors are the result of performance limitations (e.g., working memory being limited in processing capacity) or whether they genuinely exclude a mental logic.

Three main types of reasoning task are *deduction*, *induction*, and *probability judgement*. Deduction is the drawing of a conclusion from a set of premises; induction is the drawing of a general rule on the basis of one or a limited number of instances; and probability judgements involve a statement about the likelihood of an event occurring. As an example of deductive reasoning, for the premises:

If I pass my exams I'll study psychology at university
If I fail my exams I'll go into politics and become Prime Minister
I've passed my exams

the valid, if unfortunate, conclusion is that I will study psychology at university.

As an example of the problems that can arise with inductive reasoning, Wason and Johnson-Laird (e.g., see Johnson-Laird, 1988) presented subjects with the series of digits '2 4 6' and asked them to discover the underlying rule through the production of additional examples. Most subjects set about *confirming* the possible rule 'even numbers increasing by two' by generating large numbers of positive instances of the rule, instead of attempting to *disconfirm* the rule by generating negative instances such as '7 8 9'. Had they done so, they would have eventually discovered that the rule was 'any three increasing numbers'. This confirmatory bias is one of the many biases that are evident from studies of reasoning. Other biases have been examined in an elegant series of studies by Kahneman and Tversky (e.g., Kahneman, Slovic and Tversky, 1982). For example, the availability bias leads subjects to say that more words begin with the letter 'R' than have 'R' in the third letter, because it is easier to generate words beginning with 'R'. In a similar manner to the biases introduced by schemata in memory, these reasoning biases can be quite benign in their effects and even on occasion lead us to be blissfully ignorant of our faults. However, under other circumstances the same biases can lead depressed individuals to conclude that they are insignificant and that life in not worth living (see section on Cognitive Therapy below and Chapter 2).

Emotion. Cognitive psychologists were long accused of ignoring the question of emotion, a problem that probably arose because of a view that emotion is somehow more primitive than cognition, given that it was long thought that it was language and reasoning that distinguishes us from the beasts. In fact, the full range of our emotional reactions requires the full range of the cognitive apparatus; although there may be undifferentiated states of a positive or negative emotional tone, the further interpretation of such a state depends on the range of cognitive and social factors available to the individual. Following a number of other theorists Oatley and Johnson-Laird (1987) have argued that there are a set of 'basic emotions' such as sadness, anxiety, anger, happiness, and disgust. These emotions typically arise at different points in our working towards particular goals and plans; for example, happiness can arise if sub-goals towards a main goal are achieved, whereas sadness can arise if an important goal or role is lost or has to be abandoned.

One of the crucial questions that many of the chapters in this book will address is what the relationship is between the range of normal experience of emotion and the emotional disorders. The answers are, of course, many and varied. For example, the same affect-laden thought or impulse can be experienced as perfectly normal by one individual or be experienced as a desperately unwanted intrusion in an obsessional-compulsive individual (see Chapter 6); the individual prone to depression may have lost the only role or goal that really mattered and life feels meaningless as a consequence (see Chapter 2); or an individual who has learned to repress anger as a child may have problems in developing intimate adult relationships because of problems in expressing hostility (see Chapter 7).

Cognitive therapy. The relationship between cognitive psychology and cognitive therapy is minimal when compared to theory and therapy in psychoanalysis and behaviourism. Theory and therapy in psychoanalysis and behaviourism are very closely connected, whereas cognitive therapy and cognitive psychology have developed almost independently of each other; thus, it would be feasible to derive a cognitive-based therapy from current cognitive science that contrasted with cognitive therapy on most points, or, more optimistically, it may be possible to bring cognitive therapy closer to cognitive science (Power, 1989).

The details of cognitive therapy will be spelt out in subsequent chapters so they will only be summarized here. The theory has been developed by Beck (e.g., 1976) and is based on the idea that dysfunctional schemata arise in childhood typically in problematic parental relationships. These schemata normally remain dormant until later in life when a negative life event or stress occurs which activates the schemata. For example, if the schemata are focused on the need to feel loved by everybody and the first serious relationship goes wrong, the individual is likely to become depressed. As a consequence of these activated schemata, the individual becomes overwhelmed with negative automatic thoughts (see Figure 1.2) such as 'I am unlovable', 'Nobody has ever really loved me', and so on, thoughts which lead the individual into a state of depression.

The therapy itself has four main components:

1) Education. The depressed or anxious individual may have little information about depression or anxiety, or may have mistaken information such as a belief that a panic attack is the same as a heart attack (see Chapter 3). One of the useful features of cognitive therapy is the fact that individuals are provided with information about the condition they are experiencing and about the procedures used in cognitive therapy.

2) Goal-setting and graded activities. Many depressed individuals withdraw from their normal activities, and the resultant inactivity may help to maintain the state of depression (see Chapter 2). One of the key strategies of both cognitive therapy and behaviour therapy is the identification of what these activities might be, and then setting activities or homework to be carried out between clinical sessions. The activities typically begin with easier ones and then gradually build up to more difficult ones in order to lessen the chance of failure early on.

3) The identification of negative automatic thoughts. A key step in cognitive therapy is helping the individual to identify the negative automatic thoughts that

Figure 1.2: An outline of Beck's cognitive theory of depression

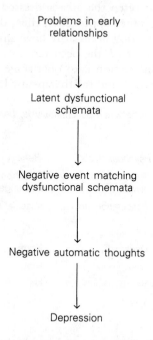

are intimately connected with feelings of depression and anxiety (see Figure 1.2 above). These may be identified in the clinical sessions themselves, for example, by asking the individual to role-play a difficult encounter, or they can be identified as homework by asking the individual to keep a diary of such thoughts in the situations in which they arise. Once identified, the individual is then encouraged to test their validity, to question them, and to check for the evidence for and against.

4) Challenging dysfunctional schemata. The identification and challenging of negative automatic thoughts leads into the final phase of cognitive therapy which is challenging the dysfunctional schemata that underlie the negative thoughts. In depression, these core beliefs typically centre around the need to be loved or the need to do well at all costs. The depressed individual tends to take a one-sided view of past achievements in love and work and may feel hopeless about the possibility of any future success; although some of these views may well be realistic, the problem for the therapist is to disentangle the genuine failures from the imagined ones, so that individuals can take a more balanced view of themselves and their future (see Chapter 2).

Psychoanalysis, Behaviourism, and Cognitive Psychology: Some Comparisons and Contrasts

The purpose of the three previous sections was to outline some of the basic principles of psychoanalysis, behaviourism and cognitive psychology, and to give a sense of the therapies that are associated with them. It will be evident from the presentation that often the area addressed by one approach is very different from that of the other approaches; thus, does the demonstration of classical conditioning in the dog necessarily have any bearing on the existence of a dynamic unconscious, or on the occurrence of perceptual biases in *homo sapiens*? The purpose of this section is to offer some points of comparison and contrast on both the theoretical and the therapeutic levels.

Figure 1.3: Some comparisons between psychoanalysis, behaviourism, and cognitive science

	Psychoanalysis	Behaviourism	Cognitive Science
Main Analogy:	Thermodynamic laws	Telephone exchange	Computer
Philosophy:	Associationism	Associationism	Constructivism + Neo-associationism
Role of unconscious:	Dynamic	None	Cognitive
Role of environment:	Low	High	Medium
Developmental stages:	Yes	No	Yes
Focus on relationship in therapy:	Yes	No	Some (recently)

The first question that can be asked is whether there is a basic analogy that underlies each of the three approaches. Figure 1.3 shows that the original analogy that Freud used for psychoanalysis was based on the laws of thermodynamics (see Power and Brewin, 1991). These laws were one of the mainstays of nineteenth century science; they relate to the fact that energy cannot be gained or lost in a system, though it can be transformed from one type to another. By analogy, Freud considered that psychic energy should follow the same rules as physical energy, and the Principle of Constancy (see p. 6) was one such rule. The underlying analogy for behaviourism is that of the telephone exchange; dial the right input and you get the desired output. In contrast, the analogy for cognitive psychology is that of the computer; thus, the computer consists of hardware (the actual cogs, valves, transistors, microchips or whatever the computer is built from), software (the programs that can be run on the hardware), and the implementation rules for how a particular piece of software runs on a particular piece of hardware. Whereas the telephone exchange should give a consistent input-output relationship because the relationship is defined by the hardware, the relationship for the computer is more complex because the action taken by the computer depends on the software or program that is currently running; thus, dialling '999' on a British telephone exchange should normally connect with the emergency services, but typing in '999' on a computer could lead to the number '999' being entered in a word-processing file, or to a connection being made with another terminal, or the Starship Enterprise moving into Inter-Galactic Space.

Cognitive science emphasizes that it is not the stimulus but the interpretation of the stimulus that is important.

Related to the question of the basic analogy is the question of the underlying philosophy of the three approaches (see Figure 1.3). Both behaviourism and psychoanalysis share similarities in their philosophical roots, in particular, in their origins in associationism. The basic laws of learning by association were adumbrated by the British Empiricist philosophers from the seventeenth century onwards, who outlined many of the basic principles long before behaviourism. The main question was under what conditions might two 'ideas' become linked together, and spatial contiguity, temporal contiguity, and similarity or resemblance were considered the main ingredients. Freud also adapted these laws for psychoanalysis, and the free association technique is explicitly derived from this philosophical basis. The emphasis in cognitive science (see Figure 1.3) is partly on the mind being much more active or 'constructive' in mental processes, in contrast to the passive mechanistic associations that are considered in behaviourism and psychoanalysis. Nevertheless, as Figure 1.3 expresses, cognitive science also has a strong influence of associationism and some of the latest computer modelling incorporates a recent version of associationism (see Boden, 1988, or Johnson-Laird, 1988, for excellent introductions to these issues).

The other comparisons presented in Figure 1.3 summarize some of the points detailed in the earlier discussion of each approach. The role of the unconscious in psychoanalysis and cognitive science is seen very differently; psychoanalysis emphasizes the motivating force of the unconscious in relation to drives and drive-related impulses, whereas cognitive science follows a different tradition derived from Helmholtz' work on perceptual processes. In Skinner's radical behaviourism there is no role for a psychological unconscious, because it is the organism's internal physiology that plays a casual role in behaviour; in methodological behaviourism (which accepts that there could be internal mental states that play a causal role in behaviour) the question of the conscious or unconscious status of such states would be seen as a scientific red herring, because neither type would be seen as the proper study of science. This emphasis in behaviourism on the observable and the measurable and its rejection of unobservable mental states is summed up in the following joke recounted by Phil Johnson-Laird (1988): Did you hear the one about the two behaviourists making love? Afterwards one of them turned to the other and said 'That was fine for *you*, but how was it for *me*?' (p. 18).

Further points in Figure 1.3 show that environmental factors play a greater role in behaviourism than in either cognitive science or psychoanalysis. Obviously, the details differ from theory to theory, but current environmental factors on average play a lower role in psychoanalytic theories. Both psychoanalysis and cognitive science consider that there may be stages in development, even though the focus in psychoanalysis is on psychosexual and emotional development, whereas the focus in cognitive science is on conceptual development, for example, in relation to language and reasoning ability. Because behaviourism focuses on laws of learning that are seen to be general both across species and throughout individual development, behaviourists have rejected the need for models that include developmental stages.

A final contrast in Figure 1.3 is on the role of the therapist-patient relationship in therapy. At one extreme, psychoanalysis would see the whole therapeutic relationship and in particular the transference relationship (see earlier) as central to therapeutic change. At the other extreme, there are behaviour therapists who say that therapy can be done as effectively by a computer or a self-help manual as a therapist (e.g., Marks, 1987). Cognitive therapy seems to be in a grey area in between; in its earlier short-term form it de-emphasized the therapeutic relationship, but in its recent extension to more difficult problems, the therapeutic relationship is being seen to play a more important role (e.g., Beck and Freeman, 1990).

The points presented in Figure 1.3 emphasize that in many ways the three main approaches in clinical psychology contrast with each other in terms of theory and therapy. However, we believe that while these differences exist, there is considerable scope for theoretical and practical integration between the three approaches. As an illustration of the potential for integration consider the two mainstays of psychoanalysis and behaviour therapy, transference and exposure treatment respectively. Surely such different ways of working could not be integrated? In fact, the mechanisms of both seem to be very similar; thus, both involve the arousal of intense emotion in the patient, the emotion derives from prior learning particularly in childhood, and the emotion needs to be worked through so that the patient responds more appropriately in the critical situations. As discrepant therefore that the different approaches seem, we hope that this book will illustrate that often similar conclusions are reached even though the starting points are very different. In addition to the considerations of theory and technique, there is the issue of 'horses for courses'; thus, different approaches will appeal to different people be they clients or therapists, and a host of social and individual characteristics will influence such appeal.

Figure 1.4: Further comparisons between psychoanalysis, behaviourism, and cognitive science

	Psychoanalysis	Behaviourism	Cognitive Science
Theoretical adequacy	medium	low	medium/high
Empirical usefulness	low	high	medium/high
Clinical usefulness	high	high	medium

In Figure 1.4 we have attempted to present an alternative way of comparing the three approaches. For example, although behaviourism has proven itself to be of high clinical and empirical use, its theoretical adequacy is now known to be low. In contrast, psychoanalysis has proven to be of high clinical usefulness for some groups in some settings, but of low empirical usefulness.

Additional Models in Psychology

There are many approaches other than those falling under the umbrellas of psychoanalysis, behaviourism and cognitive science that must be considered in the understanding of adult psychological disorders. Two such approaches that will be repeatedly encountered throughout this book are the *biological/medical* and the *social* approaches. Brief introductions therefore will be given to these approaches. A third approach, that of *humanism*, has had a considerable impact in the area of counselling and a number of its principles have filtered through into the practice of other therapies. However, there has been little theoretical development in this area to account for the origins and development of specific adult problems; this will be evident from a reading of the remaining chapters. We will not attempt therefore to provide an introduction to this approach (the interested reader should see for example, Mearns and Thorne, 1988).

Biological/Medical Models

The basic tenet for the biomedical approach is that disorders result from pathogenic physical processes of external or internal origin in relation to the organism. External pathogens include invasive agents such as harmful organisms and toxins which when introduced into the body can cause disease and temporary or permanent physical damage. Typical invasive agents include viruses, bacteria, and fungi which cause a wide range of common and not-so-common illnesses. Physical trauma may also cause temporary or permanent damage to the organism. Pathogenic processes of internal origin can, for example, result from genetic defects and natural ageing processes; thus, in the condition phenylketonuria (PKE) a simple genetic defect leads to the inability to metabolise a particular amino acid found in certain food products and can lead to the death of a newborn if not diagnosed. At the other end of the lifecycle normal ageing processes also lead to the death of the organism due to the physical deterioration of a range of tissues and internal organs.

A number of psychiatric conditions are the result of pathogenic physical processes of external or internal origin. For example, in so-called multi-infarct dementia an internal series of strokes lead to the increased death of brain matter and consequent general intellectual and personality impairments in the sufferer. Psychoactive drugs taken either deliberately or accidentally can lead to a range of psychological problems (see e.g., Chapters 4 and 9). And there are a number of harmful organisms that can also lead to psychiatric problems; one of the classic historical examples being tertiary syphilis which was originally called General Paralysis of the Insane (GPI) but was subsequently found to result from spirochaetal infection. The recognition of conditions such as GPI to be of infectious origin led to the development of effective treatment methods, so that unlike the Victorian asylum whose wards contained many such individuals our present-day mental health facilities rarely if ever see such individuals. However, these specific successes can sometimes lead to wild goose chases, for example, for *the* virus or *the* gene that causes schizophrenia (see Chapter 9) and the proposal of simplistic biomedical models for complex psychological disorders.

A more sophisticated type of biomedical approach is provided by so-called diathesis-stress models. The diathesis part of the model refers to a permanent physical vulnerability of the body which makes it more vulnerable to particular diseases, for example of invasive origin (the 'stress'). A classic example in the history of medicine was the recognition that tuberculosis arose from an interaction between an inherited vulnerability and the tubercule bacillus; thus, not everybody who is infected with the bacillus develops tuberculosis, only those with an inherited vulnerability. In relation to psychiatric disorder, diathesis-stress models have been proposed for a number of conditions that have included psychosomatic disorders such as gastric ulcer, myocardial infarctions, and eczema, and conditions such as schizophrenia (see Chapter 9) and certain types of severe depression (see Chapter 2). In these disorders, the interaction between a permanent physical vulnerability and some form of physical or psychosocial stress forms the central part of the model. In fact, diathesis-stress models are now commonplace, not only in the biomedical approach, but in a range of psychological and social models also, though the diathesis or vulnerability factor is expressed at a psychological (e.g., sensitivity to the experience of loss) or social level (e.g., a lack of social support from other individuals) rather than at a physical level.

One health warning that must be added to this discussion of biomedical models is that they provide reductionistic accounts of psychological disorders, in the sense that psychological phenomena are seen to be caused by physical pathogenic processes. For example, in the case of depression negative thoughts would be treated as symptoms caused by an underlying physical process or illness, in contrast to Beck's cognitive therapy (see p. 14) in which such thoughts are considered to be the cause rather than consequence of depression. Suffice it to say that although some psychological problems may be reducible to physical levels of explanation (with GPI discussed earlier one such success), the general cognitive approach to psychology emphasizes that many psychological processes are not reducible to solely physical terms. In other words, your chemistry might be perfectly okay but that doesn't necessarily stop you from having a hard time.

Social Models

Throughout the remaining chapters contributors will refer to a wide range of social factors that can influence the onset and course of psychological disorders (see Cochrane, 1983, for an overview of the social approach); factors such as the size of the individual's social network, the amount of support available, paid employment, criticism of the individual by significant others, and the presence of problems in significant others. Typically, one or two such social factors may be included in many examples of essentially psychological models. In some instances more complex models are presented which are primarily social; in these examples specific social factors may be seen in the context of the individual's culture and lifestyle (see Chapter 2); thus, the effect of the presence or absence of paid employment, for example, varies according to a number of interacting factors that include social class, cultural values, lifestage, and gender, therefore a model that considered employment independently of such factors can be regarded as overly simplistic. When the usefulness of psychological approaches to treatment is assessed, social factors need to be considered. Thus psychological approaches can often be improved by an integration with a social approach, though this is rarely achieved.

The application of a different type of social model to psychological disorders is illustrated by a number of family therapy approaches (see Chapter 8). The extension of general systems theory to social groups such as families and organisations demonstrates the potential for pathogenic processes at a social level, processes which cannot be simply reduced to a psychological level of explanation. Dramatic examples are presented in the family therapy literature in which the 'ill' member of the family is 'cured' only for another member of the family to become 'ill' in turn (see Chapter 8). Although the focus of this book is on the psychological level of explanation, we hope that the chapters on family and marital problems will serve as a reminder that no person is a 'psychological island' immune from the effects of others, and that there may be pathogenic social systems for which the appropriate intervention is social rather than psychological.

Final Remarks

This chapter stands as a basic introduction to the broad range of psychological disorders that will be discussed in subsequent chapters. Many of the basic concepts will of necessity be repeated in order to illustrate their application to the psychological problem in question. We must reiterate however that different problems have come to be dominated by different approaches; for example, simple phobias and obsessive-compulsive disorders are dominated by the behavioural approach, anxiety and depression by the cognitive approach, and it is no surprise that family problems have become dominated by family-systems approaches. In addition to the type of problems being considered, therapists and researchers also have their own preferences according to their own personalities: preferences which will be evident in a number of the chapters. Nevertheless, most practising clinicians subscribe to the pragmatic eclecticism which adapts the type of approach that they take according to a mixture of problem type, therapist and patient factors, and available resources. Our understanding of what constitutes good theory and good therapy for psychological problems is far too impoverished for any one approach to claim that it presents a complete answer; as the history of psychology shows, such claims fall flat on their face far too often!

Recommended Reading

General

ATKINSON, R.L., ATKINSON, R.C., SMITH, E.E., BEM, D.J. and HILGARD, E.R. (1990) *Introduction to Psychology* (10th Ed.), New York, NY: Harcourt Brace Jovanovich.

Generations of psychology students have grown up on this classic introductory text which has plenty of editions left in the old horse yet.

Specific

BROWN, D. and PEDDER, J. (1991) *Introduction to Psychotherapy: An Outline of Psychodynamic Principles and Practice* (2nd Ed.), London, UK: Tavistock.

Probably the best introduction still to psychoanalytic principles and to the practice of psychotherapy in general.

CLARE, A. (1980) *Psychiatry in Dissent* (3rd Ed.), London, UK: Routledge.

In the chair, on the couch, under the volcano — wherever you find yourself, Britain's number one media psychiatrist excels with this balanced view of psychiatry.

COCHRANE, R. (1983) *Social Creation of Mental Illness*, London, UK: Longman.

A very readable introduction to social factors in psychological disorders.

GREGORY, R.L. (1981) *Mind in Science: A History of Explanations in Psychology and Physics*.

A tour de force that links the history of mind, science, and technology.

JOHNSON-LAIRD, P.N. (1988) *The Computer and the Mind*, London, UK: Fontana.

One of the best introductions to cognitive science written by one of its finest proponents.

RACHLIN, H. (1991) *Introduction to Modern Behaviourism* (3rd Ed.), New York, NY: W. H. Freeman.

A good solid introduction to basic behavioural principles.

References

BECK, A.T. (1976) *Cognitive Therapy and the Emotional Disorders*, New York, NY: Meridian.

BECK, A.T. and FREEMAN, A. (1990) *Cognitive Therapy of Personality Disorders*, New York, NY: Guildford Press.

BODEN, M. (1988) *Computer Models of Mind*, Cambridge, UK: Cambridge University Press.

BREUER, J. and FREUD, S. (1895/1974) 'Studies on Hysteria', In *The Pelican Freud Library*, **3**, Harmondsworth, UK: Penguin.

BROADBENT, D.E. (1958) *Perception and Communication*, New York, NY: Pergamon Press.

BRUNER, J. (1983) *In Search of Mind: Essays in Autobiography*, New York, NY: Harper & Row.

CASEMENT P. (1985) *On Learning from the Patient*, London, UK: Tavistock.

ERIKSON, E.H. (1963) *Childhood and Society*, (2nd Ed.), Harmondsworth, UK: Penguin.

FREUD, A. (1937) *The Ego and the Mechanisms of Defence*, London, UK: Hogarth Press.

FREUD, S. (1895/1966) Project for a Scientific Psychology, in *Standard Edition of the Complete Psychological Works of Sigmund Freud*, Vol. I, London, UK: Hogarth Press.

FREUD, S. (1923/1984), 'The Ego and the Id', *In the Pelican Freud Library*, **2**, Harmondsworth, UK: Penguin.

FREUD, S. (1926/1979), 'Inhibitions, Symptoms and Anxiety', *In The Pelican Freud Library*, **10**, Harmondsworth, UK: Penguin.

GAY, P. (1988) *Freud: A Life for Our Time*, London, UK: Dent.

GLEICK, J. (1988) *Chaos: Making a New Science*, London, UK: Heinemann.

GRUNBAUM, A. (1984) *The Foundations of Psychoanalysis*, Berkeley, CA: University of California Press.

JOHNSON-LAIRD, P.N. (1988) *The Computer and the Mind: An Introduction to Cognitive Science*, London, UK: Fontana.

JONES, M.C. (1924) 'A laboratory study of fears: The case of Peter', *Pediatric Seminary*, **31**, pp. 308–315.

KAHNEMAN, D., SLOVIC, P. and TVERSKY, A. (1982) *Judgement Under Uncertainty: Heuristics and Biases*, Cambridge, UK: Cambridge University Press.

MARKS, I. (1987) *Fears, Phobias and Rituals*, Oxford, UK: Oxford University Press.

MEARNS, D. and THORNE, B. (1988) *Person-Centred Counselling in Action*, London, UK: Sage.

MOWRER, D.H. (1939) 'A stimulus-response analysis of anxiety and its role as a reinforcing agent' *Psychological Review*, **46**, pp. 553–565.

NEISSER, U. (1967) *Cognitive Psychology*, New York, NY: Appleton-Century-Crofts.

OATLEY, K. and JOHNSON-LAIRD P.N. (1987) 'Towards a cognitive theory of emotions' *Cognition and Emotion*, **1**, pp. 29–50.

PENROSE, R. (1989) *The Emperor's New Mind: Concerning Computers, Minds and the Laws of Physics*, London, UK: Vintage.

POWER, M.J. (1989) 'Cognitive therapy: An outline of theory, practice and problems', *British Journal of Psychotherapy*, **5**, pp. 544–556.

POWER, M.J. and BREWIN, C.R. (1991) 'From Freud to cognitive science: A contemporary account of the unconscious', *British Journal of Clinical Psychology*, **30**, 289–310.

POWER, M.J. and CHAMPION, L.A. (1986) 'Cognitive approaches to depression: A theoretical critique. *British Journal of Clinical Psychology*, **25**, pp. 201–212.

RACHMAN, S.J. (1990) *Fear and Courage*, (2nd Ed.), New York, NY: W.H. Freeman.

SELIGMAN, M.E.P. (1971) Phobias and preparedness, *Behavior Therapy*, **2**, pp. 307–320.

SELIGMAN, M.E.P. (1975) *Helplessness*, San Francisco, CA: W.H. Freeman.

WATSON, J.B. and RAYNER, R. (1920) 'Conditioned emotional reactions', *Journal of Experimental Psychology*, **3**, pp. 1–14.

WOLPE, J. (1958) *Psychotherapy by Reciprocal Inhibition*, Stanford, CA: Stanford University Press.

Chapter 2

Depression

Lorna Champion

A depression is a low point, a sinking down, a reduction in output of strength, vigour or productivity. From a psychological perspective, everyone at some time in his or her life experiences low moods. These low points are often described by using words such as sorrow, sadness and despair, or by words that mean the absence of something good, such as hopeless, restless, uneasy and unhappy. Low points in mood often occur when an experience threatens or results in the loss of some valued person, object or idea.

The pervasiveness of depression as it is described above is clear. However, depression also refers to a serious disorder which can disrupt all areas of a person's life so that he or she cannot work or maintain relationships. In some cases depression can be life threatening because of the risk of suicide. Of those people diagnosed as clearly suffering from clinical depression in a psychiatric context, about 15 per cent will eventually commit suicide, and a higher proportion (up to 40 per cent) will make suicide attempts (see Paykel, 1989).

Clinical depression is regarded by many as a disease. However, there is no consensus regarding exactly how depression should be distinguished from unhappiness, and many regard the so-called clinical state as the extreme end of a continuum (see Arieti and Bemporad, 1978; Kendell, 1976). Little attention has been given to the study of unhappiness as opposed to depression. It is clear that most depressed people are unhappy, but it is not so clear that most unhappy people are depressed. In this chapter on depression as a psychological problem in adult life, the focus is on a disorder that involves depressed mood and a range of other symptoms which, taken together, will have an adverse effect on the person's ability to function in important areas of his or her life.

Defining Depression as a Disorder

Depression is the most commonly presented psychiatric disorder and has been of great interest to the medical profession since Hippocrates first described melancholy over 2,000 years ago (Gilbert, 1984). The classification of depressive disorder into various types has received a great deal of attention from psychiatry. The emphasis on classification is important, as different causal factors have been proposed for the different types of depression. These different causal factors have implications for the type of model used to explain and treat the disorder in clinical practice. Before going on to consider the main classifications, the symptoms of depression will be defined.

The Symptoms

Depressed mood is the most central symptom and a prerequisite for diagnosis. In addition there will be some or all of the following main symptoms:

- Sleep disturbance — usually insomnia, particularly with a tendency to wake much earlier than desired in the morning
- Appetite disturbance — usually a loss of the desire to eat and/or weight loss
- Excessive tiredness
- Decrease in sexual interest
- Loss of interest in usual activities
- Slowness in thinking and, in more severe cases, in movement
- Feelings of self-condemnation
- Thoughts of suicide and suicide attempts

In addition to the main symptoms outlined above, depression often includes variation in mood throughtout the day (diurnal variation), with the mood usually being lowest or most depressed in the morning.

Guilt is also a common experience; this feeling may be intense and to others will seem out of proportion with the 'crime'. Often minor misdeeds that occurred long ago will become a focus for intense guilt. In some severe cases delusions of persecution and more rarely hallucinations will occur. Anxiety often exists with depression and can include panic symptoms. Fear of losing one's mind or going mad can be a consequence of the self-perceived deficits in the depressed person's performance. These deficits may be in sharp contrast to the often highly efficient performance of the depression-prone person when he or she is not depressed (see section on depressive personality). Having outlined the main symptoms, those classification issues which have implications for the usefulness of the various treatment models will be described.

The Classification of Depression

First, a lot of attention has been given to the distinction between *endogenous* or *psychotic depression* and *reactive* or *neurotic depression*. From a practical point of view these two sets of complex terms can be understood as a way of distinguishing between the most severe disabling depressive states and the usually milder but often more chronic depressions. A diagnosis of endogenous or psychotic depression will usually be made where the symptoms are more severe, especially sleep and appetite disturbances; generally, more symptoms will be present. There is likely to be a major disruption in the person's ability to function in the normal everyday tasks of his or her life. In this type of depression, in contrast to the neurotic type, the person is more likely to perceive his depressed state as a distinct change from his usual self and will complain more of a loss of pleasure in all activities (Winokur, 1981).

The endogenous or psychotic diagnosis is also regularly applied where there is a marked distortion of the ability to perceive reality, especially if there are any hallucinations or delusions in which the content refers to the individual's badness as a person. In those cases where there are hallucinations or delusions the label of psychotic rather than endogenous will often be used.

Endogenous depression is defined as having an onset unrelated to upsetting or unpleasant events, the cause supposedly coming from within the person. This proposed lack of reaction to external stress is in stark contrast to the neurotic/reactive type where the onset of disorder is usually linked to a stressful or upsetting event. The preponderance of more physical disturbance in those depressions labelled as endogenous, such as the severe disruption of sleep and appetite, often with serious weight loss and many somatic symptoms, has made this more severe type of depression a focus for biological theories of causation and treatment.

The inaccessibility of the severely depressed person to attempts at communication is one reason that this type of depression is more often considered unrelated to events in the person's life. Such a person is simply less likely to tell others about what has happened or to be able to think in a meaningful way about what may cause his or her distress. A case example of this was a very severely depressed man in his seventies. He had been highly successful in his work and family life prior to the onset of his disorder. He was hospitalised for depression and was suffering from a host of severe physical symptoms. He could give no reason for his state of despair and seemed to present a classic picture of endogenous depression. After several weeks of attempting to talk to this man, he mentioned that his only son, who had had a glowing career and young family had died quite suddenly from cancer. Following this event, but some time before the onset of the depression, the patient had sold his large family home, because he thought it too great a burden for him and his wife to manage. Just before the onset of his depression he had learned that this house was to be a nursing home for the elderly. He said he could not bear the thought that so many others would spend their last years in his beautiful house while he would have to end his days in a small flat which he now felt it had been a mistake to buy. He did not connect these events with his depression; he felt that because he had been so fortunate in life, he had no justification for feeling so bad, either about the loss of his son, or his regret about his home. He had never mentioned any of these problems to the doctors and nurses who had cared for him, because he said he could see no point in doing so.

Investigators, who have gone to some length to find out if those patients who are classified as endogenously depressed had experienced an event, have almost always found that they have (e.g., Arieti and Bemporad, 1978; Brown and Harris, 1978; Thomson and Hendrie, 1972). Endogenous depression, therefore, can no longer be defined by the absence of external events, but can only be defined by the presence of more severe symptomatology.

Those depressions that are given the label of neurotic/reactive, although often milder in terms of symptoms, are not always so. The sufferer is likely to be aware of what may have contributed to the depression, often an event involving some kind of significant loss, or the threat of loss. Common examples may include the ending of a love relationship, or the loss of a valued job. Sometimes depression will occur in the context of more chronic stress; there may have been no major event, but instead a minor incident which triggers a feeling of hopelessness about the situation. Examples of this more chronic stress would be: an unhappy, conflict-ridden marriage, caring for several very young children in inadequate housing, or an unsatisfactory work situation where there seems to be no hope of improvement. The work of Brown and Harris (e.g., Brown and Harris, 1978) provides a host of such examples in their study of women living in the community.

Life events or more chronic stressors may make a greater contribution to the onset of depression when they occur in that domain of the person's life in which he or she has most invested, reflecting a sense of selfworth or positive value (see Brown, 1989). Arieti and Bemporad (1978) have pointed out that, for women, this is more often in the domain of personal relationships, whereas for men it is more often in the work domain. This is obviously a generalisation and each case needs to be assessed individually.

To return to the distinction between severe and mild types of depression; it is important to point out that in the milder type of depression thinking will be negative, but individuals will be able to think about their situation and talk about it in a reasonable way. So the label of neurotic/reactive is usually given when there is no major distortion in the ability to perceive reality. In most cases, it is possible to make contact and form a relationship with such a person. This ability to relate to others is essential for many of the psychological treatment approaches which will be outlined below. For this reason many practitioners would only regard those with this milder depression as suitable for most psychological approaches.

The description of the distinction between the two types of depression outlined above is a gross simplification. There is no consensus on the definition. As Winokur (1981) points out, while it is possible to provide general descriptions of the two types, it is difficult to separate clearly and precisely the neurotic/reactive from the psychotic/endogenous type with regard to both severity and the specificity of symptoms. The interested reader is referred to Kendell (1976); in this review he assesses the evidence for separate distinct types of depression and concludes they can best be viewed on a continuum of severity.

There is insufficient space to consider the various other ways in which depression may be usefully subdivided. It can be useful to include the following: a consideration of the course of the disorder, that is, how long the episode lasts; the chances of recurrence; and how the symptoms may relate to more stable features of the person's character or personality. The interested reader is referred to Gersh and Fowles (1979) and Paykel (1989).

There is one type of depressive disorder that does seem to be distinct, called *bipolar disorder* or *manic-depressive disorder*. The term bipolar distinguishes it from all the other types which are unipolar; in bipolar disorder there are two extremes of mood as opposed to only one. Mood can be excessively high or excessively low. Severe bipolar disorders include periods of being manic. Mania can be regarded as the opposite of depression: there will be feelings of elation, usually a great deal of activity, sometimes to the point of exhaustion or collapse. The person will feel powerful, grand, on top of the world. Although this may sound a pleasant state, it is not generally so. There can be a loss of contact with reality in mania; sometimes when this occurs the person can run up huge debts from spending sprees and make major decisions which, in a more normal mood, would be regarded as disastrous.

Bipolar depression is clearly distinguished from other type of depression by the presence of manic episodes. Research has shown that there is likely to be a clear genetic contribution to its development, evidence for which is lacking in other types of depression (see McGuffin and Katz, 1989). The relative importance of biological factors, including genetic factors in the causation of depression, is a highly complex and a much researched area. In general, the more severe types of depression are considered to have a greater degree of biological causation than the milder more neurotic types. Current thinking and research does not point towards any one clear factor as the cause but rather sees the biological contribution as one of various vulnerabilities, which if they come together will then result in an episode of depression in the at-risk person (see Chapter 1). This idea of multiple causal factors applies to the genetic contribution too; it is clear that even severe depression is not due to the presence of a single defective gene. Depression does tend to run in families, but it is most important to remember that this does not mean the cause is genetic. Families usually have many things in common aside from their genes: the way they relate to others, the way they cope with stress, the kind of environment they live in and so on. (The interested reader is referred to the following references: Gilbert, 1984; Herbst and Paykel, 1989; McGuffin and Katz, 1989.)

The Prevalence of Depression

Depression is one of the most common adult psychological problems. Carefully conducted community surveys, which attempt to assess the rate of clinically significant depression, reveal rates of between 3 per cent and 7 per cent of the general population (see Paykel, 1989). Approximately 3 per cent of the general population are treated by their GPs for depression, but it is generally thought that about half of the cases presenting depression to a GP go unrecognised as such (Goldberg and Huxley, 1980). About 1 per 1,000 of the general population are admitted to hospital annually with depression, while about 3 per 1,000 are referred to a psychiatrist. A large community survey conducted in inner London estimated that seven out of ten women and four out of ten men will have at least one clinically significant episode of depression by the time they are 65 years of age (Bebbington, *et al.*, 1989). This last figure raises the important issue of the difference between men and women regarding the rate of depression. Overall, women are about twice as likely as men to suffer from depression. This difference applies regardless of how prevalence is assessed; it applies to both rates in the community and hospital admissions (see Cochrane, 1983). Depression is also more common amongst those in the lower social class groups, and amongst the unmarried as compared to the married. The study of the prevalence of depression in different social groups has made important contributions to our understanding of the disorder. Explaining these differences is an important challenge for the various models and theories of depression that have been developed. Differences in the rates of depression in various social groups are discussed in more detail in the section below on social models.

Finally, it is necessary to consider depression in relation to life stage. Depression can occur in childhood and in adolescence (see Rutter, 1986). It is of interest that before the age of 15 boys are more likely to be treated for depression than girls (Cochrane, 1983). A first episode of depression can occur at any age in adult life; the milder neurotic/reactive depressions tend to begin earlier, usually between the ages of 20 and 40. The onset of these disorders may be gradual and often occurs in those with a vulnerable personality (Akiskal, *et al.*, 1980). Early adult life is a demanding period during which many transitions need to be negotiated: for example, gaining independence from family, establishing oneself in the domains of work, love relationships and child rearing. Each of these transitions will place considerable demands on the person who may be susceptible to depression in the face of stress (see Maughan and Champion, 1990). The course of a disorder that begins early in adult life may be chronic, with fluctuations occurring in severity of symptoms according to the demands placed upon the individual. The more severe types of depression, often labelled as endogenous, tend to have an onset later in life, usually around mid-life or later and will often occur in individuals who have apparently coped well with their life. When thinking about the onset of depression, it is important to consider the major transitions that are likely to characterise each life-stage. Negotiating major transitions may put a person at an increased risk for depression. Winokur (1981) states that on average a depressive episode lasts between 4 and 9 months, although obviously the length of an episode will be affected by whether treatment is received and how successful this is.

Having outlined some of the main issues to consider about the various models and theories of depression, we can now go on the consider each main approach in turn.

Cognitive Models

Cognitive approaches to both the understanding and treatment of depression represent the most recent major development in the area from a psychological perspective. The work of Aaron Beck (e.g., Beck *et al.*, 1979) has been the most influential; his ideas will therefore be considered in some detail. This approach regards the main causal factor in depression as a disorder of cognition; this means that there is a problem with the person's perception and thinking (see Chapter 1). Beck regards the depressed person's thinking as excessively negative. Such individuals view themselves, the world and the future in a negative way. The theory proposes that, in the course of development, people acquire knowledge about themselves and the world in general; this knowledge is stored in the form of stable mental structures called schemata. It is these schemata, which can also be regarded as beliefs or assumptions, that form the basic structures a person uses to perceive, understand and think about the world (see Chapter 1). The schemata of the depressed person are constructed in such a way that they generate a negative bias when interpreting experience. One feature of these schemata is that they generate what Beck terms negative automatic thoughts. It is these automatic thoughts which cause depressed mood. These thoughts are called automatic because the person does not make a conscious decision to think such thoughts. The thoughts just come into the person's mind and may not even be noticed by the person; the truthfulness of the content of these thoughts is not questioned. Because the meaning of the thought is negative, it has an adverse effect on the person's performance or enjoyment of experience.

The theory states the following sequence: A critical incident will occur in a person's life which will often be an event involving loss; this critical incident will activate the dysfunctional assumptions and will generate negative automatic thoughts which in turn produce depression (see Figure 1.2).

An example of this process can be demonstrated in the case of someone we shall call Ann. Ann had been brought up by caring, but highly critical parents. Her attempts to please her parents always seemed unsatisfactory in some way. She frequently experienced feelings of being unloved and rejected. Ann found that trying hard at her work led to success, and approval by her parents. Work came to seem more controllable and rewarding for Ann than relationships.

Experiences such as those described above are likely to lead to a dysfunctional assumption of the form 'unless I am successful in my work, I am worthless and unloveable'. This assumption was of little trouble to Ann while she was being highly successful in her work. However, a disagreement led to a loss of a hoped-for major promotion. Following this experience, Ann came to feel she was unable to cope with responsibility; she could not find the energy to apply for other jobs, even though she knew this might help to improve her situation. It was at this stage she became depressed. She was not particularly aware of what she was thinking, but when asked to reflect, she reported thinking such automatic thoughts as 'I know I'm no good' and 'I'm useless, I'm a failure.' Ann did not question the truthfulness of these thoughts, but was only aware of not being able to do anything to make herself feel better.

The model of depression outlined above has generated a form of treatment called cognitive therapy (see also Chapter 1). An important assumption made by the model is that people are capable of examining their thinking in a logical, rational, scientific way. This means that they can be objective in their assessment of themselves and the world around them. The cognitive therapist sets out to help the depressed person by explaining the model outlined above and then works with the client to demonstrate exactly how, in his or her particular case, excessively negative thinking is contributing to a depressed state. Clients are asked to describe in great detail the events of their day (this is often done by diary keeping); at each point a recording is made, the automatic negative thoughts are identified, and the client's belief in these thoughts is assessed. The therapist works with the client to help him or her to challenge or question the truthfulness of the thoughts, carefully weighing up the evidence on the basis of what the client knows and has previously told them. The aim of this process is to enable the clients to begin to think about themselves, the world and their future in a less distorted way, and replace the negative bias with a more realistic, logical, rational assessment.

This brief account does not do justice to cognitive therapy for depression which involves a whole range of other techniques for helping the depressed person to change. Many of these techniques are aimed at directly recording and changing the person's behaviour, particularly increasing the amount of rewarding experiences the person has on a daily basis. These techniques and the theory behind them are more accurately termed behavioural than cognitive. Although there is a definite cognitive element to them, they are not unique to cognitive therapy. The interested reader is referred to Kovacs and Beck (1978) for an account of the theory and to Beck, *et al.* (1979) for a complete account of cognitive therapy and its techniques.

The unique contributions of Beck's cognitive model can be summarised as follows: a disorder of cognition is a primary causal factor in depression. This disorder of cognition includes an excessively negative bias in processing information about the self, the world and the future. People are capable of logical assessment of their thoughts and can be trained to think in a more rational, less biased way. Therapy is regarded as a collaborative process between therapist and client. The therapist shares his or her model of the disorder with the client and therefore the client's understanding and acceptance of the model is important.

The account above has concentrated on Beck's model. However, a number of other models and theories of depression could also be regarded as cognitive because they place considerable emphasis on the role of processes such as perception and thinking. Examples of these theories include those with a strong developmental element and basis in psychoanalytic ideas (e.g., Arieti and Bemporad, 1978) and those models originally based on strict behavioural principles, for example, the learned helplessness model. When the latter model was applied to depression in humans it was necessary to expand the theory to take into account how individuals perceived their helplessness. It was found that it was the person's perception of his or her helpless state in a given situation that resulted in depression rather than the helpless situation *per se.*

Beck's model and its therapy have been criticised on a number of grounds, for example on the adequacy of the cognitive theory on which it is based (see Power and Champion, 1986) and on the difficulties and desirability of changing people's beliefs (see Marzillier, 1986).

The Behavioural Model

Behavioural psychology and behaviour therapy have produced models of depression and methods of treatment. There are a whole range of different approaches within this school of thought and the interested reader is referred to Williams (1984) for a full account of these. In this section, the main principles of the behavioural approach to depression will be outlined, concentrating on its unique contribution.

In general, behavioural models claim that depression comes about because the person is receiving inadequate or insufficient positive reinforcement or reward from his or her environment. If the person's behaviour is changed so that an increase in the amount of positive reinforcement or reward is received, the depression will decrease. So the focus of this approach is on behaviour change. Some models, for example Ferster's (1973) operant model, argue that a careful analysis needs to be carried out to determine the function of the depressed person's behaviour. Such an analysis involves assessing what the person is getting out of behaving in the way he or she does. For example, the passive behaviour of the depressive may be a way of avoiding punishment or criticism. Such passive behaviour may have been learned because it was more reinforcing than active behaviour which was experienced as punishing. For example, a depressed person may have ceased to talk to his wife because he has learned from experience that talking to her elicited a critical response. Because he does not talk to her, he cannot ever experience any positive reinforcement from the behaviour so it is not reinstated. It is not difficult to see how this process can gradually generalize to produce a very impoverished environment where the depressed person engages in less and less activity that has the potential of providing any positive reinforcement.

In behavioural terms the behaviour of the depressed person has been learned (see Chapter 1); therefore, the task of treatment is to provide an environment where more adaptive, non-depressed behaviour can be learned by ensuring that such behaviour receives optimum reinforcement. The example of the husband and wife is a social one; other theorists, for example Lewinsohn (1974) have proposed that the main problem in depression is a lack of response-contingent positive social reinforcement. In ordinary language this means that the person's actions in social situations do not produce any rewards. This may be because the person never really enters into social situations in the first place, or because the depressed person's behaviour is such that it fails to produce a rewarding response from those with whom he or she interacts. Lewinsohn proposes that in treatment the therapist needs to establish the following:

- The number of activities or experiences that are potentially reinforcing for that person
- The availability of resources in the person's environment to make reinforcing activity possible
- The extent to which the person has the skills to elicit those behaviours that will be reinforcing; this usually means social skills.

As with many other originally purely behavioural theorists, Lewinsohn has since gone on to propose a much broader theory encompassing cognitive and biological ideas (see Lewinsohn, *et al.*, 1985). The clearest example of how the behavioural approach to depression can be useful, but inadequate as a complete explanation of the disorder in humans, is shown by the model termed *learned helplessness*.

Learned Helplessness

The theory of learned helplessness (see Seligman, 1975) was developed following a series of laboratory experiments in which dogs in one group were given inescapable electric shocks. The behaviour of these dogs was compared to another group who were given the chance to learn how to avoid the shocks. The dogs in the first group showed severe learning deficits on subsequent learning tasks. The behaviour of the dogs in the inescapable shock group showed a pattern not unlike depression; they were lethargic and did not make attempts to learn. The essential causal factor in producing this state of helplessness was the uncontrollability of the stimulus, in this case shock. In other words, there was no contingency between the animal's response and the outcome the animal achieved; no matter what they did to try to avoid the shock they still received it. This state of helplessness was thought to be similar to depression, and a huge amount of research was conducted to assess the validity of the theory in humans. The learning tasks used to induce helplessness in humans usually involved some form of impossible reasoning problems and, fortunately, not inescapable electric shock! (See Abramson, Seligman and Teasdale, 1978).

The results of this research showed that it was possible to induce a state of dysphoria by exposing people to helplessness experiences in a laboratory setting. However, it became clear that in order for depression to occur, *how* the person perceived the negative experience was crucial. Therefore, Abramson, *et al.* (1978) proposed a new model which they termed *reformulated helplessness*. This reformulation involved the addition of a cognitive level of explanation which included an analysis of the attributions a person makes for his or her experience of failure. This model can be summarised as follows:

1 The model does not account for all types of depression; it is therefore a sufficient but not a necessary condition for depression.
2 The person learns to expect that a highly aversive state of affairs is likely to occur (positive state of affairs unlikely).
3 The person expects that he or she will be able to do nothing about the likelihood of this aversive state of affairs occurring.
4 The person possesses a maladaptive attributional style.

A maladaptive attributional style in this sense means that when a negative event is experienced it is attributed to factors which are internal, stable and global. When a positive event is experienced it is attributed to external, unstable, specific factors. So if we take the event of failing an exam, for example, the attribution the person makes for this failure will determine whether or not he or she becomes depressed. An example of an internal, stable, global factor is intelligence; intelligence is internal to the person, stable in that it will not change over time, and global in that it is likely to affect most tasks the person performs. If the failure of the exam is attributed to lack of intelligence, this will more likely lead to depression than if the failure is attributed to a particularly difficult set of questions which the person had not been taught how to answer. In this latter case the attribution is made to an external factor, namely the difficulty of the paper; this attribution is also unstable in that another exam paper is not likely to be so difficult; it is specific because the problem of difficulty in this case concerns only exam papers and not all lifes challenges.

The reformulated model of learned helplessness has been further developed and refined and is now called the *hopelessness theory*; the interested reader is referred to Abramson, Metalsky and Alloy (1989) for further details.

Psychodynamic Models

As an approach to depression psychoanalysis presents a range of models or theories rather than just one unitary view (see Arieti and Bemporad, 1978; Coyne, 1985). Salient features of the approach are that it places emphasis on unconscious factors and has a great deal to say about early development and how this can create vulnerability to depression in adult life. A good place to begin is Freud's (1917) paper 'Mourning and Melancholia'. In this paper Freud made the link between mourning and depression. He argued that in both states something is lost, but in depression what is lost is often less clear. The loss in depression may be a more abstract concept, such as the failure of a valued plan or the loss of a cherished idea or ideal. Because this approach places great emphasis on the importance of the unconscious and defense mechanisms that prevent painful or unacceptable thoughts and ideas from entering consciousness, it is possible that a person may not be consciously aware of loss, instead he or she is aware of feeling hopeless and depressed.

Freud states that a major difference between mourning and depression is that the latter involves a lowering of self regard and self denigration; this can be seen as an attack on the self. In mourning it is the world which has become poor and empty, but in depression it is the ego itself. Freud proposed the following sequence to explain one common way in which depression can develop.

1   The person experiences a disappointment, for example with a loved one.
2   The loved one cannot be abandoned as worthless and the affection transferred to someone else, perhaps because the loved one is felt to be needed as a child needs a mother.

3 Instead of abandonment, the person identifies with the other and internalises him/her. In psychoanalytic terms this would be described as the introjection of the object as part of the ego.
4 Because the loved one is now felt to be a part of the self or ego, the attacks on the self can be understood as denigration and attacks against the lost or disappointing person.

This sequence of events presents an early psychoanalytic formulation of depression which has been both expanded on and criticised by a number of more recent psychoanalytic theorists (e.g., Bibring, 1953). However, before moving on to consider more recent ideas, Freud's formulation is important in drawing attention to the following. First, the difficulty depressed individuals have in giving up what they have lost. There appears to be an intense need to maintain the ideal situation, whether this is a loved person, a goal, aspiration or quality of the self. It is as if the person cannot survive without his/her cherished ideal; there is little or no intrinsic sense of selfworth or value aside from the attainment of the ideal (see Arieti and Bemporad, 1978).

Second, there is the idea of repressed hostility in depression, a phenomenon that will be apparent to anyone who has been exposed to a severely depressed person. Indeed depression itself can be seen as an indirect and unconscious way of expressing hostility. This aspect of the account could be considered to solve the riddle of suicide in depression. The depressive really wants to kill or attack the person who has caused his or her sense of disappointment or abandonment. Because this person is now felt to be a part of the self, by killing the self, the depressive kills the person who has caused the hurt.

Third, the loss of energy in depression and the withdrawal of interest from the external world can be explained by the absorbing and exhausting nature of the conflict set up in the person's inner world. The conflict being brought about by the perceived discrepancy between the actual situation and the wished for situation which cannot be abandoned.

More recent psychoanalytic formulations (see Bibring, 1953) have emphasised the importance of the helplessness of the ego as the central mechanism in causing depression. It is argued that depression is the emotional expression of a state of powerlessness of the self to achieve or live up to the strongly held wishes. Such wishes may include the following; the need to be worthy and loved, to be strong and secure and to be good and not aggressive or destructive. Bibring states depression results from the tension between these aspirations, which are felt to be essential for the survival of the self, and the ego's acute awareness of its perceived (but not necessarily real) helplessness and incapacity to live up to them. The person becomes tired of the struggle and gives up, withdrawing from the external world and in extreme cases wishes to die. In contrast to Freud's formulation, Bibring argues that it is the ego's awareness of its helplessness which in some cases forces it to turn the aggression away from what has caused its suffering onto the self. In other words, the turning of the aggressive impluses against the self is secondary to the breakdown in self-esteem.

All psychoanalytic theorists see the origin of the situation described above to be in a developmental context. Particular emphasis is placed on the earliest experiences of feeding in the infant because it is at this stage in development that the organism really is quite helpless without the adequate care of another person (usually a mother). At this early stage of development the infant does not have the necessary understanding of the world to know that food will come soon or that the lack of comfort is not a permanent state but only a temporary one. How much deprivation and frustration an infant has to experience, how this is handled by the infant's caretakers, and how well the infant can tolerate these experiences will all contribute to how helpless the infant feels. In situations of loss in adult life, psychoanalytic theory argues that there is a temporary regression in which the feelings of these much earlier experiences of loss and helplessness are experienced again. Therefore, how individuals cope with loss, whether or not they become helpless and depressed, will depend to some extent on how they coped with these earlier losses and disappointments. How such resilience is conceptualised varies according to the particular psychodynamic theory, but to put it very simply, resilience will depend on the extent to which a person was able to internalise good experiences; good experience should enable a person to tolerate or withstand the inevitable bad experiences of loss and disappointment without feeling helpless. However, it is important to emphasise that the needs for love and care and the meeting of basic needs extends well beyond earliest infancy, and it is likely that any experiences of extreme helplessness may well contribute to later vulnerability to depression (see Bowlby, 1988). Conversely, the experience of a positive loving relationship later on in development may lead to greater resilience to depression by the suggested process of internalisation (see Bowlby, 1988). Indeed, one way in which psychoanalytic psychotherapy may work is to provide a kind of repetition of the parent-child relationship with the hope that the patient can internalise a better experience of a caring and understanding other than he or she had done previously. This internalisation of the therapeutic relationship should have a beneficial effect on self-esteem and so increase resilience to depression.

There is not space here to provide a detailed account of psychoanalytic approaches to treating depression. The unique features of this approach are that emphasis is placed on the therapeutic relationship and on working in the transference (see Chapter 1). In contrast to Beck's cognitive therapy, the psychoanalytic therapist would not explain directly about distortions in perception. Instead, distortions in perception would be drawn to the patient's attention using interpretation of material the patient presented. Many interpretations would address how such distortions influenced the patient's perception of the therapist. In this way, the psychoanalytic therapist helps the patient to work through difficulties and conflicts in the here and now of the therapeutic situation. Links would also be made with the patient's past experiences of significant others, relating to both conscious or unconscious memories or conflicts. Psychoanalytic theory provides a framework which informs the therapist about the possible nature of unconscious conflicts in depression.

The Depressive Personality

The idea of vulnerability has already been briefly considered in relation to genetics and social factors. The cognitive model also suggests a type of cognitive vulnerability and indicates how that may have developed. It is clear to some therapists and researchers who have worked extensively with depressed people that many of these people have a certain type of personality. This sort of personality can be seen as providing a kind of fertile 'soil' in which, given the necessary conditions, the 'seed' of depressive disorder will be more likely to grow.

Psychoanalytic approaches to depression have gone to great lengths to describe the personality type of the depression-prone person; attention is paid to what may have contributed to the development of this vulnerability from birth onwards. In contrast, other approaches, particularly the behavioural approach, have given very little attention to this area. The idea of personality is important because biological and social factors interact with the personality and influence if, when and how depressive disorder develops. Only a very brief account can be given here of the main characteristics of the depressive personality. A clear and useful account is given by Anthony Storr (1979).

A central feature of the depressive personality is the absence of a secure sense of self-worth or built-in sense of self-esteem. This characteristic may not be at all obvious to an observer when the person is not depressed. What may be more obvious in many cases is that the person is compliant and reticent in stating opinions. Because the depressive does not have a built-in sense of self-esteem, he or she needs constantly to be obtaining it from the external world. This will be manifested in over-anxiety to please, to fit in and to be successful and achieve. Popularity and achievement are essential requirements because this is the only way any confirmation can be obtained. Storr states 'It is impossible for the depressive to be indifferent to what others think of him, since repeated assurance of their good opinion is as necessary to his psychic health as are repeated feeds of milk to the physical well-being of infants.' (Storr, 1979, p. 99) To be in such a position makes a person excessively vulnerable to criticism and makes being assertive in the face of opposition a very risky, enterprise. For these reasons, those with depressive personalities may be regarded as 'nice', but often will not gain the respect that they deserve or feel is due to them for the considerable efforts they make on others' behalf. They are likely to feel resentment and hostility because of this, but be unable to express it for fear of rejection and loss of the other's good opinion. It is not difficult to see how this state of affairs can lead to a vicious circle of over-compliance, leading to more resentment and then increased attempts to conceal resentment by more over compliance and so on.

The picture of the depressive personality portrayed above presents a view of the more passive type, however, the same basic lack of self-esteem can manifest itself as far from passive. Some individuals will reach a point in development when they come to see that success can relieve feelings of worthlessness. In this case ceaseless striving will replace passivity. In many capable individuals, such striving can lead to considerable success and acclaim in the external world. Winston Churchill provides an excellent example of someone who was prone to depression and did suffer at times from quite severe depressive disorder, but for most of his life presented as anything but passive and helpless. This picture can be seen as a kind of overcompensation for feelings of inadequacy. All is well for such a person, if the external world is providing a focus for what may otherwise remain inner conflicts. Such a person is particularly prone to a depressive disorder following a success as well as a failure, because success can be felt to be a loss; that is, loss of a goal or something to strive for. Once the goal is obtained, the person is back to a basic feeling of being not worthwhile, or being empty.

Biological Models

This book is about psychological models of adult disorders and does not attempt to cover biological explanations. However, no consideration of the causes and treatment of depression would be complete without some mention of biochemistry and the action of anti-depressant drugs.

Drugs to treat depression entered the public arena in the late 1950s and have been the focus of much publicity since that time. Increasing numbers of people have gone to their general practitioner expecting effective drug treatment for depression. Indeed for most people anti-depressant medication will be the first treatment received. It is only usually after this has been initiated that other psychological treatments will be offered either in conjunction with drugs or because, for one reason or another, the drug treatment has proved unsatisfactory (WHO, 1989).

A Brief Summary of the Action of Anti-depressive Drugs

In the late 1950s, evidence gradually came together to suggest that there was a link between mood disorder and the level of monoamines in the central nervous system. The main substances implicated were noradrenaline (NA) also called norepinephrine (NE), dopamine (DA) and 5-Hydroxytryptamine (5-HT), also called serotonin. Noradrenaline and dopamine are both catecholamines. Serotonin is an indolamine. Two pieces of evidence implicated this link. First, reserpine, a drug used to treat hypertension, was found to produce a lowering of mood and symptoms similar to depression in a small proportion of patients treated. It was known that reserpine produced a lowering of the levels of NA, DA and 5-HT in the central nervous system. In contrast, another drug, iproniazid, used to treat tuberculosis, sometimes produced a raising of mood, or symptoms opposite and incompatible with depression. Iproniazid was known to increase levels of NA, DA and 5-HT in the brain. A vast amount of research has been conducted to establish the validity of this hypothesis and to establish exactly how these neurotransmitters are regulated leading to levels being raised or lowered. Other neurotransmitters such as acetylcholine have also been implicated. No attempt will be made here to go into the mechanisms involved in the action of these neurotransmitters, the interested reader is referred to the following references: Gilbert (1984), Willner (1985), Montgomery (1989).

The main groups of anti-depressant drugs, namely the monamine oxidase inhibitors (MAOIs) and the trycyclic anti-depressants, work on the basic hypothesis that increasing the levels of NA, DA and 5-HT will alleviate the symptoms of depression. These two main groups of drugs and lithium, which is the most widely used treatment for manic-depressive disorder, all have different mechanisms of action for achieving an increase in the levels of these neurotransmitters in the central nervous system. Attempts have been made to establish if certain amines are more important than others in producing specific symptoms. For example, DA has been associated with a lack of pleasure, whereas 5-HT has been especially linked with sleep disturbance. Overall, this search for specificity has not as yet proved very successful, this may be at least in part because improvement in mood can be achieved by many different routes, with improvement in one symptom having a beneficial effect more generally. (See Willner, 1985 and Montgomery, 1989)

The most widely used anti-depressant drugs are those from the trycyclic groups such as imipramine and amytryptaline. This group of drugs is generally preferred to the MAOIs, as this latter group can be more dangerous, producing a hypertensive crisis if certain common foods like cheese, which contain tyramine, are consumed. Biopolar depression or manic-depressive disorder is almost always treated with lithium. This treatment is usually continuous once the diagnosis is made; patients are required to have blood levels of the drug checked every two months or so. It is important to note from a psychological perspective that anti-depressant drugs do not have an immediate action, but need to be taken in the correct dosage over many days or sometimes weeks before they have a therapeutic effect. Side effects are common and these may be very unpleasant and reduce compliance in many patients. Whilst drug treatment is usually the first treatment offered to those presenting with depression, it is not effective for everyone; this is due, at least in part, to the problems with compliance in taking the drugs correctly over a long period of time. In addition to these considerations, many people do not feel a chemical solution to their depression is desirable and taking drugs can increase a feeling of helplessness or being trapped in a dependence which they do not like or fully understand. Current approaches to anti-depressant medication suggest that drugs should be continued for at least six months after recovery from depression and that only after this time should the medication be reduced gradually. For those with a recurrent disorder where there has been more than one episode of depression in the past five years, long term or permanent medication is often considered (WHO, 1989).

Considering the information presented above, practioners using psychological treatments for depression will often be working with people who are on medication for depression. In this case, and for those who have received apparently unsuccessful drug treatments for depression, it is often important to know about the side effects anti-depressant drugs produce; sometimes these can be a source of distress and mistaken for symptoms of the disorder. In addition, the patients' attitude to the drugs, their understanding of how they may work and why they have to take them, may need to be integrated into a psychological approach to treatment.

Finally, drug treatments and other physical treatments such as electro-convulsive therapy (ECT) are often the treatment of choice, and sometimes the only reasonable option in cases of very severe depression, where the person is not capable of entering into any kind of relationship with a therapist or complying with any treatment regime which requires their understanding or active participation. The desirability of drug treatment is likely to be influenced by many factors including life-stage and the attitudes of the person concerned. Very elderly patients who are severely depressed may find many of the psychological treatments unacceptably demanding and so be more appropriately treated with drugs. In cases of very severe depression physical treatments are often used as a first stage, helping to reduce the severity of symptoms, so that more demanding treatment approaches can be used once there has been some improvement. Simple behavioural techniques can be used with quite severely depressed patients with a view to gradually helping them to increase their range of activities. Again, after some progress has been made more demanding cognitive approaches can be attempted. Psychotherapy using an analytic approach is likely to be a long-term treatment, generally this type of treatment will have to be modified during the most severe phases of a major depression; the therapist needs to be much more active than he or she would normally be.

Social Models

So far in this chapter we have considered models of depression that focus on behaviour, cognition, biology, and early experience. Most of these models have mentioned the experience of loss as a precipitant of depression. However, none of these models have had very much to say about the contribution of social factors in the person's environment, or about the broad influences of sex, class, race, culture and life stage.

Social models of depression see the cause of the disorder as primarily of social origin (see Brown and Harris, 1978; Brown, 1989). In other words, depression can be caused by upsetting or unpleasant experiences in the person's social world. These experiences may be acute life events, such as the loss of a valued friend or partner, or more long term experiences of adversity, such as living in damp, crowded housing conditions for a long period with no obvious hope of ever being able to move. The models considered so far have emphasised the experience of helplessness and the lack of a sense of control over one's environment as a major cause of depression. It is not difficult to see how certain social conditions or certain social roles can produce a greater likelihood of this experience than others.

Before moving on to consider a specific social model for depression, it is important to point out that the rates of depression differ between certain social groups; these differences do not apply to the biopolar disorders. First, there is a dramatic sex difference in the rates of depression; women are about twice as likely as men to be diagnosed as having major depression (Weissman and Klerman, 1985; Cochrane, 1983). There is no space here to go into all the possible explanations that have been proposed for this difference. Many of these explanations are biological, including endocrine or genetic factors. However, biological explanations are undermined by the finding that the sex difference is not consistently found when other, more social, comparisons are made. To give one example, divorced and widowed men have higher rates of depression than single or married women. It is, in fact, only amongst those who are married that the large excess of women over men is to be found (Cochrane, 1983).

Recent research has suggested that having children may be the crucial factor in accounting for the higher rate of depression in women (see Gater, Dean and Morris 1989). It is important to point out that the excess of depression in women who have had children is not adequately explained by the occurrence of the mild dysphoria that occurs immediately after childbirth or the more severe postpartum psychosis. The severe and relatively rare disorder of postpartum psychosis occurs immediately after childbirth and appears to have a distinct aetiology linked to biological changes (see Kumar and Brockington, 1988). Indeed recent research suggests that there is little evidence that women are at increased risk for the more commonly occurring types of depression immediately following childbirth (O'Hara and Zekoski, 1988). It is important to point out that in general women with children are at increased risk for depression when compared to those without children. The problems of selecting a control group to make these comparisons precisely are considerable (see O'Hara and Zekoski, 1988).

In order to explain the sex difference in rates of depression, it is necessary to look at social explanations, including those that relate to women's social roles and the stress these roles may cause. Various social explanations have been put forward; these include sex discrimination, the early role socialisation of girls to be more helpless and powerless than boys, the greater acceptability for women in our society to express depression than men. Some sociologists have argued that women's greater vulnerability to depression lies in the types of roles women are expected to fulfil (see Gove and Tudor, 1973); roles such as the carer for young children, cleaner, housewife, working mother, etc. The work these roles demand is not highly valued in our society, it is often not paid or poorly paid, there are no fixed hours and generally very poor conditions of service. For many women, especially those who are poor and have few material or social resources, the experience may produce the feelings of being trapped and helpless that are so characteristic of depression.

A well developed and influential social approach to depression is presented by Brown and his colleagues (Brown and Harris, 1978; Brown, 1989). Over the past twenty years, this research on the social origins of depression has proposed increasingly complex models of the cause of depression and has also implicated the role of social factors in recovery. The approach has many similarities with the other approaches already outlined; for example, the role of early experience is emphasised; a range of vulnerability factors are identified; and specific events are defined which immediately precede or trigger the onset of disorder. The unique contribution of this approach is that all the aspects mentioned are defined in social terms. Adversity in the social world is seen as the cause of the internal changes in biology, cognition and behaviour which are characteristic of depression.

The work of Brown and his colleagues focuses exclusively on women, but many of the basic ideas about the social causation are likely to apply to men, albeit in slightly different ways due to their different social circumstances (see Brown, 1989; Bebbington, *et al.*, 1981; Bolton and Oatley, 1987). Earlier research (see Brown and Harris, 1978) clearly shows that in an inner city sample, working-class women are more likely to suffer from depression than middle-class women. Working-class women are also much more likely to have experienced a life event with severe long-term threat or a major difficulty. A severe event is one which was considerably unpleasant or upsetting for the women concerned, and had a negative threatening aspect which was still evident after about two weeks from the event's occurrence, for example the death of a parent, child or other very close relative; the loss of a job with no immediate prospect of another one; news of eviction, etc. A major difficulty is an upsetting or unpleasant social situation that has been going on for at least two years, for example very poor housing conditions; chronic, serious illness in a household member; unemployment of the main 'breadwinner' in the family. These two types of stressors, severe events and major difficulties, are termed *provoking agents*. The research showed that these provoking agents were much more likely to have occurred in the group of women who had become depressed than in the group that were not depressed. For those women who had become depressed in the past year, 89 per cent had experienced a provoking agent in the nine months before the onset of the depression. In the normal group, only 30 per cent had experienced a provoking agent in the same time period (see Brown and Harris, 1986).

In addition to establishing the importance of provoking agents, the model was further refined to include a number of other social factors that were found to be associated with an increased risk of depression, if a provoking agent occurred. These factors were called *vulnerability factors*, and included the following: having several young children at home; not having employment outside the home; lacking an intimate and confiding relationship with a husband or partner.

Further research has attempted to replicate the above findings in different samples. This research has confirmed the importance of provoking agents in preceding the ontset of depression. Only one vulnerability factor has been consistently identified across studies. This factor is the absence of a confiding relationship with a partner (see Brown, 1989; Campbell, *et al.*, 1983; Parry and Shapiro, 1986; Bebbington, *et al.*, 1984). The importance of social support more generally, in protecting against depression in the face of stress, has been the focus of a great deal of recent research; the interested reader is referred to Cohen and Wills (1985) and Brown (1989).

The social model outlined above, including some of the more recent developments (see Brown, 1989), can be summarised as follows; vulnerability to depression and the onset of a depressive disorder are regarded as the result of adverse experiences in the environment rather than the result of internal faults, such as those of biology or cognition. Adverse social experiences can occur early in life; one example is the lack of adequate parental care in child-hood. This lack of care is then associated with an increased risk of continuing adversity later, such as early pregnancy (see Harris, *et al.*, 1986; 1987). Sex, class, culture and life stage are all important factors in assessing the type of social vulnerability that is likely to be implicated in an increased risk of depression. There is more than one route by which these early adverse social experiences can have their effect (see Maughan and Champion, 1990); Two examples could be: first, the continuation of external stress; second, a negative effect on internal resources such as the adequate development of self-esteem. To give one example of this second route, a failure to establish an adequate degree of self-esteem may make it more difficult to establish and sustain supportive relationships in adult-life; these problems may also increase the risk of experiencing unpleasant and upsetting events in the area of relationships (see Champion, 1990). It is at this point in discussing the refinements of a social model that it becomes clear that the model is not entirely social, but includes many aspects of the person, such as cognition, behaviour and almost certainly biology and genetics. So, finally, this chapter will briefly consider how each of the models described can be usefully integrated to provide a more complete understanding of depression.

Integration

The aim of this chapter has been to introduce the reader to the subject of clini-cal depression and to impart some basic knowledge about the main models or approaches to understanding the causes of the disorder and its treatment.

By now, it should be clear that while each approach represents a different angle and emphasises different causal factors, there are a great many similarities between the approaches. Taken together, all the approaches outlined empha-sise the many facets of this complex disorder. In practice, most researchers and clinicians will consider biological, genetic, cognitive, behavioural and social factors when thinking about depression. Which aspect takes precedence will depend on the aims of the particular study or clinical intervention in question.

Some of the strengths and weaknesses of each of the approaches will be considered below: first, the cognitive approach is useful in that it forces us to think about how depression represents certain types of distortion in percep-tion. This approach points out that there can be a marked discrepancy between the objective and the subjective view of the same event and that this discre-pancy can create problems. However, the psychoanalytic approaches would argue very much the same, but from a different theoretical perspective. The psychoanalytic approach is helpful in the following ways: it provides a detailed framework for explaining how the misperceptions may have come about and forces us to think about depression in a developmental context. In addition, the idea that much of what governs our perception and behaviour in depression is unconscious is an important contribution of this approach. Both the cognitive and psychoanalytic approaches can be informed by the social approach, regarding the types of external circumstances that are associated with both vulnerability to depression and to the onset of the disorder itself. Biological approaches provide another level of explanation and description. They are especially useful in increasing our understanding of the most severe disorders.

All approaches provide methods of treatment, some of which will be more suitable than others for certain types of depression and certain individuals. Behavioural and biological approaches are likely to be especially useful for the initial treatment of the most severe depressions. Cognitive and psychoanalytical approaches generate different types of treatment which may appeal to different types of practitioners and clients. Behavioural and cognitive compared to psychoanalytic approaches to treatment are relatively short-term. This can offer advantages in terms making less use of limited resources of time and money. There is not much research which genuinely addresses all the approaches considered here, however, there is a move towards integration especially of the social and biological approaches (see Bebbington and McGuffin, 1989).

No attempt has been made here to consider the relative effectiveness of the different approaches to the treatment of depression. This is a highly complex and controversial area. The outcome of any treatment will be influenced by a host of different factors including, for example, the severity of the disorder, the characteristics of the depressed person and so on. In addition, how outcome is assessed presents a complex problem. A number of studies have demonstrated that cognitive therapy can be at least as effective as drug treatment in the acute phase of depression and that cognitive therapy may be more effective than drugs in preventing relapse. The interested reader is referred to Williams (1989). Psychoanalytic approaches tend to report their effectiveness by clinical case studies. An example of these for both severe and mild depression can be found in Arieti and Bemporad (1978). Finally, in the spirit of integration, a recent, large scale study was conducted to assess the comparative effectiveness of two different types of brief psychological treatment and drug treatment for outpatients with major depressive disorder (see Elkin *et al.*, 1989). The results of this research showed few clear differences in the overall effectiveness of the different treatments.

Recommended Reading

COYNE, J. (1985) *Essential Papers on Depression*, New York, NY: New York University Press.

See pages 1–22 for a general introduction. This book includes reprints of key papers on all the models covered in this chapter.

GILBERT, P. (1984) *Depression: From Psychology to Brain State*, London, UK: Lawrence Erlbaum.

A good general introduction is provided in Chapter 1 (pp. 1–20). This book is strongest on biological models, although it covers all approaches.

HERBST, K. and PAYKEL, E. (1989) *Depression: An Integrative Approach*, Oxford, UK: Heinemann.

This book provides up-to-date reviews of all the main models and issues in depression. This is not an introductory text.

ARIETI, S. and BEMPORAD, J. (1978) *Severe and Mild Depression: The Psychotherapeutic Approach.* London, UK: Tavistock.

This book provides a good general introduction and an in-depth look at psychoanalytic ideas. There are many case examples in this book.

WILLIAMS, J.M.G. (1984) *The Psychological Treatment of Depression: A Guide to the Theory and Practice of Cognitive-behaviour Therapy*, London, UK: Croom Helm.

WILLNER, P. (1985) *Depression: A Psycho-biological Synthesis*, New York, NY: Wiley.

A good book on biological aspects of depression.

References

ABRAMSON, L., METALSKY, G. and ALLOY, L. (1989) 'Hopelessness depression: A theory-based subtype of depression', *Psychological Review*, **96**, pp. 358–72.

ABRAMSON, L., SELIGMAN, M. and TEASDALE, J. (1978) 'Learned helplessness: critique and reformulation', *Journal of Abnormal Psychology*, **87**, pp. 49–74.

AKISKAL, H., ROSENTHAL, T., HAYKEL, R. *et al.* (1980) 'Characterological depression', *Archives of General Psychiatry*, **37**, pp. 777–83.

ARIETI, S. and BEMPORAD, J. (1978) 'Severe and mild depression: the psychotherapeutic approach', London, UK: Tavistock.

BEBBINGTON, P., HURRY, J. TENNANT, D., *et al.* (1981) 'Epidemiology of mental disorders in Camberwell', *Psychological Medicine*, **11**, pp. 561–79.

BEBBINGTON, P., KATZ, R., McGUFFIN, P., *et al.* (1989) 'The risk of minor depression before age 65: results from a community survey', *Psychological Medicine*, **19**, pp. 393–400.

BEBBINGTON, P. and McGUFFIN, P. (1989) 'Interactive models of depression: the evidence', in HERBST, K. and PAYKEL, E. (Eds) *Depression: An Integrative Approach*, Oxford, UK: Heinemann.

BEBBINGTON, P., STURT, E., TENNANT, C. and HURRY, J. (1984) 'Misfortune and resilience: a community study of women', *Psychological Medicine*, **14**, pp. 347–63.

BECK, A., RUSH, A., SHAW, B. and EMERY, G. (1979) *Cognitive Therapy of Depression*, New York, NY: Wiley.

BIBRING, E. (1953) 'The mechanism of depression', in GREENACRE, P. (Ed.) *Affective Disorders: Psychoanalytic Contribution to Their Study*, New York, NY: International Universities Press.

BOLTON, W. and OATLEY, K. (1987) 'A longitudinal study of social support and depression in unemployed men', *Psychological Medicine*, **17**, pp. 453–60.

BOWLBY, J. (1988) *A Secure Base: Clinical Applications of Attachment Theory*, London, UK: Routledge.

BROWN, G. (1989) 'Depression: a radical social perspective', in HERBST, K. and PAYKEL, E. (Eds) *Depression: An Integrative Approach*, Oxford, UK: Heinemann.

BROWN, G. and HARRIS, T. (1978) *The Social Origins of Depression: A Study of Psychiatric Disorder in Women*. London, UK: Tavistock.

BROWN, G. and HARRIS, T. (1986) 'Establishing causal links: the Bedford College studies of depression', in KATSCHNIG, H. (Ed.) *Life Events and Psychiatric Disorders: Controversial Issues*, Cambridge, UK: Cambridge University Press.

CAMPBELL, E., COPE, S. and TEASDLE, J. (1983) 'Social factors and affective disorder: an investigation of Brown and Harris's model', *British Journal of Psychiatry*, **143**, pp. 548–53.

CHAMPION, L. (1990) 'The relationship between social vulnerability and the occurrence of severely threatening life events', *Psychological Medicine*, **20**, pp. 157–61.

COCHRANE, R. (1983) *The Social Creation of Mental Illness*, London, UK: Longman.

COHEN, S. and WILLS, T. (1985) 'Stress, social support and the buffering hypothesis', *Psychological Bulletin*, **98**, pp. 310–57.

COYNE, J. (1985) *Essential Papers on Depression*, New York, NY: New York University Press.

ELKIN, I., SHEA, T., WATKINS, J.T., *et al.* (1989) 'National Institute of Mental Health treatment of depression collaborative research program', *Archives of General Psychiatry*, **46**, pp. 971–82.

FERSTER, C. (1973) 'A functional analysis of depression', *American Psychologist*, **28**, pp. 857–70.

FREUD, S. (1917) 'Mourning and melancholia', *The Standard Edition of the Complete Works of Sigmund Freud*, **14**, pp. 243–58, London, UK: Hogarth Press.

GATER, R., DEAN, C. and MORRIS, J. (1989) 'The contribution of childbearing to the sex difference in first admission rates for affective psychosis', *Psychological Medicine*, **19**, pp. 719–24.

GERSH, F. and FOWLES, D. (1979) 'Neurotic depression: the concept of anxious depression', in DEPUE, R. (Ed.) *The Psychobiology of the Depressive Disorders*, New York, NY: Academic Press.

GILBERT, P. (1984) 'Depression: From psychology to brain state', London, UK: Lawrence Erlbaum.

GOLDBERG, D. and HUXLEY, P. (1980) 'Mental illness in the community: the pathway to psychiatric care', London, UK: Tavistock.

GOVE, W. and TUDOR, J. (1973) 'Adult sex roles and mental illness', *American Journal of Sociology*, **78**, pp. 812–35.

HARRIS, T., BROWN, G. and BIFULCO, A. (1986) 'Loss of parent in childhood and adult psychiatric disorder: the role of lack of adequate parental care', *Psychological Medicine*, **16**, pp. 641–59.

HARRIS, T., BROWN, G. and BIFULCO, A. (1987) 'Loss of parent in childhood and adult psychiatric disorder: the role of social class position', *Psychological Medicine*, **17**, pp. 163–83.

HERBST, K. and PAYKEL, E. (1989) *Depression: An Integrative Approach*, Oxford, UK: Heinemann.

KENDELL, R. (1976) 'The classification of depressions: a review of contemporary confusion', *British Journal of Psychiatry*, **129**, pp. 15–28.

KOVACS, M. and BECK, A. (1978) 'Maladaptive cognitive structures in depression', *American Journal of Psychiatry*, **135**, pp. 525–33.

KUMAR, R. and BROCKINGTON, J. (Eds) (1988) *Motherhood and Mental Illness 2: Causes and Consequences*, London, UK: Wright.

LEWINSOHN, P. (1974) 'A behavioural approach to depression', in FRIEDMAN, R. and KATZ, M. (Eds) *The Psychology of Depression: Contemporary Theory and Research*, New York, NY: Winston-Wiley.

LEWINSOHN, P., HOBERMAN, H., TERI, L. and HAUTZINGER, M. (1985) 'An integrative theory of depression', in REISS, S. and BOOTZIN, R. (Eds) *Theoretical Issues in Behaviour Therapy*, New York, NY: Academic Press, pp. 331–59.

MARZILLIER, J. (1986) 'Changes in depressive beliefs; An analysis of Beck's cognitive therapy for depression', *Advances in Cognitive-Behavioural Research and Therapy*, **5**, pp. 89–113.

MAUGHAN, B. and CHAMPION, L. (1990) 'Risk and protective factors in the transition to young adulthood', in BALTES, P. and BALTES, M. (Eds) *Successful Aging: Perspectives from the Behavioural Sciences*, Cambridge, UK: Cambridge University Press.

McGUFFIN, P. and KATZ, R. (1989) 'The genetics of depression and manic-depressive disorder', *British Journal of Psychiatry*, **155**, pp. 294–304.

MONTGOMERY, S. (1989) 'Developments in anti-depressants', in HERBST, K. and PAYKEL, E. (Eds) *Depression: An Integrative Approach*, Oxford, UK: Heinemann.

O'HARA, M. and ZEKOSKI, E. (1988) 'Postpartum depression: a comprehensive review', in KUMAR, R. and BROCKINGTON, I. (Eds) *Motherhood and Mental Illness*, London, UK: Wright.

PARRY, G. and SHAPIRO, D. (1986) 'Social support and life events in working class women: stress buffering or independent effects', *Archives of General Psychiatry*, **43**, pp. 315–23.

PAYKEL, E. (1989) 'The background: extent and nature of the disorder', in HERBST, K. and PAYKEL, E. (Eds) *Depression: An Integrative Approach*, Oxford, UK: Heinemann.

POWER, M. and CHAMPION, L. (1986) 'Cognitive approaches to depression: a theoretical critique', *British Journal of Clinical Psychology*, **25**, pp. 201–12.

RUTTER, M. (1986) 'The developmental psychopathology of depression: issues and perspectives', in RUTTER, M., IZARD, C. and READ, P. (Eds) *Depression in Young People: Developmental and Clinical Perspectives*, New York, NY: Guildford Press, pp. 3–30.

SELIGMAN, M. (1975) *Helplessness*, San Francisco, CA: W.H. Freeman.

STORR, A. (1979) *The Art of Psychotherapy*, London, UK: Secker and Warburg/Heinemann.

THOMPSON, K. and HENDRIE, H. (1972) 'Environmental stress in primary depressive illness', *Archives of General Psychiatry*, **26**, pp. 130–32.

WEISSMAN, M. and KLERMAN, G. (1985) 'Gender and depression', *Trends in Neuroscience*, September 1985, Amsterdam, Neth.: Elsevier.

WHO (1989) 'Pharmacotherapy of depressive disorders: A consensus statement by WHO Mental Health Collaborating Centres', *Journal of Affective Disorders*, **17**, pp. 197–8.

WILLIAMS, J.M.G. (1984) *The Psychological Treatment of Depression: A Guide to the Theory and Practice of Cognitive-behaviour Therapy*, London, UK: Croom Helm.

WILLIAMS, J.M.G. (1989) 'Cognitive treatment for depression', in HERBST, K. and PAYKEL, E. (Eds) *Depression: An Integrative Approach*, Oxford, UK: Heinemann.

WILLNER, P. (1985) *Depression: A Psycho-biological Synthesis*, New York, NY: Wiley.

WINOKUR, G. (1981) *Depression: The Facts*, Oxford, UK: Oxford University Press.

Chapter 3

Anxiety

Margie Callanan

Introduction

The Nature of Anxiety

Anxiety is a common form of reaction that every person experiences to a greater or lesser extent during his or her lifetime. The term anxiety is one that is as much a part of the lay person's vocabulary as it is the clinician's. Defining the concept of anxiety is, therefore, not a simple task. People may describe themselves as anxious when they are anticipating an important examination, or an important job interview. Those who report experiencing fear when left alone in the dark may also describe themselves as anxious. On the other hand, anxiety may be diagnosed when general functioning is at a level below usual competence and is accompanied by physical symptoms such as tension headaches. Do all these experiences refer to the same concept? Is anxiety to be defined as excessive worrying? Does it involve a fearful reaction?

Without a fear reaction, which is frequently an element of anxiety, we would not survive very long. It is the fear reaction that drives us to avoid danger, for example, getting out of the path of an oncoming train; or fighting a threatening figure; or fleeing from a potentially hazardous element. Research into how anxiety is described (that is, by the sufferer) suggests that fear is a basic, fundamental discrete emotion that is universally present across ages, cultures, races and species. Anxiety, therefore, has a clear functional value in the evolutionary sense and is vital to survival. It also seems to be a feature of being successful; thus, classic laboratory studies have shown that moderate levels of anxiety can lead to optimising task performance and that too much or too little anxiety leads to worse performance (Yerkes and Dodson, 1908). The performance of athletes, entertainers, executives and students might therefore suffer without the presence of some anxiety.

Anxiety, in the simplest sense, is a form of response or reaction. Its existence in the individual does not necessarily denote abnormality. Anxiety can, however, be much more than a normal, helpful, reaction in a challenging situation: it can become intolerably destructive. As with many other conditions, whether it is regarded as a disorder depends on the extent of its negative impact on thinking and behaviour and on how much it interferes with the person's daily life. The reaction of anxiety is on a continuum from normal, even desirable, to a severe disruption in ability to function as desired or expected. The concept of anxiety has been studied along this continuum, and it is the disorder of anxiety, its more destructive presentation, which concerns this present chapter.

The Features of Anxiety

What are the main features of anxiety? Fear and worry would seem to be important elements to its make-up: one is worried because one fears that something undesirable will happen; or one is anxious because one is frightened of something. Though fear is considered a dominant feature in the syndrome of anxiety, there is general agreement that a number of other emotions may be present, including distress or sadness, anger, shame, guilt and interest or excitement. A different combination of these emotions will operate in different situations and across time (Izard, 1977). This makes it difficult to talk about anxiety in a precise way.

Definition, therefore, is particularly important with the concept of anxiety as it encompasses a range of reactions and can refer to a range of possible experiences. A precise definition is not universally agreed; presented here are the main elements that may be observed in clinical cases of the anxiety syndrome.

Anxiety may be defined as an unpleasant emotion that is characterised by feelings of dread, worry, nervousness or fear. This emotion may be experienced in response to particular events, situations, people or phenomena; it may also be experienced in *anticipation* of such stimuli. The stimulus may be external, for example a storm, or internal. An internal stimulus might be a belief that is negative, for instance that one's ability is inadequate or one's health is poor. This unpleasant emotion is often accompanied by a sense of helplessness, so that the individual does not feel in control of the situation or his/her response to it. In addition, the individual may experience physical symptoms such as sweating, over-breathing, an increased heart-rate, nausea or dizziness. In an attempt to deal with the distress and discomfort the individual will usually make efforts to avoid the situation that is believed to excite these feelings. This avoidance behaviour is a common characteristic in the syndrome of anxiety. The main elements of the present definition, therefore, may be summarised as follows:

- an unpleasant emotion such as dread or fear
- in response to particular external or internal events
- accompanied by feeling out of control
- with the experience of uncomfortable physical symptoms
- resulting in an effort to avoid the stimulus event

In an attempt to illustrate the syndrome defined above let us consider the case of a 26-year-old young man, here referred to as Jack, who was described by his GP as severely anxious. Jack works as a magazine photographer, and his job performance is successful to the extent that his input is increasingly demanded at executive-level meetings. In these meetings he would sweat profusely and experience feelings of panic. Jack described other physical symptoms such as his heart 'thumping loud and fast' and he was suffering frequent headaches. He reported feeling a sense of dread whenever he was due to attend a meeting and, eventually, he began to worry about these meetings even when none were due to take place. Jack felt out of control of the situation: he did not want to lose credibility by refusing to attend the meetings, and he could not control his response to the situation. He began to devise ways of avoiding the meetings but continued to worry about the possibility of having to attend one some day. This worry began to affect his usual work.

In the case described above, Jack's anxiety could be described as a response to an external stimulus, the executive meeting. However, it could also be described as a reaction to an internal stimulus. The internal stimulus might be Jack's lack of belief in his ability to take part in executive-type decisions: he may have believed that he was leaving his real area of expertise, photography, and attempting an unfamiliar role. The physical symptoms experienced in the meeting may have served to further undermine his already negative self image.

There is one further element that is often mentioned when defining clinical cases of anxiety — the extent to which it interferes with daily life. This element is not strictly necessary to warrant a diagnosis of anxiety, but it is often the reason for the individual presenting in the consulting room for help. If Jack, in the case cited above, had not experienced interference in his usual work-performance he may not have presented for help. Jack's fearfulness in the face of executive meetings was not as great as his fear of losing his job.

Fear, according to evolutionary theory, is a basic innate emotion while anxiety is for the most part learned. Barlow (1988) recommends acknowledging the distinction between fear and anxiety. However, it would seem generally acknowledged that fearfulness is a dominant feature in anxiety.

Phobias are usually categorised under anxiety states, as the main element of a phobia is one of fear. Phobia is the name given to an irrational fear of objects (e.g., trains), situations (e.g., open spaces), animals or phenomena (e.g., thunderstorms). A phobia may be very specific, for example, a snake phobia, or it may be general and take the form of fearing any situation which requires interaction with a number of people (a social phobia). In the usual presentation of the phobic state, the individual will manifest anxiety when he or she is brought into contact with a phobic stimulus (that is, the feared object or situation).

As mentioned previously, a common feature of the phobic state or anxiety presentation is avoidance behaviour. This is the term given to behaviour where the objective is to avoid a particular object, place or situation. Generally this avoidance behaviour takes place in the absence of any rational or obvious reason for the activity, although the origin of the avoidance is a deep fear. Thus a person who is afraid of open spaces, an agoraphobic, will avoid any such situation which is likely to bring contact with open spaces.

Generalised anxiety is the term usually used to describe an anxious state which does not have as its focus any particular object or situation. Individuals who describe themselves as worrying excessively about most, even minor, events to the extent that normal functioning is interfered with or reduced, are considered to be suffering from generalised anxiety. In some cases, this state of generalised anxiety may include presentation of physical symptoms, such as tension pains or diarrhoea.

The 'anxious personality' is a term used to refer to someone who is identified as a 'worrier', worrying about most events to some degree, be they major or minor. In this individual anxiety is considered to be a character trait: it permeates thinking and behaviour though not necessarily to a destructive degree. For example, the 'anxious personality' would not view a major life-change as a stimulating challenge, but rather something to worry and fret about. This anxiety trait has been measured by questionnaires such as the Middlesex Hospital Questionnaire and is generally used to support the notion that 'emotionality' or 'nervousness' may be hereditary.

It is suggested that the difference between the 'anxious personality' and the individual with a severe anxiety state is one of quantity: the main elements are the same, but severity and interference are greater in the latter. There is, however, no evidence to suggest that the clinical anxiety syndrome is hereditary. While it has been observed that families of patients suffering with anxiety are more prone to fearfulness or excessive worrying (Crowe, *et al.*, 1983), this finding argues as well for learning as for genetics. Barlow (1988) suggests that the anxious personality may be the ' "platform" for panic' (p. 174), so that the presence of this trait makes the individual more susceptible to triggers of acute panic or anxiety. Evidence from clinical cases, albeit anecdotal, presents inconsistent support for this notion. Some anxiety syndrome patients report having always been 'rather a worrier', while others state that they were 'never inclined to fret' before their current anxiety state developed.

Spielberger (1966, 1972, 1985) considers anxiety a personality trait that determines how external or internal stimuli are appraised. In other words, the appraisal of threat, in Spielberger's model, will be a function of one's level of *trait anxiety*. He distinguishes *trait anxiety* from what he terms *state anxiety*, considering the latter to be a transitory emotional state. The personality trait of anxiety may lead the individual to be anxiety-prone. According to Spielberger's state-trait model, if the individual frequently experiences state anxiety then s/he has a strong trait anxiety. This model enables one to distinguish between common anxiety reactions and more intense and consistent anxiety. The model also supports, to some extent, Barlow's (1988) notion of the 'anxious personality' being more vulnerable to triggers that produce acute anxiety or panic. However, the causes of individual differences in trait anxiety remain unexplained.

Anxiety as a Disorder

The disorder 'anxiety' appeared for the first time in the seventh revision of the International Classification of Diseases (ICD-7) in 1955, and its categorisation was influenced by contemporary theoretical conceptions of anxiety disorders (Barlow, 1988). The current ICD (ninth revision) groups anxiety disorders, including panic states, under the general heading of 'anxiety states'. Thus, anxiety is officially classified as a disorder, though the listing does not provide a good descriptive account of its possible features.

Anxiety becomes destructive and warrants the description of disorder when it is prolonged, perceived by the sufferer to be out of his or her control and when it begins to result in behaviour or symptoms that reduce normal or desired functioning. Many people will describe a phobic reaction to something in their environment, for example an irrational fear of, and consequent attempts to avoid, spiders. However, a phobic disorder is diagnosed when such irrational fears begin to affect behaviour and decision-making to an extreme extent. Thus, a spider phobic warrants the diagnosis of a disorder when the individual requires all rooms to be thoroughly checked before entering them. As may be imagined, this extreme fear could interfere with normal or usual functioning to a great extent.

Anxiety sufferers are often unaware of the cause of their condition. One of the aims of treatment is to provide an explanation of the condition as increased understanding helps to control the sufferer's fear of the unknown.

How Anxiety Develops

The nature versus nurture controversy runs through theories of the origin of anxiety, as indeed it does through all theoretical attempts to explain human behaviour and processes (see Chapter 1). The nature perspective is that our responses are primarily genetically coded in our physical and biological make-up. One may be predisposed to overreact to potential threat in the environment and, thus, may be biologically vulnerable to developing anxiety.

The nurture argument is that we are born as a *tabula rasa* (a blank sheet), and we learn every movement, thought and belief from that moment. Vulnerability to developing anxiety is primarily a social factor: repeated negative events, observed or experienced, teach the individual to anticipate failure and, thus, lead to an anxious state. Behavioural theories of anxiety acquisition are based on the nurture paradigm: we learn to be anxious, we are not born that way.

Cognitive and psychodynamic theorists combine nature and nurture as an explanation for anxiety acquisition. They acknowledge physiological vulnerability, a predisposition to experience events in a way that influences perceptions, thoughts and, consequently, experiences. Psychological vulnerability to anxiety is thought to be related to attributions with regard to the intense arousal or response experienced. If the arousal is unpredictable, that is, it could happen at any time, and one is unable to explain it, then one is likely to feel more out of control and become anxious. Biological vulnerability then coincides with a social or psychological vulnerability to develop anxiety.

The Prevalence of Anxiety

Many individuals each year seek help for what is broadly construed as anxiety or nervousness. The prevalence of generalised anxiety in the United States, on the basis of the Epidemiologic Catchment Area survey, is 4 per cent (Barlow, 1988). This finding suggests that anxiety disorders represent the single largest mental health problem in America. Studies in Britain have also been conducted and reveal that the percentage of the population presenting with an anxiety disorder consist of a majority of females. As part of a national survey in the British Isles, Burns and Thorpe (1977) interviewed 963 agoraphobics: it was found that 88 per cent were women. The explanations put forward for this finding relate to culture, developmental differences, coping mechanisms and endocrinology. It is suggested that it may be more culturally acceptable for females to express fear, that males are taught to be 'tough' and overcome avoidance behaviour in early development. On the other hand, the sex difference may be explained by the fact that coping styles are different for men and women. Females may cope with anxious states by using avoidance behaviour and males by using alcohol. While these coping responses are maladaptive in both sexes, they result in different categories of diagnoses being applied to males and females. The endocrinological explanation suggests that females may be biologically more susceptible to panic: it is acknowledged that hormonal levels, which tend to be more variable in women, can affect mood state and so may affect perceptions of threat in a negative way. It may be that a combination of these factors operate to produce the data demonstrating that more women present with anxiety than men.

Anxiety Presentation/Secondary Anxiety

Anxiety presents itself in the consulting room in a variety of guises:

- a specific phobia may be cited as the main problem
- inability to cope, at work or at home, may be the major difficulty experienced
- worries about health may be reported, along with aches and pains that have been found to have no medical basis
- recent major loss or trauma may be reported as the overwhelming difficulty
- depression may be cited as the main problem
- obsessive and repetitive behaviour may be the main presenting problem

Anxiety can be secondary to another major disorder: for example, although excessive alcohol consumption can be a maladaptive response to anxious states, it is also known that drinking makes the person more susceptible to anxiety and symptoms associated with anxiety (see Chapter 4). Another example is the individual with a diagnosis of schizophrenia who may experience extreme anxiety as a result of a delusional view: for instance the person may fear that an outside force of some kind will control his or her movements (see Chapter 9). In these cases, the primary presenting problem is not an anxiety state; anxiety is considered to be secondary to the main disorder.

Any condition of which the individual is aware, and which reduces the ability to function normally or as desired, may produce some anxiety. It may be considered almost inevitable that one would worry if one were ill in any way, and as such, anxiety would be expected to be present to some degree. However, this secondary anxiety could develop to a stage that is debilitating by itself, that is, detrimental to functioning and interfering with the management of any other disorder present. In some cases secondary anxiety will require treatment and attention. For example, a young woman undergoing treatment on a sub-fertility program became very anxious about her general health and the possible success of the intervention. This anxiety resulted in muscle tension and physical responses that interfered with the sub-fertility treatment. It was necessary to help her reduce tension and develop strategies to cope with her fearful thinking.

Theories of Anxiety

Outlined here are some of the major approaches which attempt to account for the origin and maintenance of anxiety. The approaches outlined constitute those responsible for the commonest approaches to treatment currently utilized in the disorder of anxiety.

Biological Theory of Anxiety Acquisition

While most theorists acknowledge the role of neurobiology in both anxiety and emotion, some consider it to be a primary factor in the origin and maintenance of such states. Eysenck proposes a biological theory of personality that is based on different levels or intensities of cortical arousal (1967). Positive or pleasant emotions are associated with moderate levels of arousal while negative or unpleasant emotions are associated with arousal that is either too high or too low. This, according to Eysenck, motivates individuals to seek moderate levels of arousal and to avoid extremes. Level of cortical arousal at resting state, that is, when one is not emotionally or physically aroused, is biologically determined and therefore varies across individuals. Extravert personalities are postulated to have a low level of arousal at resting state and are thought to seek out higher levels of arousal. Introvert personalities will find their optimal levels of arousal at a much lower level of stimulation according to Eysenck's theory.

It is postulated that neurotic individuals possess the characteristic of intense nervous system activity and very slow rates of habituation (that is, poor or slow learning ability). Without the ability to habituate it will take an individual a long time to become accustomed to something and intense nervous system activity means that the individual's response level is strong. Thus, anxiety is seen as resulting largely from the interaction of individual cortical arousal level and nervous system reactivity. Anxious individuals are thought to have both high resting levels of cortical arousal and high auto-nomic nervous system activity.

What has become known as the 'fight or flight syndrome' is an attempt to explain anxiety in terms of nervous system reactivity. As in most biological explanations there is a strong evolutionary factor: it is stated that human beings developed a physiological reaction to external danger signals that was designed to enable the individual to fight with great strength or flee with speed. This kind of reaction was appropriate when human beings were hunters in a world populated with numerous larger, free-roaming creatures. The human system attempted to maximise survival by developing a physiological reaction that optimised successful combat with these larger and stronger creatures. Essentially, in response to a danger signal the body emits adrenaline. This activates four main physical responses: heart-beat is increased to pump blood more effectively to muscles; breathing quickens in order to take more oxygen into the blood; energy is redistributed within the body, away from the head and trunk and out to the limbs; and, finally, in the face of increased bodily activity, it is necessary for the cooling system to be activated and so sweating occurs. The four physical reactions described are frequently reported by patients suffering anxiety: increased heart-beat or breathing, fluttering in the stomach or dizziness and excessive sweating (see case example in the Introduc-tion to this chapter).

The danger signals in today's society do not normally require this intense physiological reaction for us to cope effectively. However, when our system detects a signal of danger it instinctively reacts with the 'fight or flight syndrome'. This nervous system activity produces physical sensations that alarm the individual further. This added fear of symptoms increases the level of danger perceived by the physical system. This is hypothesised to be the biological basis of what is termed a panic attack: a vicious circle of fear producing symptoms which increase fearfulness and escalate or maintain the physical distress. The biological theorists postulate that this physical distress becomes associated with particular phenomena and so explain the acquisition of irrational fear. Drug treatment may be used to reduce the system's reactivity and relaxation therapy may be used to enable the individual to learn to control the physical response. While behavioural associations are acknowledged in the biological account of the acquisition of fear, and negative-thinking patterns recognised, the biological theorists see the primary factor to be the nervous system and its reactivity.

Behavioural Theory of Anxiety Acquisition

Behavioural theories of the acquisition and maintenance of anxiety are based on theoretical explanations of how we learn. To understand the concepts employed by behaviourists to describe the origin of anxiety it is necessary to consider the two main learning theories known as *Classical Conditioning* and *Operant* or *Instrumental Conditioning* (see Chapter 1).

Classical conditioning. This theory originated with the work of Ivan Pavlov early this century, who was studying salivation in dogs. In the course of these experiments Pavlov observed that not only did the dogs salivate in response to the presence of food but also in response to whatever they strongly associated with food. So, for example, a bell would ring just before the dog was presented with food; eventually the animal learned to associate the sound of the bell with food and so would salivate in response to hearing it (before seeing or smelling the food itself). The dog was, therefore, *conditioned* to expect food whenever he heard the bell. In this example the food is what is known as the *unconditioned stimulus*, while the bell with which it was paired is the *conditioned stimulus*. Salivation in response to food is the *unconditioned response* and in response to the bell it is known as the *conditioned response* (see Chapter 1 for further details).

To understand how classical conditioning theory attempts to explain how one learns to be anxious, let us take the example of a road traffic accident and the responses that might occur in this situation. Let us imagine that a bus has collided with a car and one of the bus occupants panics and is made very worried or anxious by the event. This bus occupant may strongly associate buses with this feeling of panic or anxiety. Thereafter, upon seeing a bus or entering a bus this person becomes frightened or worried. In this example the road traffic accident is the unconditioned stimulus (UCS) and the bus occupant's panic is the unconditioned response (UCR). The bus itself, having been strongly associated with the anxiety experienced by the occupant, becomes the conditioned stimulus (CS) which can now produce the conditioned response (CR) of anxiety.

The strength of the fear acquired (the CR) relies on the number of associations between the CS and the UCS and also on the intensity of the experience of fear. Certain conditions have been found to increase the likelihood of anxiety of fear developing: confinement is one (Eysenck and Rachman, 1965) and would be a factor offered to explain the single-event learning that occurred in the collision example mentioned above: the bus occupant was confined within the bus at the time of the collision and could not avoid the danger. Repeated presentation of the CS may also lead to increases in responsiveness. Through repeated presentation the person becomes sensitised to the stimulus and so we have the process of sensitisation.

Extinction of a conditioned response is said to occur when the CS is repeatedly presented without the UCS: for example, when travelling on the bus does not lead inevitably to a collision. The CR will occur at first, but with repeated presentation of the CS (and the absence of the UCS) the magnitude of the CR diminishes. Thus the association between the CS and the CR is extinguished.

Habituation is another frequently used term within the learning theory paradigm. The habituation process is similar to that of extinction in that it refers to a breakdown in association, but in this case between the UCS and the UCR. Repeated experience of the UCS causes the strength of the UCR to reduce and eventually be extinguished. To remain with the bus collision example: the bus occupant gets so used to collisions that s/he no longer responds to them with panic or fear. The process of habituation has been used to explain behaviour observed during wartime: people became so used to air raid sirens that they no longer feared them and sometimes did not heed them at all.

The second process which attempts to explain how anxious responses arise is termed *operant* or *instrumental conditioning* (see Chapter 1). In this process the individual involved is considered to be *instrumental* in determining what happens. The individual (for example, the unfortunate bus occupant) learns that avoiding the CS (the bus) reduces the CR (anxiety): avoidance behaviour, therefore, results in feeling secure and so this behaviour is reinforced. The *reinforcement* is the avoidance behaviour and the *reinforced response* is a feeling of security or a reduction in anxiety. Therefore, it is postulated that a two-process learning has occurred: the bus occupant has learned to associate buses with an anxious feeling and has also learned that avoiding buses results in feeling secure. Behaviour patterns, such as avoidance of the fear-provoking object, which successfully reduce fear are likely to be repeated and increase in strength. This two-factor learning theory was proposed by Mowrer (1939) to explain the origin and maintenance of anxiety.

Evidence for the conditioning theory of fear acquisition was drawn from a number of sources, including studies of the development of anxiety states in combat soldiers and clinical observations (for example, dental phobias). But the strongest and most systematic evidence was drawn from a multitude of experiments on laboratory animals. However, whether laboratory experiments on animals can be generalised to non-laboratory situations with humans is debatable: the demonstration that fear can be induced in animals by a conditioning paradigm, in a contrived environment, does not necessarily indicate that this is how animals or humans ordinarily acquire fears.

The evidence that combat soldiers developed fears and anxieties as a result of traumatic incidents (e.g., Flanagan, 1948) seemed consistent with conditioning theory. However, conditioning theory does not account for why only a small number of combat soldiers developed these fears: many who had the same experiences did not acquire lasting fears. Furthermore, fears that develop gradually (for example, social fears) cannot be traced to specific occurrences and so often are not fully accounted for by conditioning theory.

The failure of people to acquire fears in theoretically fear-provoking situations (such as air raids) is one of the major criticisms of the conditioning theory of the development of anxiety. It has been found that it is difficult to produce conditioned fear reactions in human participants, even under controlled laboratory conditions. The notion of habituation and the addition of sensitisation are offered by learning theorists as a resolution to these criticisms (Watts, 1979).

In theory, any object should be able to become a CS but Seligman (1971) showed that this was not the case. The notion of preparedness was postulated to explain why some stimuli were more likely to become conditioned (Seligman, 1971). Seligman explained the non-random distribution of the fear of spiders and snakes, for instance, with the notion that these insects/reptiles are *prepared stimuli*. He suggests that human beings are predisposed to develop strong, persisting fears of them. This preparedness, it is proposed, combined with the right conditioning process will result in the development of anxiety. However, clinical data tell us that a significant amount of phobic people recount histories that cannot be accommodated by conditioning theory. It is argued that some fears may be induced by information-giving, from society and parents.

Behavioural theorists propose that another way that one can learn to be anxious is by observing significant others in our life and basing our behaviour on theirs. This form of learning is termed *modelling*: one models the behaviour and reactions of another. This vicarious learning process is offered by conditioning theorists as a resolution to criticisms of the theory with regard to why some people do not develop fears when they might be expected to. It is suggested that fears can be reduced by vicarious processes, such as modelling, in the same way that they can be learned (Rachman, 1968). For example, in therapy the technique of the therapist walking unafraid into the feared situation is often used to model the safety of such an activity to the patient. In group work, patients watch other sufferers overcome fears and model their behaviour on this success.

Conditioning theory cannot easily account for disorders where it is not possible to clearly identify the conditioned stimuli, for example in generalised anxiety. It is proposed that secondary gain may be a factor here: reinforcement may be given for displaying fear. For example, the husband of a woman with generalised anxiety may, through his concern for her, pay her a lot more positive attention. This increase in attentiveness may unwittingly reinforce her behaviour.

Conditioning theory as an explanation for the development of fears has resulted in a number of treatment procedures subsumed under the title of *behaviour therapy*. Behaviour therapy's main objective is to break the association between the CS and the CR; thus the frightened bus occupant is repeatedly exposed to or presented with buses, but hopefully without the recurrence of a collision (that is, the UCS). The hoped for result is that the bus occupant will learn that buses are not inevitably associated with collisions and the fear and anxiety (the CR) will reduce and disappear. This is the process of extinction mentioned above. It is an attempt to desensitize the individual to the CS. Systematic desensitization often includes instructions to the individual on how to relax. This process has been termed *reciprocal inhibition* (Wolpe, 1958) and is a term borrowed from physiology. The reciprocal inhibition process is where one physical or emotional state (for example, relaxation) will inhibit another (anxiety). Thus in systematic desensitization the repeated events of evoking small amounts of fear and immediately suppressing them with relaxation will result in fear reduction (that is, therapeutic benefit). It assumes an incompatible relationship between relaxation and fear. However, it has been noted in some studies that there can be failure to extinguish a response (Rachman, 1990) and in spite of exposure to the stimulus the fear did not reduce. Conditioning theorists attempt to explain this with the notion of sensitisation.

A further criticism that arises from clinical studies is the lack of synchrony between emotional and behavioural responses: in fact one study demonstrated remarkable desynchrony. On the clinical application of desensitisation to reduce fear it was found that a person, whose behaviour had markedly improved, did not report feeling any better (Rachman, 1990). It is postulated that cognitive factors may operate also to maintain fears, and the notion of secondary gain is offered as one reason to explain such findings.

It is proposed by behaviourists that the individual learns to be anxious via a number of possible processes, such as the strong association of reactions or feelings with an event or place, or reinforcement of particular behaviours within a certain context, or by observation of the reactions of significant others in one's life.

Cognitive Theory of Anxiety Acquisition

Cognitive theorists postulate that the primary factor in the origin and maintenance of anxiety is the thinking process: cognitions, that is one's thoughts, determine one's reactions (Beck, 1985). According to *cognitive theory*, it is the way an individual appraises a situation and thinks about it that determines the emotional and physical response to that situation; it is acknowledged that two individuals can undergo exactly the same process of events and yet, because they view the situation differently, each will have experienced a very different impact.

According to cognitive theorists, one is anxious because of perceived threat. It seems clear, at a simple level, that if we perceive a particular phenomenon in a very negative way, we are more likely to be adversely affected by it; we are more likely to worry and more likely to feel apprehension.

A number of cognitive processes have been described attempting to explain the development and maintenance of an anxiety state. Some of these processes incorporate physiological factors and behavioural factors; these factors are considered in terms of their effect on thinking, but it is the cognitions themselves that are considered to have the primary impact on emotional reactions.

It is postulated that if the individual has a negative view of his/her physiological response, anxiety will increase as will negative thinking. Negative attributions to the physiological response, for example interpreting faster breathing rhythms as being *unable* to breathe, will result in intense anxiety. This misinterpretation model is based on Clark, *et al.*'s (1985) cognitive model of panic states. The objective of therapy, based on this model, is to reproduce the feared physical sensations in the consulting room so that a non-catastrophic interpretation of the symptoms may be encouraged. For example, the patient is instructed in hyperventilation and is encouraged to observe the effects of overbreathing. These effects are then compared to the experience of a panic attack, and the patient is guided to the conclusion that hyperventilation contributes to the symptoms experienced. The patient is then instructed in a breathing technique to control hyperventilation. The objective is that the patient learns that these sensations are not due to an impending medical crisis and, in addition to learning a strategy to control the symptom, changes the negative attributions previously held.

Beck's (1985) model of the cognitive processing proposed to be involved in the production of the anxiety syndrome may be broken down into three steps: *primary appraisal, secondary appraisal* and *reappraisal.* These terms were first used by R.S. Lazarus (1966) and are employed by Beck to describe his cognitive theory of the anxiety state. The primary appraisal is the first impression in which the individual assesses the potential threat. This may be reinforced or modified by a preexisting *cognitive set.* The cognitive set is basically how one is predisposed to think; for example, if one is thinking negatively about one's environment then one is likely to have a predisposition to make negative assessments. Beck argues that it is during the primary appraisal that one assesses whether the threat directly affects one's vital interests. The result is that vital interests are affected then the individual has what Beck calls a critical response. This critical response may be produced by a range of situations, from a potential future disaster to an immediate threat to life.

While the primary appraisal is taking place the individual is making a secondary appraisal and is assessing possible resources for dealing with the potential threat. Secondary appraisal is where the individual is evaluating internal resources for protecting or deflecting the possible damage that might result from the threat. The example Beck uses to illustrate primary and secondary appraisal is that of a youngster confronted with a bully in the playground: the youngster not only assesses the size and harmfulness of the bully but also assesses the resources at hand for protection or flight. Beck postulates that the level of anxiety experienced is dependent on these two appraisals: in the case of a phobic state, for example, primary and secondary appraisal of going out alone may result in negative assessments with regard to potential harm and the individual's own ability to cope. However, it is often observed in the clinical setting that an agoraphobic will go out with a trusted significant other. The secondary appraisal in this case results in a positive assessment of resources to cope because of the presence of a caretaker.

Beck states that the cognitive appraisal of the individual is not applied in any conscious way; rather the appraisals and reappraisals occur automatically. The third stage, reappraisal, is where the individual estimates the severity of danger and as a result may have what is termed a hostile response: whether the individual reacts with flight (due to anxiety) or fight (due to anger) depends on the level of self-confidence. A hostile response may also occur if the individual perceives that s/he is trapped, in which case the fight reaction results from anxiety rather than anger.

Self-confidence is considered to be a key factor in the appraisal of threat and may be affected by external factors such as the assistance of a caretaker: agoraphobics' confidence in their ability to cope is increased if someone they trust accompanies them into the feared situation. Positive thinking is considered to increase one's sense of self-efficacy, or self-confidence and negative thinking can reduce one's belief in one's ability to cope. Our thinking is, therefore, postulated to affect how we react in threatening situations. Our reactions, in turn, can affect our performance in the situation and this performance will feed back to either confirm or reduce self-efficacy.

This feedback loop, or vicious circle, may be illustrated by considering an individual in the act of public speaking. The individual may be concerned to make a good impression and so a good performance is of the utmost importance: the cognitive set may now predispose the individual to be critical of his or her own performance. If the person estimates that there is a good chance of getting it wrong, and is feeling inadequate with regard to coping with this possibility, then anxiety will occur. If, during the speech, this person makes a slip, this flaw in performance increases anxiety, which in turn increases the potential to make further mistakes. Eventually there may even be an audience reaction to these mistakes; this also feeds into the vicious circle to increase anxiety.

Anxiety is maintained within the vicious circle until an appraisal of the situation takes place that restructures the perception of the threat. If the public speaker decides that his flaws in performance are not important and may not even be noticed, then his cognitive focus has shifted from negative to positive and anxiety is likely to reduce. A reduction in anxiety can result in more positive appraisal and less likelihood of flaws in performance. Cognitive therapy in the case of anxiety focuses on negative thinking (especially negative appraisals) and attempts to shift this to a more positive appraisal: this is known as *cognitive restructuring*. Cognitive restructuring is a therapeutic approach that may also be used with depressed patients though it would not generally apply to specific contexts as in the case of an anxious patient.

People generally accept that, while it may be difficult, it is possible to change behaviour. Most people, at some point in their lives, attempt to give up a bad habit of one kind or another. When it comes to how we think, however, there is often a belief that thinking is involuntary and therefore cannot be changed. 'That's how I think. I can't help it!' is often heard both inside and outside the clinician's consulting room. In fact, it is argued that we learn to think in much the same way as we learn to behave: our perceptions and cognitions are shaped by experience. As may be seen from the vicious circle described above, it is possible for our thinking to shape our experiences and so change how we think can be important. It may be said that while we cannot change the world, we can perhaps affect how it impacts on us by changing how we think about it. For example, if we were to think always of the possibility of threat without taking into account the probability of it, we would be likely to be continuously anxious (as almost anything is possible). Most irrational thinking focuses on possibilities and uses this to justify the cognitive activity and the consequent behavioural activity. For example, if one feared that the roof would fall in and considered the possibility alone, then that fear would not be easily argued away (ceilings do fall in — it is possible). However, most individuals consider the probability of the roof caving in and quite rightly assess the danger as minimal given the very low probability of occurrence. Appraisals of potential threat, therefore, need to take into account probability as well as possibility.

Physiological factors are also taken into account in the cognitive theory of anxiety states. Beck recognises anxiety as complex responses with evolutionary, biological, emotional and cognitive components. It is acknowledged that the most basic emotions are innate, survival oriented responses to an environment that has changed greatly over the course of evolution.

The locus of the problem in anxiety disorders is where reality is continually interpreted as dangerous. Information about oneself, the world and the future is continually processed in a distorted way as dangerous. Consequently, states of anxiety are associated with automatic thoughts and images relevant to danger. These thought processes trigger physiological and emotional components of the anxiety response. It is under conditions where emotions are inappropriate or exaggerated that Beck emphasises the importance of cognitive factors. Therapy is directed at altering these automatic thoughts and the underlying misperceptions responsible for distorted processing of information.

Some cognitive theorists (for example Spielberger, 1985) view anxiety as a trait: the individual has a disposition to experience anxiety frequently or to be anxiety-prone. This view of the anxiety syndrome is primarily concerned with cognitions but relates the nature of thinking to innate and learned processes which may be predispose the individual to be more fearful. A vulnerability factor, that is the predisposition to attribute negative outcomes to anticipated events and to own physical response, is recognised as the core of the anxiety syndrome. When one feels threatened one feels more vulnerable and this affects the appraisals that are then processed.

Cognitive theory has the explanatory power to account for irrational anxiety, because the cause of anxiety is seen to reside in faulty processing of information rather than a clear, rational perception of threat. It is not unusual for individuals to report that their fears are irrational, yet this knowledge, or insight, does not stop continuous thoughts of threat and impending doom. The problem, as Beck sees it, is that there is a tendency to overestimate danger and underestimate the ability to cope. Individuals in therapy often come to realise that it is their thinking that frightens them, not the so-called feared stimulus. For example, when a patient is instructed to examine the elements of danger to them in open spaces, or in a supermarket, they are often unable to identify them: yet his/her thinking has assumed a danger element.

Psychodynamic Theory of Anxiety Acquisition

Psychodynamic theory is concerned with the unconscious. Events that have occurred early in life and which have had an impact on the individual's emotions, are stored in the unconscious and are postulated to affect the adult's functioning (see Chapter 1).

The disorder of anxiety occurs when one has thoughts or feelings that one cannot cope with, when external demands or internal impulses represent a major threat. Psychodynamic theorists postulate that anxious feelings arise from internal conflicts or impulses of which the individual is not consciously aware. In other words, the origin of the anxiety is in the unconscious, and the feeling is triggered in the present by a variety of associations. Freud stated that missing someone who is loved and longed for is the key to an understanding of anxiety. For example, early loss or separation, though not consciously remembered or thought of, may produce anxiety in the adult individual.

In psychodynamic theory anxiety is related to the persistence of remembered danger situations that seemed real at an earlier stage of development. For example, the developmentally immature fears of separation may be activated by the emergence of a symbolically linked situation currently present in one's environment. A young adult who lost his mother in childhood may have difficulty forming deep relationships with girlfriends: the psychodynamic theorist would hypothesise that this man was afraid to get close to another woman because he was afraid of the loss that might result.

In Freud's later reconceptualisation of anxiety in 'Inhibitions, Symptoms and Anxiety' (1926) one of the proposed functions of anxiety is to warn of a potential danger situation, which thereby triggers the recruitment of internal psychological and/or external protective mechanisms. The employment of effective psychological defense mechanisms is considered adaptive as it serves the purpose of protecting the individual and allowing a higher and more mature level of functioning. Anxiety may also be adaptive in recruiting help from others when there is real danger.

Sometimes defensive reactions are inadequate and lead to the formation of symptoms. The solution to the problem becomes the problem. These may include phobic or compulsive symptoms that are symbolically related to the unconscious wishes or fears that have generated the anxiety. So, for example, Freud might view anxiety about being alone in a raging storm as the possibility of unconscious separation fears. One is alone in the storm, cut off from others, rendered helpless. This may be eliciting a childhood anxiety about separation from a loved one when all those emotions would have been intensely felt.

Freud saw anxiety as the psychic reaction to danger. A situation can be defined as dangerous if it threatens a person with helplessness in the face of hazard. Anxiety is self-defeating or pathological when it is noticeable, intense, disruptive, and paralysing or when it triggers self-defeating defensive processes (also called symptoms).

All evidence for the psychodynamic theory of the acquisition of anxiety arises from clinical material, that is therapeutic contact with anxious individuals. Supporting evidence for the explanatory power of the theory is taken from reports of outcome of psychodynamic therapies which use the theory to drive the intervention employed.

Malan (1979) proposed a two-triangle model of psychotherapy in dealing with for example anxious individuals: the Triangle of Conflict and the Triangle of Person. These are represented standing on apex (see Figure 3.1): the Triangle of Conflict has at its three points defence, anxiety and hidden feeling. The Triangle of Person has other (O), transference (T) and parent (P) at its three points. 'Other' represents current or recent significant individuals and

Figure 3.1: Malan's two triangle model of therary (1979)

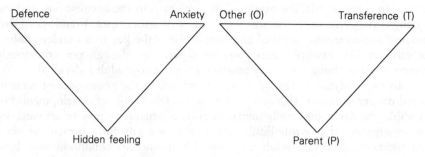

transference is a psychoanalytic term which refers to the feelings expressed towards the therapist within the therapy. It is hypothesised in psychodynamic therapy that feelings acted out with the therapist represent a transference of feelings from other important relationships in the client's life, particularly from the past (see Chapter 1). The aim of psychotherapy is to reach beneath the defence and anxiety to the hidden feeling and then to trace this feeling back from the present (O or T) to its origins in the past, usually in relation to the parents. The therapist does this by making interpretations, that is, suggesting what feelings might be hidden behind what the client is actually presenting with. The therapist enables the client to relearn how to tolerate and understand these hidden feelings within the psychotherapeutic relationship. Such relearning can lead to a reduction in the anxiety and the use of more adaptive, mature defenses; hence a reduction in symptoms. Therapy, therefore, provides a new more positive experience of how anxiety can be dealt with via this process of 'working through'.

The psychodynamic theory of anxiety acquisition offers a way of examining and understanding unusual fears and, perhaps just as importantly, provides a framework for understanding the therapist-client relationship. As with all other theories in their purist form, the psychodynamic theory does not appear to fully account for all the manifestations of anxieties and fears presented in our society.

An Integrated Model of Anxiety Acquisition?

John Bowlby's (1973) proposed model for the explanation of the development of anxiety states includes the notion that there is no single key. Instead he suggests that fear and anxiety are aroused in situations of many kinds. Basically, Bowlby's theory is an evolutionary one: fears are normal and phylogenetically determined. Ontogeny (the development of the individual) recapitulates phylogeny (the development of the human race): in other words, our development as individuals reflects the process of development the human race has been through.

Bowlby proposes that individuals have an innate propensity to make emotional bonds: once attachment is made it determines our emotional state. If the attachment is a secure one and we do not lose it at a vulnerable stage, then we are more likely to be healthy emotionally. Anxiety is seen to be related to fears of separation and an insecure attachment. Bowlby considers levels of, and susceptibility to, anxiety to be dependent on the quality of the infant-caregiver relationship in early childhood. This incorporates elements of the psychodynamic theory and also refers to a learning process with some regard to innate disposition.

More recently Bowlby (1988) states that change can go on throughout the life cycle. Therefore, there is potential to revise failures in the early relationship or to create anxiety in those who have had adequate early care. Because fear is seen to arise in a 'compound' situation, for example, being alone *and* in the dark *and* hearing strange noises, then an integrative or interactive model to explain its development might be more appropriate.

Eysenck (1976) advocated the interactive role of learning and conditioning in the formation and expression of biologically-based or innate emotions such as anxiety. There is recognition of the interaction between biological and cognitive systems, as well as the role of learning in the full expression of personality. It also seems reasonable to accept the psychodynamic theorists' view that early experience affects emotional development and the expression of these emotions.

An integrative approach in the therapeutic situation may also be more efficient with some anxious patients. When patients present in the consulting room in a state of distress because they are frightened of the physical symptoms that they are experiencing, it can be reassuring for them to have a way of understanding their body's reactions. This reassurance is often provided by explaining the 'fight or flight syndrome'. Because many of the same physiological reactions occur when running for a bus (increased heartbeat, increased breathing, maybe even sweating), it is often useful to use this analogy to reduce their fear of the symptoms. This constitutes a two-pronged attack on the patients dysfunctional state; it attends to the physical symptoms, making the patient feel 'listened to' and at the same time, it is an attempt to restructure their thinking. By shifting the negative explanation of the symptoms the therapist attempts to deal with patients' cognitions as well as their body's reactions.

When patients are in acute distress it is not always appropriate to take a purist approach and attend only to their thinking processes. Nor would it prove helpful to stop with the description of the 'fight or flight syndrome'. Using the theory of reciprocal inhibition and teaching patients relaxation techniques gives them a strategy to begin to combat their uncomfortable sensations.

In the above case, three different theories of anxiety acquisition are driving the therapist's intervention: biological, cognitive and behavioural. This is a common approach in short-term work with patients suffering panic attacks or acute anxiety. Other groups of patients may have different needs, however. For example, a patient with generalized anxiety may need to explore the underlying reasons for this state: cognitive and psychodynamic approaches provide a way of understanding and intervening with such a case. Exploring past and current relationships in the patient's life, and assessing his/her thinking processes, provides much information on what might be operating to create the anxiety.

Each approach to anxiety acquisition has unique tools to offer the therapist. For example, biological accounts of the anxious state offer patients a way of understanding what is happening to their own bodies. Behavioural techniques offer a way to begin making change and attempting to reduce the level of interference that may be caused by the anxiety. Cognitive assessment and intervention, on the other hand, provide a way of understanding and dealing with anxieties that are irrational and seem to have no single-event source. When working closely and repeatedly with someone it is important to have a way of understanding the therapeutic relationship: this is offered by the psychodynamic approach. While many approaches offer strategies for dealing with anxiety problems, the psychoanalytic therapy offers a way of exploring their source and increasing self-knowledge.

Given the range of possible presentations of anxiety, and bearing in mind Bowlby's notion that fear occurs in many forms, it would seem that the more tools available to aid understanding and intervention the better. The purist approach in research activity may be important in order to identify which tools are most effective with certain emotional states. However, as mentioned above, while anxiety presentation itself is variable, it must be borne in mind that the complexity of the human being in the consulting room is infinite. For this reason an integrative approach to treatment is often a necessity.

Recommended Reading

BARLOW, D.H. (1988) *Anxiety and its Disorders: The Nature and Treatment of Anxiety and Panic*, New York, NY: Guildford Press.

BECK, A.T. and EMERY, G. with GREENBERG, R.L. (1985) *Anxiety Disorders and Phobias: a Cognitive Perspective*, New York, NY: Basic Books.

RACHMAN, S.J. (1990) *Fear and Courage*, 2nd Edition, New York, NY: W.H. Freeman and Company.

References

BARLOW, D.H. (1988) *Anxiety and Its Disorders: The Nature and Treatment of Anxiety and Panic*, New York, NY: Guildford Press.

BECK, A.T. (1985) Chapters 3, 4 and 5 in BECK, A.T. and EMERY, G. with GREENBERG, R. *Anxiety Disorders and Phobias: a Cognitive Perspective*, New York, NY: Basic Books.

BOWLBY, J. (1973) *Separation: Anxiety and Anger* Vol. 2, London, UK: Hogarth.

BOWLBY, J. (1988) *A Secure Base: Clinical Applications of Attachment Theory*, London, UK: Routledge.

BURNS, L.E. and THORPE, G.L. (1977) 'Fears and clinical phobias: epidemiological aspects and the national survey of agoraphobics', *Journal of International Medical Research*, **5**, Supplement (1), pp. 132–39.

CLARK, D.M., SALKOVSKIS, P.M. and CHALKEY, A.J. (1985) 'Respiratory control as a treatment for panic attacks' *Journal of Behavior Therapy and Experimental Psychiatry*, **16**, pp. 23–30.

CROWE, R.R., NOYES, R., PAULS, D.L. and SLYMEN, D.J. (1983) 'A family study of panic disorder', *Archives of General Psychiatry*, **40**, pp. 1065–69.

EYSENCK, H.J. (1967) *The Biological Basis of Personality*, Springfield, IL: Thomas.

EYSENCK, H.J. (1976) 'The learning theory model of neurosis — a new approach', *Behaviour, Research and Therapy*, **14**, pp. 251–67.

EYSENCK, H.J. and RACHMAN, S.J. (1965) *The Causes and Cures of Neurosis*, London, UK: Routledge and Kegan Paul.

FLANAGAN, J. (1948) 'The aviation psychology program in the Army Air Forces, *USAAF Aviation Psychology Research Report No. 1*, Washington, DC: US Government Printing Office.

FREUD, S. (1926) 'Inhibitions, Symptoms and Anxiety, in *The Standard Edition of the Complete Works of Sigmund Freud*, **20**, James Strachey (Ed.) London, UK: Hogarth Press and the Institute of Psycho-Analysis, pp. 77–172.

IZARD, C.E. (Ed.) (1977) *Human Emotions*, New York, NY: Plenum Press.

LAZARUS, R.S. (1966) *Psychological Stress and the Coping Process*, New York, NY: McGraw Hill.

MALAN, D.H. (1979) *Individual Psychotherapy and the Science of Psychodynamics*, London, UK: Butterworths.

MOWRER, O.H. (1939) 'Stimulus response theory of anxiety' *Psychological Review*, **46**, pp. 553–65.

RACHMAN, S.J. (1968) *Phobias: Their Nature and Control*, Springfield, IL: Thomas.

RACHMAN, S.J. (1990) *Fear and Courage*, 2nd Ed. New York, NY: Freeman and Co.

SELIGMAN, M.E.P. (1971) 'Phobias and preparedness', *Behavior Therapy*, **2**, pp. 307–20.

SPIELBERGER, C.D. (1966) 'Theory and Research on Anxiety', in SPIELBERGER, C.D. (Ed.) *Anxiety and Behaviour*, New York, NY: Academic Press.

SPIELBERGER, C.D. (1972) 'Anxiety as an emotional state', in SPIELBERGER, C.D. (Ed.) *Anxiety: Current Trends in Theory and Research* **1**, New York, NY: Academic Press.

SPIELBERGER, C.D. (1985) 'Anxiety, cognition and affect: A state-trait perspective', in TUMA, A.H. and MASER, J.D. (Eds) *Anxiety and Anxiety Disorders*. Hillsdale, N.J.: Erlbaum.

WATTS, F.N. (1979) 'Habituation Model of Systematic Desensitization', *Psychological Bulletin*, **86**, pp. 627–637.

WOLPE, J. (1958) *Psychotherapy by Reciprocal Inhibition*, Stanford, CA: Stanford University Press.

YERKES, R.M. and DODSON, J.D. (1908) 'The relation of strength of stimulus to rapidity of habit formation', *Journal of Comparative Neurology and Psychology*, **18**, pp. 459–82.

Chapter 4

Alcohol and Drug Dependence

Jane Powell

Introduction

It is probably fair to say that all of us experiment with recreational drugs at some time or other in our lives. For the most part, however, these drugs are socially acceptable and do not become problematic; drinking alcohol in social situations to relax, taking caffeine in the form of tea or coffee to increase alertness, or smoking the occasional cigarette (inhaling nicotine) to calm ourselves down, are all examples or 'normal' drug use. These substances all exert 'psychoactive' effects, i.e. they alter our mental functioning via an affect on brain activity. Indeed, this is often the very reason for which we take them. They may, however, be taken in excessive amounts, and then can lead to a range of medical, social, and psychological problems.

As an example, heavy alcohol consumption is associated with damage to the liver (cirrhosis) and to the brain (alcoholic dementia, or Korsakoff's Syndrome). Over a period of frequent drinking, *tolerance* develops: the body is geared to maintaining equilibrium in its physiological processes, and therefore gradually adapts its functioning to accommodate the disturbance created by ingestion of the drug. This means that in order to achieve the original effects, the drinker must consume progressively larger quantities. Often associated with this is *physical dependence*, which arises because the adaptations made by the tolerant body means that it no longer functions normally without the alcohol; thus, for instance, when an alcoholic goes without drink for longer than usual, he or she experiences unpleasant withdrawal symptoms such as shaking, sweating, and even hallucinations. Tolerance and physical dependence characterise prolonged use of some, but not all, addictive drugs, and are often seen as significant obstacles to becoming abstinent.

Social functioning will be progressively disrupted as the drinker/drug user spends more and more time inebriated or suffering from the after-effects of drug use. At the extreme, addicts may be unable to hold down stable employment, and may become abusive or dismissive towards family and friends, eventually resulting in isolation and alienation. Lack of work creates financial difficulties, and, particularly if illicit and expensive drugs such as heroin or cocaine are used, the addict may become involved in criminal activity or prostitution. The psychological consequences can be equally grim. Having increasingly severe social and financial problems to contend with, and possibly physical ill-health as well, the addict is likely to become anxious and depressed. If, as is likely by this time, there are few people left to whom he or she can turn for emotional support, then alcohol or other drugs may be seen as a way of achieving temporary relief — and so a vicious circle is established.

There is a vast range of psychoactive drugs which can be used to excess, some illicit, but many legal. The effects they produce vary, and the consequences of heavy sustained use differ, depending partly on the particular drug and partly on personal characteristics of the drug user. Some people, for example, become intoxicated with much smaller amounts of alcohol than others, and this is influenced by their sex, their body mass, their recent daily intake of alcohol, and so on. Likewise, the likelihood that someone will turn to crime to finance drug use will be affected by factors such as opportunities for legal employment and personal moral code. Drugs can nevertheless be classified according to the psychoactive effects which they produce through their action on the central nervous system (the CNS, which includes the brain). One such classification system is described in the following section.

General Classes of Psychoactive Drug

The Royal College of Psychiatrists (1987) has listed five main categories of psychoactive drugs which are frequently misused: opiates, depressants, stimulants, hallucinogens, and minor tranquillizers. Examples of drugs falling into each category, with details of their main effects follow.

The Opiates

These include natural extracts from the opium poppy (e.g., morphine, codeine), drugs derived from these via some chemical modification (e.g., heroin), and a range of synthetic (man-made) compounds which have similar chemical structures (e.g., methadone, dihydrocodeine). Opiates are medically prescribed for pain relief, but also tend to produce pleasant mood states, and in some cases a transient euphoric 'high' or 'rush' which occurs shortly after drug ingestion. They are capable of inducing tolerance and physical dependence, and the withdrawal syndrome includes severe flu-like symptoms such as sweating, shaking, weakness, runny eyes and nose, aching, and nausea. As yet no permanent medical consequences have been directly associated with opiate use, though, as discussed below, lack of care in the way the drugs are used may lead indirectly to numerous health hazards.

General Depressants

The most common members of this class are alcohol and barbiturates, and they act by reducing (depressing) brain activity and thus decreasing mental exertion.

Early effects include decreased anxiety, and reduced control over behaviour, experienced as a relaxation of normal inhibitions and often manifest as excitability. Later, however, the sense of relaxation progresses into general sedation and eventually unconsciousness. Tolerance and physical dependence can develop, with unpleasant withdrawal symptoms which include shaking and hallucinations.

Minor Tranquillizers

These are the benzodiazepines, of which two of the most well-known are diazepam (a well-known brand-name is Valium) and nitrazepam (Mogadon). They have very similar effects to the general depressants, and are commonly prescribed for the relief of anxiety and insomnia. Over recent years, increasing attention has been drawn to their addictive potential, and whilst they were originally thought not to induce physical dependence, it is now clear that many long-term users do experience extreme physical discomfort when they attempt to cut down or stop.

Stimulants

These include, for example, cocaine, amphetamines ('speed'), and caffeine. They stimulate brain activity, leading initially to increased alertness, elevation of mood, and an enhanced sense of mental and physical energy. Heavy stimulant use can produce feelings of paranoia and occasionally frank psychosis. The existence of tolerance and physical dependence is more controversial than with the preceding classes of drug, though there is some evidence for a withdrawal syndrome characterised by general weakness and low mood (which may be severe).

Hallucinogens

Drugs falling into this category include synthetics such as LSD (lysergic acid diethylamide) and a variety of plant products such as mescalin and psilocybin ('magic mushrooms'). They accentuate sensory experience, often inducing bizarre perceptual distortions and hallucinations, and altering normal thought processes in a variety of ways. Their spectrum of effects can range from enjoyable fantasy to terrifying nightmare and dangerous delusions. Some individuals experience 'flashbacks' when drug-free, weeks or even months later, though these gradually disappear. There does not appear to be any tolerance or physical dependence.

Other Drugs

A comparatively small number of drugs do not fit into the above classification, and these include some of the synthetic 'designer' drugs (e.g., ecstasy). Three of the most widely used exceptions are nicotine, cannabis, and volatile inhalants. Nicotine is the psychoactive substance present in tobacco, and has complex effects, acting both as a stimulant and a sedative. It often induces some degree of physical dependence, though in comparison with the opiates and alcohol the physical withdrawal symptoms are mild. Cannabis is extracted from the Indian hemp plant, and has mixed depressant and hallucinogenic properties. Whilst it is clear that tolerance to many of its effects develops, there is some controversy over whether it also induces physical dependence. Volatile inhalants, such as glues, industrial solvents, and lighter fuels, can produce a wide variety and mixture of effects, including sedative and hallucinogenic experiences.

Medical Problems Associated with Drug Use

The most dramatic danger associated with use of many of the drugs listed above is the risk of fatal overdose: above a certain threshold, drug effects may be so powerful that they disable some aspects of normal body function and eventually cause death. For example, opiates can suppress the respiratory system to the point where inadequate oxygen reaches the brain. In some cases, taking the drug over a period of time can have a cumulative effect which endangers life, as in the case of smoking tobacco, which is associated with an increased incidence of lung cancer and heart disease, and heavy drinking which may lead to liver disease. In addition to hazards posed directly by the drugs themselves, there is also a long list of indirect problems arising as secondary consequences or from the way in which they are used. Many infectious diseases, for instance, can be passed on through unhygienic methods of drug administration, notably when the drug is injected and needles are shared between two or more users. Contaminated blood can be transferred in this way, leading to the spread of conditions such as hepatitis or HIV. Secondary consequences of drug use include increased risk of illness arising from reduced attention to self-care, or from inadequate nutrition. Another set of problems is associated with the illegality of certain drugs: in these cases the black market price of the drug may be high, increasing the likelihood that the user will finance his/her habit through risky criminal activity or prostitution.

Development of the Concept of Drug Dependence

Whilst media coverage often leads us to think of drug addiction as a modern day phenomenon, excessive drug use has occurred at most periods in history and in most cultures. In Victorian England, for instance, not only was alcoholism rife in the inner city slums, but opiates were used heavily in the form of laudanum, sold commercially for the relief of minor aches and pains. Prior to the eighteenth century, heavy drug use was usually considered a vice, and it was only towards the end of the nineteenth century that medical explanations which conceptualised 'inebriety' as a disease began to gain a significant foothold. These early medical models focused primarily on the phenomenon of physical dependence, identifying the onset of withdrawal symptoms as the main impediment to abstinence. This meant that substances such as alcohol and opiates, which have particularly florid withdrawal syndromes, became prototypical of addictive drugs, whilst others such as nicotine which either do not induce physical dependence or where the withdrawal symptoms are very subtle, were for a long time not considered to be addictive at all. To quote Rolleston (1926), a highly influential authority on drugs at the time, 'To regard tobacco as a drug of addiction is all very well in a humorous sense, but it is hardly accurate' (p. 963).

Increasingly, however, it has become recognised that people can develop psychological as well as physical dependence on drugs, experiencing a strong and apparently irresistible urge or 'craving' for the substance in question even when they are not in the grip of withdrawal symptoms. Indeed, in 1969 the World Health Organisation (WHO) gave greater weight to the psychological than to the physical symptoms, defining drug dependence as follows:

> A state, psychic and sometimes also physical, resulting from the interaction between a living organism and a drug, characterized by behavioural and other responses that always include a compulsion to take the drug on a continuous or periodic basis in order to experience its psychic effects, and sometimes to avoid the discomfort of its absence. Tolerance may or may not be present (p. 6).

There have been numerous hypotheses regarding the underlying causes of psychological dependence, each with their own implications for treatment. On the one hand it has often been suggested that certain personality traits may be associated with proneness to addiction; as yet there is no convincing evidence that this is so. Other theories focus on particular drug effects which the individual experiences, and conceptualise psychological dependence as an inability to cope with the void that cessation of drug use would leave. Whereas psychoanalytic models may postulate that the drug serves crucial symbolic functions, cognitive-behavioural formulations emphasise very practical needs such as dealing with stress, or acceptance within a particular sub-culture. This theoretical framework will be discussed at greater length later.

As it has been recognised that addiction to drugs is largely a psychological phenomenon, parallels have been drawn with other types of compulsive behaviour such as gambling or over-eating, and it is now common to hear the term 'addiction' applied to these behavioural abnormalities; similarly, the word 'workaholism' has been coined to describe what is perceived as pathological over-working. This terminology assumes that these superficially diverse behaviours are maladaptive responses to a range of underlying needs, dependence on drugs representing just one example of such a general process.

Approaches to Understanding and Treating Addiction

The Pharmacological Approach

It may at first sound counterintuitive that the problem of addiction to drugs should be treated by drugs. However, there are a number of pharmacological treatments which have already been found useful, or whose potential useful-ness is currently being explored. First, as discussed earlier, many addictive substances induce a state of physical dependence, such that if the addict misses a dose he experiences a physically uncomfortable set of withdrawal symptoms. This presents an early obstacle to quitting, and various types of drug may be prescribed in an attempt to help the addict through this stage. The drugs used vary according to the particular addictive substance, but the principles are similar for most substances. Taking opiate dependence as an example, many addicts find it impossible to stop all at once and so request help with a graduated reduction, where the dose is tapered off over a period of time. This period may be anything from a few days to several months, depending on the addict's preference and the policy of the prescribing physician. With small reductions, the intensity of the withdrawal discomfort is not so great; however, compared with a sudden cessation of drug use the symptoms will last for longer. An opiate addict can be transferred to any form of opiate for with-drawal purposes, since all opiates have similar effects. However, some types, such as methadone, have longer-lasting effects than others, such as heroin or morphine, and doctors often prefer to prescribe the former type because it does not need to be taken so frequently in order to allay withdrawal symptoms. Methadone also tends not to produce the euphoric effects that heroin does, and this is often given as another reason for transferring the addict to methadone. The main alternative to the graduated reduction method is to stop all opiate use at once, and to prescribe non-opiate drugs for a short period to provide symptomatic relief. Clonidine, for instance, can help to alleviate some opiate withdrawal symptoms such as sweating and shaking, and thus make the withdrawal syndrome easier to endure. This method has the advantage of minimising the duration of discomfort whilst reducing its overall severity; however the drugs used may produce side effects, thus limiting their usefulness. A fuller discussion of these withdrawal regimes is available in Ghodse's (1989) book.

Whilst help with physical withdrawal undoubtedly makes it easier for many addicts to actually become abstinent, it is far from a complete 'cure' for addiction. Hunt *et al.* (1971) reviewed the literature on relapse to drug use, and found that whether the substance in question was opiates, alcohol, or nicotine, about 70 per cent of addicts used drugs again within six months of successful detoxification. A more recent study by Gossop *et al.* (1987) with opiate addicts who completed detoxification in an in-patient setting revealed that the majority used at least once within six months of leaving and about 50 per cent became re-addicted within this period. Another form of pharmacological treatment has therefore been directed at protecting the addict after detoxification. One example here is the use of a drug called naltrexone in opiate addiction, which works to replace the drug. All drugs exert their effects by attaching themselves to receptors within the body — rather like putting a plug in a socket in order to run an electrical appliance. It follows, therefore, that if the receptors are already occupied then the incoming drug cannot plug itself in, and is eventually excreted from the body without having had any effect. Naltrexone is known as an *opiate antagonist*, because it attaches itself to the same receptors as opiates. It does not appear to produce any addictive effects in its own right, and if taken by a detoxified addict will 'block' the action of any opiates taken subsequently. This may therefore protect the addict against succumbing to a momentary impulse to use opiates, since he knows that he will not achieve the desired effect. For the addict who continues to take naltrexone on a regular basis, it potentially encourages him to develop a lifestyle within which drugs have no place. Each dose of naltrexone blocks the opiate receptors for a limited period of time, however, so that if the addict is really determined to use he or she simply has to wait until the naltrexone has passed out of his system. Similarly, alcoholics can take a drug called disulfiram (or Antabuse) which interacts with any alcohol which is consumed and causes nausea and vomitting. Clinical experience to date suggests that these treatment methods are primarily useful for a circumscribed set of highly motivated addicts, including professionals whose career development depends on remaining drug-free and women whose children are likely to be taken into care if they relapse.

Psychological Models

The social learning theory perspective. Social Learning Theory (SLT; Bandura, 1977) has its origins in the behavioural principles of *instrumental* learning (Skinner, 1938). In essence, this analyses animal and human behaviour in relation to its consequences: a behaviour which leads to a rewarding outcome tends to be repeated, whilst one which is punished tends to be avoided in future (see Chapter 1). The more frequently and/or intensely the behaviour is rewarded, the more habitual it becomes, and the more frequent or intense the punishment, the greater the likelihood it will be avoided. The application of this framework to understanding drug dependence is straightforward if we define dependence operationally as an excessive tendency to engage in drug-taking behaviour. This implies that the rewards to the addict are so salient, and sufficiently reliable, that he or she has become motivated to take the drug progressively more often in order to achieve these effects, eventually reaching a point where the desire overwhelms all else. Likewise, the decision to try and break a habit can be seen as reflecting the strength of its punishing outcomes. Since most habits produce mixed effects, some pleasant and others aversive, the addict may find him/herself in an *approach-avoidance conflict*, where motivation fluctuates between wanting to use and wanting to stop. Most of us can identify with such ambivalence, which accompanies many important transitions in our lifestyles.

As discussed earlier in this chapter, different classes of drug exert quite disparate pharmacological effects, so that the rewards which have contributed to development of the addiction will vary from drug to drug. The particular effects which are most powerfully rewarding will differ between individuals according to their personal needs and desires, which in turn will depend on some combination of their past experience (learning history), basic personality traits, and current life circumstances. To illustrate this, let us consider two people (Jack and Jill) both addicted to heroin. Heroin is an opiate and, as we saw earlier, has the dual effects of producing a transient euphoric 'high' and of alleviating emotional distress through its more protracted sedative action. Jack has used heroin recreationally about once a month for two years, and has always enjoyed the relaxation it produces. However, six months ago his girlfriend left him for another man, and he has become very depressed and anxious about the future. Such an intense reaction is typical of Jack: his parents divorced when he was a child, and since then he has been highly sensitive to perceived rejection. He has few other friends to help him through this difficult period, and has begun to use heroin on a daily basis because it gives him a short-term escape from his distress. If he seeks help in overcoming his addiction, it will be crucial to address his particular vulnerability to depression, since it is otherwise likely that when it recurs in the future it will put him at renewed risk of turning to drugs.

Jill, by contrast, considers herself to be a generally relaxed person with no current sources of worry, but enjoys the 'high' she experiences after injecting heroin. Although she, too, began to use recreationally, her social circle is now comprised predominantly of other drug users, and she has lost touch with non-using friends. Her intermittent use has therefore escalated to the point where she, like Jack, is taking heroin every day; she has become physically dependent, and she feels she would be lost without the excitement and social life attached to her drug use. The issues she faces in becoming drug-free are clearly very different from those faced by Jack, as discussed in more detail below.

Another basic principle of instrumental learning theory is that a specific behaviour will be more rewarding in some contexts than others, and that individuals are able to learn to distinguish favourable from unfavourable contexts. In theoretical terms, features which distinguish these contexts are known as *discriminative stimuli* (DS). Referring back to the two addicts described above, Jack will have learned that heroin use is more rewarding when he is feeling low in mood than when he is happy, and depression will have become a DS which triggers the response of drug use. Jill, on the other hand, may have learned that heroin is particularly exciting when used in company but not so thrilling when she is on her own: in this case, drug-using acquaintances will have become DS for her use.

Social Learning Theory (SLT) is an elaboration of instrumental learning theory which emphasises the important contribution of cognitive processes to goal-directed behaviour in humans. Whilst learning theory has its origins in the analysis of animal behavior, SLT enables these same principles to be applied to the understanding of human activity by taking into account our much more complex perceptual and reasoning skills. For instance, we do not need to experience the outcomes of every action directly in order to modify our behaviour, but can learn through observing other people or listening to what they say. Similarly, the significance of a particular occurrence will be perceived differently from one individual to another, depending on personality, learning history, alertness, etc., and the panoply of cognitive processes involved in perception will thus influence the impact that an event has on overt behaviour. The application of SLT to the understanding and treatment of addictive behaviours has been formalised by Alan Marlatt in a model which he has labelled 'Relapse Prevention' (Marlatt and Gordon, 1985). The RP model concentrates particularly on the factors which will influence the success or failure of an addict who attempts to become abstinent, but there is a great deal of overlap with processes which may be involved in the initial development of an addiction. The model is too complex to discuss completely here, and the interested reader is referred to the references by Marlatt himself, given at the end of this chapter. However, the main principles are as follows:

For any addict, there will be a range of DS for drug use. If, after becoming drug-free, he encounters one of these stimuli, then he will be at high risk of a lapse to drug use. The presence of one or more DS thus constitutes a *high-risk situation*. So, if Jack is feeling depressed or Jill meets one of her drug-using contacts, the likelihood that they will take drugs is increased. Marlatt argues that a cognitive process is involved here, the DS arousing *positive outcome expectancies* and thus triggering a motivation to use drugs. However, the ability of the addict to survive this threat to his abstinence will be influenced by various other factors including the strength of his motivation not to use, his knowledge of alternative strategies for coping with the situation, and his *self-efficacy*, i.e., his belief in his personal control or ability to master the situation. A shortfall in any one of these factors will increase vulnerability to relapse, as illustrated in Figure 4.1 below.

Figure 4.1: *A social learning theory model of relapse to addictive behaviour*

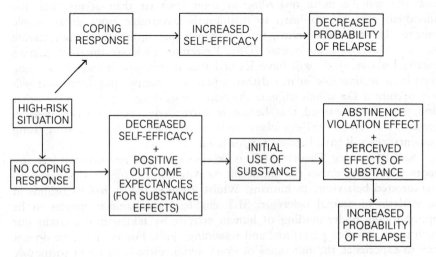

Taken from Cummings, Gordon and Marlatt (1980). Reprinted with kind permission of Pergamon Press.

For example, Jack may know in principle that an alternative strategy for combatting low mood is to listen to a favourite piece of music. If, however, he has temporarily lost sight of his reasons for wanting to stay drug-free (a common problem in treatment), he may be insufficiently motivated to try this strategy and may therefore go straight for the easier option of drug use. Likewise, if his self-efficacy is very low and he feels that he does not have the strength within himself to apply the effort that is needed to let the music work, then he is likely to dismiss it as a possibility. It is essential, then, that intervention not only focusses on equipping the addict with adequate strategies but also addresses the personal resources which allow him/her to use them effectively. Conversely, a high degree of self-efficacy combined with strong motivation to remain abstinent may be insufficient if the addict does not have the knowledge or skill to resolve the situation in some other way. Thus, for instance, Jill may be determined not to use again, and may feel confident in her ability to resist, but may nevertheless lapse when she meets a friend who urges her to use with him because she has not thought through or practiced how to resist this kind of social pressure. The fewer alternatives that an individual has accessible for dealing with a situation, the more salient his positive outcome expectancies for drug use will become.

The outcome of the high-risk situation, and the way in which the individual interprets it, has important consequences for his future progress. If he has successfully resisted drug use, and attributes this to his personal ability, then his level of general self-efficacy will be raised and he will feel more confident in his ability to handle future threats successfully. This increased self-efficacy will, as discussed already, make it more likely that he will attempt alternative coping strategies in other high-risk situations, and thus improve his chances of long-term abstinence. Assume, for instance, that Jack sees his ex-partner with another man. Instead of resorting to heroin use to block out his distress, he goes away for a long weekend to visit his sister, and to his surprise has an enjoyable time and is able to put the incident to the back of his mind. He returns feeling good about himself and optimistic that he will be able to help himself through future stresses in an equally constructive way. Whilst such a process may happen spontaneously, the fact that Jack has a deeply ingrained tendency to construe things negatively means that he will probably need substantial help and support in learning to approach his life in such a positive manner. This is consequently a central focus of his treatment.

By contrast, if he did in fact lapse, either because he was inadequately prepared with coping strategies or because he lacked the self-efficacy to try them out, then he may be at risk of a full-blown relapse to addictive use. Again, however, cognitive factors are important. Marlatt has identified one particularly destructive process, the *abstinence violation effect*. Here, the individual sees that his drug use is incompatible with his previous determination to remain abstinent ('cognitive dissonance'), and resolves this dissonance by assuming that some intrinsic personal quality makes abstinence impossible for him ('personal attribution'). He may tell himself, for instance, 'Addiction is a disease I have, which I can't shake off — so there's no point in trying any more.' Such an interpretation will clearly undermine his resistance to future temptations. A more productive assessment of a lapse would be to identify circumstantial factors which made it difficult to resist, permitting contingency plans for the future to be developed. Viewed in this way, lapses can be used as learning experiences.

There is a substantial amount of evidence to support the general principles of the RP model. By way of example, Cummings, *et al.* (1980) found that alcoholics, smokers, opiate addicts, gamblers, and overeaters were particularly likely to lapse when they experienced negative emotional states: 35 per cent of all lapses were identified as having been preceded by negative mood, with a further 16 per cent following some form of interpersonal conflict, and another 20 per cent being attributed to social pressure. These findings are consistent with the view that addictive behaviour is often engaged in because of its effectiveness in escaping stress, and suggest therefore that stress situations may be particularly risky to recent 'quitters'. Adding further weight to this, Litman, *et al.* (1984) assessed detoxified alcoholics prior to their discharge from hospital, and found that those who identified a wider range of strategies for dealing with stressful situations were likely to remain abstinent for at least six months.

What are the implications of the RP model for treatment? From the foregoing discussion, it is evident that there is no single treatment or educational package which can be applied identically with every client. Rather, the therapist must be aware of the many different factors which can influence attitudes to and expectations about use of a wide variety of drugs, and be willing to approach each individual's dependence with a mind free of assumptions about underlying factors. Within the broad theoretical framework, there are least four elements to developing an individual treatment, as follows:

1   Detailed assessment of the addict's personal risk factors and existing coping resources. Intervention will start with a reasonably extensive assessment, but information will continue to emerge throughout the treatment.
2   Helping the addict to identify alternative strategies for avoiding or coping with risk situations. These strategies may comprise both cognitive aspects (e.g., talking oneself through difficult issues, or challenging inappropriate assumptions) and behavioural aspects (e.g., taking up new leisure pursuits, or learning how to relax physically).
3   Enhancing the addict's self-efficacy and skill in using alternative strategies, for instance by assisting him to practise them and thereby identify potential difficulties so that these can as far as possible be ironed out.
4   Preparation for how to deal with a lapse. This might entail discussion of the abstinence violation effect, together with the development of a structured plan of what to do in such an eventuality (e.g., contact a particular person, go somewhere private for a period of reflection).

All of these four elements can take many different forms, depending on characteristics of the therapist, the patient, and the resources available. Most general cognitive-behavioural methods (see, for example, Kanfer and

Goldstein, 1986) are readily applicable within this field, and Marlatt and Gordon's (1985) book offers suggestions for approaching more specific problems such as the abstinence violation effect. The highly interactive nature of this type of intervention, where the therapist and patient work together to identify problem areas and evaluate different coping strategies, should generate a supportive atmosphere for the patient's efforts at change: this is clearly a vital component of the treatment process. Since the aim is for abstinence and psychological well-being in the long-term, beyond the limited duration of formal therapy, it is important that the patient should also be helped to establish durable social support outside the treatment setting, whether in the form of developing new non-drug-using relationships or of attending peer support groups such as Alcoholics/Narcotics Anonymous (see pp. 84–6).

The classical conditioning model.   Classical conditioning is the form of learning most closely associated with the work of Pavlov. His best-known demonstrations were with dogs, showing that when the sound of a bell reliably preceded the arrival of their food, they eventually began to salivate when they heard the bell (see Chapters 1 and 3). In the normal course of events, the smell and taste of food tends to elicit this reaction automatically (as an *unconditioned reflex* or UCR) whilst the sound of bells does not. Pavlov therefore deduced from his experiments that animals can learn about associations between two stimuli, so that one becomes a signal that the other is about to occur and triggers an anticipatory physical reaction. These learned reactions are largely involuntary, and are termed *conditioned reflexes* (CR); the stimuli that trigger them are referred to as *conditioned stimuli* (CS). The interested reader is referred to Gray's (1979) book for a more detailed description of classical conditioning principles.

The relevance of this type of learning to addiction was first suggested by an American physician, Abraham Wikler, who observed that several opiate addicts whom he had detoxified experienced renewed physical discomfort when they returned to the areas in which they had formerly bought and used drugs. Their symptoms resembled those of withdrawal, including for instance watering eyes and a runny nose. Wikler's explanation is shown schematically in Figure 4.2 (p. 82).

Briefly, the model is as follows: The withdrawal syndrome is a UCR which occurs when the drugs are metabolised by the body and lose their effect. Most addicts experience withdrawal symptoms repeatedly in the course of their addiction, since there are often delays in finding the drug, which means that the symptoms begin before the addict succeeds in procuring his next dose. Since the addict will react to the onset of symptoms by looking for and using drugs, a whole range of environmental cues may potentially become associated with the experience of withdrawal, including the places where the drugs are bought and used, and stimuli which are regularly present in those settings, such as drug-using paraphernalia (e.g., needles and syringes), fellow drug users or dealers, and so on. Through classical conditioning, these cues can become CS capable of eliciting withdrawal-like symptoms as CR. If this is true, then detoxification from opiates is not enough to ensure abstinence, because when

Figure 4.2: *Wikler's model of the role of classical conditioning in relapse*

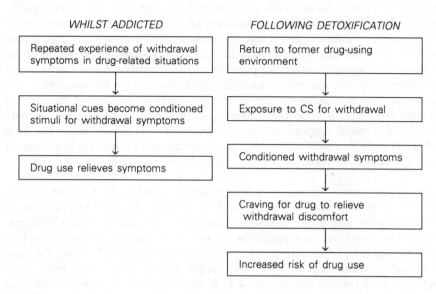

the detoxified addict encounters one of these cues his body will still react with the conditioned withdrawal response. This may put him at risk of relapse, as he knows that the quickest way of alleviating the symptoms is to take drugs. Wikler has therefore argued that the CR may elicit drug craving; clearly, whether or not a lapse actually ensues will be influenced by other factors such as determination to stay drug-free, possession of alternative coping strategies, drug availability, and so on.

A number of studies have yielded support for this analysis. First of all, experiments with animals and with humans have demonstrated that it is possible to produce classical conditioning of withdrawal symptoms in the laboratory. O'Brien, *et al.* (1975) studied current (i.e., non-detoxified) opiate addicts, and manipulated the onset of their withdrawal symptoms by giving them naloxone (an opiate antagonist drug which immediately displaces opiates from their receptors, thus causing the addict to experience withdrawal symptoms). Simultaneously with administration of the naloxone, an unusual odour was presented. This was repeated several times, in order to produce an association between the odour and the onset of withdrawal. In a subsequent test trial, the odour was presented in the absence of naloxone. Over half of the subjects still reacted with withdrawal symptoms, indicating that for these subjects the odour had indeed become a CS for a conditioned withdrawal response.

It has furthermore been shown in many studies that addicts react very differently from non-addicts when they are exposed to drug-related cues. For instance, Teasdale (1973) showed opiate addicts pictures of drug stimuli and neutral stimuli, and found that their ratings of withdrawal-like symptoms were much higher during exposure to the drug-related material. Other experiments, with both opiate addicts and alcoholics, have shown that physiological responses (e.g., heart rate, temperature) are greater to drug stimuli than to neutral stimuli, with non-addict control subjects tending to show little or no reaction. O'Brien and his colleagues in Philadelphia asked subjects to give ratings of their craving for drugs, and again found substantial elevations when drug-related material was presented. More details of these experiments can be found in O'Brien *et al.*'s (1986) review.

Several variations on Wikler's original theory have been proposed. Siegel (1983) has put forward an alternative explanation for the withdrawal-like symptoms elicited by drug-related cues, arguing that they are, in fact, conditioned *opponent processes* (OP). He has cited evidence that when drugs cause changes in normal physiological processes, the body reacts by producing effects opposite in direction to the drug effects, thereby suppressing them. These so-called opponent processes are adaptive, because they provide protection against potentially dangerous effects. For example, if a drug slows respiration rate, then at an extreme level breathing may stop altogether. The body's OP would be to *increase* breathing rate, counteracting the drug effect and protecting life. Siegel's view is that the OP which occur after drug ingestion can become conditioned to environmental cues, so that a detoxified addict may experience conditioned OP when he encounters drug-related cues. Because OP are the reverse of direct drug effects, they appear very similar to withdrawal symptoms.

In addition to the conditioned withdrawal and conditioned OP theories, there is also evidence that at least some individuals show conditioning of the direct drug effects. Thus, O'Brien's team has consistently found a minority of their subjects reporting an opiate-like 'high' during exposure to drug-related material. There is also clinical evidence of conditioned drug-like effects in the form of 'needle-freak' behaviour: some intravenous drug users report that if they are unable to find a supply of their drug, they will inject water instead and achieve some degree of pleasure or alleviation of withdrawal from this. It is plausible that conditioned drug-like sensations could also trigger craving in detoxified addicts via a 'priming' effect — effectively, whetting the appetite for a bigger, better effect.

Regardless of which type of symptom becomes conditioned, if it gives rise to a subjective desire or craving to use, and/or actually increases the likelihood of a lapse to drug use, such reactions should clearly become a target of intervention. Although there is little direct evidence as yet that addicts who experience such reactions have higher relapse rates, a number of studies suggest that the responses can be eliminated through a treatment based on conditioning principles, known as cue exposure. This involves exposing the addict to drug-related material, but restraining him from actual drug use so that the conditioned associations between the cues and drug effects are gradually weakened and eventually extinguished. In other words, the cue ceases to be a signal that drug effects are about to occur, and the anticipatory response (the CR) therefore dies away.

Bradley and Moorey (1988) exposed two opiate addicts and a solvent abuser to drug-related cues, and observed that their subjective craving gradually waned over the course of the exposure (*within-session habituation*; see Figure

Figure 4.3(a): Within-session habituation of craving ratings

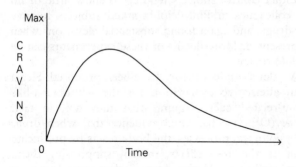

Figure 4.3(b): Between-session habituation of craving ratings

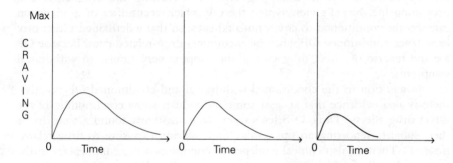

4.3a). A number of single-case reports have demonstrated that when addicts are exposed to the same stimuli for several consecutive sessions, the magnitude of subjective craving experienced declines from one session to the next (*between-session habituation*; see Figure 4.3b). Thus, Blakey and Baker (1980) worked with six individual alcoholics, systematically exposing them to situations associated with drinking and encouraging them to resist actually having an alcoholic drink. They found that the level of craving reported did drop from one session to the next, and five of the six patients managed to remain abstinent for at least two months. Their subsequent progress is uncertain, as further follow-up was not carried out. Likewise, O'Brien's team has conducted cue exposure treatment with opiate addicts (Childress, *et al.*, 1986) and found between-session habituation of craving, as have Bradley and Moorey (1988). Cue exposure therefore appears to hold promise as an approach to one aspect of addiction, and could provide a useful complement to the broader SLT approach which focuses on other underlying motives for using drugs.

The disease model. This discussion would not be complete without at least brief consideration of an opposing conceptualisation of addiction, that it is a disease (i.e., a disorder, presumed or known to have an organic cause, and largely beyond the individual's control; see Chapter 1). The most prominent advocate of this view is the Alcoholics Anonymous (AA) organisation. The disease model began to develop in the early 1900s, and reflected a transition from the prevalent perception of addiction as a vice. AA's original argument was that some people have a physical allergy to the intake of alcohol which causes them to react to a single drink with an intense craving for more, so that they have abnormal difficulty in limiting their consumption. The 'allergy' component of this argument has, scientifically unsupported, receded, but the more general concept of addiction as a 'disease of the will' has gained in strength and been broadened to apply to other forms of addiction. There is now a host of organisations associated with AA, including Narcotics Anonymous (NA) for other drug users, Gamblers Anonymous (GA), and various groups such as Al-Anon which provide contact for families of addicts. The remainder of this discussion will focus on AA as an example of the stance taken by all these groups.

In the absence of any known physical cure for the underlying disease process, AA has adopted a spiritual framework, calling on addicts to subjugate their own will to that of a 'higher power' which imposes a set of rules for structuring beliefs and behaviour. The 'higher power' is not necessarily identified as God, although some individuals with pre-existing religious convictions may well do so. When an addict engages with AA, he progresses through a set of twelve steps, each of which involves recognition and acceptance of a new spiritual/moral code. The addict effectively commits himself to a new way of life, one aspect of which is abstinence, and is given massive support for this conversion by the other AA members. There are various levels of support, via regular meetings held in the community, individual contact, and residential treatment where addicts progress through a very structured programme and move through levels of seniority in a rigid hierarchy. Deviation from the rules of the programme is harshly penalised, and the addict may be required to move *down* a tier in the hierarchy, or even be expelled. When addicts have completed the programme, there is often a system of half-way houses to facilitate their transition to a drug-free life in the community.

Alongside its spiritual emphasis, AA also encourages its members to use a range of strategies to help themselves in conforming to the new code of abstinence. These overlap noticeably with the practical interventions of the RP model, and include various cognitive manoeuvres, such as calling to mind the benefits of abstinence, or the aversive consequences of drug use, and behavioural tactics such as the avoidance of certain risky situations (e.g., pubs).

Whilst AA claims great success for its methods, very little scientific evaluation has been conducted. One of the problems in interpreting statistics concerning the progress made by addicts involved with AA or NA is that many of those who find it difficult or impossible to remain abstinent drop out of the treatment programmes. This means that those who complete the programmes tend to be the ones who remain drug-free, a pattern which is too easily taken as meaning that the programme has produced the success. In fact, of course, it may equally well mean that those who have the personal resources to succeed are better motivated to persist with their AA involvement; with AA and with psychological/medical interventions alike, success comes most easily for those who have fewest areas of personal weakness to begin with.

Integration

The most obvious conflict between the approaches outlined above lies in the fundamental disagreement between the disease and the SLT models concerning the degree of control an individual has over his addiction. AA argues that addiction is a disease over which, by definition, the individual has little control; the SLT model sees it as largely reflecting inadequate resources for coping with life without drugs, and stresses that the addict can actively take control by acquiring the resources, psychological or material, which will enable him to remain abstinent. The two theories are diametrically opposed, then, in the view which they encourage an addict to take of himself — victim or master. In terms of practical guidance, however, there is much overlap. Both approaches recommend a range of practical coping strategies for avoiding or dealing with the temptation to use, and clinically there is often a good working liaison between them. Thus, a psychologist applying SLT principles might well recommend a client to attend AA for the contact with successful abstainers, who will both provide a new non-using social network and serve as encouraging role models. Likewise, AA often values the specialised help psychologists can offer the individual in learning strategies which will aid him in adhering to their abstinence-oriented philosophy. Ultimately, of course, the approach which proves of most practical use to any individual addict will be strongly influenced by his/her personal preferences and belief system. Some individuals find themselves alienated by the quasi-religious framework promoted by AA, whilst others may be so psychologically vulnerable and lacking in social support or self-confidence that the SLT emphasis on personal mastery seems unrealistic and the affiliation offered by the AA disease model much easier to identify with.

The pharmacological approach is complementary to the other frameworks, which deal primarily with the difficulties of long-term abstinence. Too often, pharmacological treatments are identified with a very narrow 'medical' model, which sees addiction as a disease rooted exclusively in physical dependence. This represents an injustice to the majority of doctors working in the area who, through hard clinical experience, are well aware not only that withdrawal is merely the first step towards sustained abstinence, but also that the clinical effectiveness of any withdrawal regime depends on the psychological preparedness of the addict and the resources he has to draw on to tolerate these first difficult days. Indeed, the development of post-detoxification pharmacological treatments (naltrexone, disulfiram) is clear testimony to medical recognition of the more persistent impact of psychological needs and desires.

Thus, GPs often work in collaboration with other professionals to develop a structured plan for helping the addict through both the immediate difficulties of detoxification and the longer-term problems of remaining drug-free. So, for instance, the SLT model of addiction recognises the relevance of well thought-out reduction regimes in enabling people to tolerate the discomfort of detoxification. The emphasis, however, is on identification of psychological factors which may help or hinder the course of any withdrawal regime, with therapeutic input directed at developing necessary resources. On the basis of such an assessment, therapists working within this framework might well liaise with the prescribing physician to negotiate a withdrawal programme most likely to suit the individual patient (e.g., a short, sharp reduction versus a gentle, protracted one). Similarly, the idea of prescribing a pharmacological substance as a block to impulsive drug use originates as much in the psychological as in the medical analysis. The psychologist would, however, ideally couple the drug treatment with sessions for identifying any high-risk situations experienced during this period and helping the client to develop appropriate coping strategies.

Although the conditioning model of addiction has been derived from a different branch of learning theory, it too is easily accommodated within an overarching SLT model. Thus, it is possible that classical conditioning may account for a significant proportion of the craving experienced by detoxified addicts; but whether or not they respond to their craving by actually using drugs is one of the central concerns of SLT. Whilst one intervention is to extinguish conditioned responses via cue exposure, an alternative approach is to help the addict develop a repertoire of strategies to counteract the impulse to use. Furthermore, it is plain that conditioning cannot account for all of the temptations to use drugs, with social pressure, for instance, being another important influence. Even the firmest believer in cue exposure would currently see this as but one component of intervention.

Although these approaches to addiction seem to hold considerable promise for our future understanding of the mechanisms underlying drug and alcohol dependence and for offering effective rehabilitation, it is important to realise that systematic evaluation is urgently needed. The AA approach has very little scientific basis, and there is as yet no objective evidence that their framework actually does improve outcome. The underlying assumptions of the SLT and conditioning models have been better researched, and have received substantial support, but evaluation of their treatment implications is at a very preliminary stage. The same is true of the pharmacologically based treatments: although they have in general been shown to be medically safe, there is still little to indicate, for instance, whether one withdrawal regime is preferable to another, whether certain regimes are better suited to particular client groups, and so on. These limitations in our knowledge partly reflect the relative recency with which concepts of dependence have developed, and, with increasing social and political interest, it is to be hoped that more resources will be invested in identifying which treatments are effective as well as at simply increasing service provision.

Recommended Reading

GHODSE, H. (1989) *Drugs and Addictive Behaviour*, Oxford, UK: Blackwell Scientific Publications.

A useful overview of assessment and treatment of drug addiction from a variety of perspectives, and a good source of information regarding pharmacological issues specific to particular classes of drug.

GRAY, J.A. (1979) *Pavlov*, Glasgow, UK: Fontana.

A readable introduction to the history and principles of classical conditioning.

KANFER, F.H. and GOLDSTEIN, A.P. (Eds) (1986) *Helping People Change: A Textbook of Methods*, 3rd Ed. New York, NY: Pergamon.

This edited volume includes several chapters describing cognitive-behavioural interventions, many of which may be employed in the Social Learning Theory (SLT) approach, helping addicts acquire new skills or resolve problems which have contributed to sustaining their drug dependence.

MARLATT, G.A. and GORDON, J.R. (1985) *Relapse Prevention: Maintenance Strategies in the Treatment of Addictive Behaviors*, New York, NY: Guilford Press.

A well-written and detailed account of the SLT approach to addiction.

ORFORD, J. (1985) *Excessive Appetites: A Psychological View of Addictions*, Chichester, UK: Wiley.

A fascinating account of developments in the concept of dependence, this book considers differences and similarities between approaches to a range of addictive behaviours, including gambling, eating, and sexuality alongside substance use.

ROYAL COLLEGE OF PSYCHIATRISTS (1987) *Drug Scenes: A Report on Drugs and Drug Dependence*, London, UK: Gaskell.

A concise book summarising the basic issues in drug dependence, which also considers the socio-political dimension.

References

BANDURA, A. (1977) *Social Learning Theory*, Englewood Cliffs, NJ: Prentice-Hall.

BLAKEY, R. and BAKER, R. (1980) 'An exposure approach to alcohol abuse', *Behaviour Research and Therapy*, **18**, pp. 319–25.

BRADLEY, B.P. and MOOREY, S. (1988) 'Extinction of craving during exposure to drug-related cues: three single case reports', *Behavioural Psychotherapy*, **16**, pp. 45–56.

CHILDRESS, A.R., McLELLAN, A.T. and O'BRIEN, C.P. (1986) 'Abstinent opiate abusers exhibit conditioned craving, conditioned withdrawal, and reductions in both through extinction', *British Journal of Addiction*, **81**, pp. 655–60.

CUMMINGS, C., GORDON, J.R. and MARLATT, G.A. (1980) 'Relapse: Prevention and prediction', in MILLER, W.R. (Ed.) *The Addictive Behaviours*, New York, NY: Pergamon Press.

GOSSOP, M., GREEN, L., PHILLIPS, G. and BRADLEY, B. (1987) 'What happens to opiate addicts immediately after treatment: A prospective follow-up study', *British Medical Journal*, **294**, pp. 1377–80.

HUNT, W.A., BARNETT, L.W. and BRANCH, L.G. (1971) 'Relapse rates in addiction programs', *Journal of Clinical Psychology*, **27**, pp. 455–59.

LITMAN, G.K., STAPLETON, J., OPPENHEIM, A.N., PELEG, M. and JACKSON, P. (1984) 'The relationship between coping behaviours, their effectiveness and alcoholism relapse and survival', *British Journal of Addictions*, **79**, pp. 283–91.

O'BRIEN, C.P., O'BRIEN, T.J., MINTZ, J. and BRADY, J.P. (1975) 'Conditioning of narcotic abstinence symptoms in human subjects', *Drug and Alcohol Dependence*, **1**, pp. 155–23.

O'BRIEN, C.P., EHRMAN, R.E. and TERNES, J.W. (1986) 'Classical conditioning in human opioid dependence', in GOLDBERG, S.R. and STOLERMAN, I.P. (Eds) *Behavioural Analysis of Drug Dependence*, Academic Press.

ROLLESTON, H. (1926) 'Medical aspects of tobacco', *The Lancet*, **1**, pp. 961–65.

SIEGEL, S. (1979) 'The role of conditioning in drug tolerance and addiction', in KEEHN, J.D. (Ed.) *Psychopathology in Animals*, New York, NY: Academic Press.

SKINNER, B.F. (1938) *The Behaviour of Organisms*, New York, NY: Appleton-Century-Crofts.

TEASDALE, J.D. (1973) 'Conditioned abstinence in narcotic addicts', *International Journal of the Addictions*, **8**, pp. 273–92.

WORLD HEALTH ORGANISATION (1969) The 16th report of the WHO expert committee on drug dependence. WHO Technical Report Series No. 407. Geneva: WHO.

Chapter 5

Eating Disorders

Jean Mitchell and Helen Fensome

Anorexia Nervosa

Historical Overview

Although English language references to anorexia nervosa can be found in seventeenth century medical writings, the disorder was first described in detail in 1873, by Sir William Gull in England, and Dr Lasegue in France. Their two independent publications described a condition (named 'anorexia nervosa' by Gull) whereby young females were apparently anorexic in the absence of any observable organic illness. These individuals typically became hyperactive, were preoccupied with their bodies being thin, and would refuse food, even though severe emaciation and amenorrhoea (cessation of menstruation) were often consequences of their actions. Both Gull and Lasegue stressed the fact that they considered anorexia to be a psychological rather than a physical disease.

Historically, debate has focused on the issue of whether or not anorexia nervosa represents a distinct clinical entity, or whether it is a variant of other psychiatric illness, such as depression, schizophrenia, obsessive-compulsive disorder and hysterical disorder. A further debate has centred on whether or not anorexia nervosa represents a nonspecific symptom of a group of disorders linked only by the fact that significant weight loss occurs as a result of emotional problems. However, the contemporary viewpoint is that there is a syndrome of primary anorexia nervosa which has characteristic signs and symptoms that distinguish it from other causes of weight loss (Garfinkel and Garner, 1982).

What is Anorexia Nervosa?

Russell (1970) provided the following general definition of anorexia nervosa:

1 Behaviour leading to marked loss of body weight. A studied avoidance of foods considered to be of a fattening nature. Often but not

invariably the subject resorts to additional devices which ensure a loss of weight: self-induced vomiting or purgation, or excessive exercise. Occasional bouts of overeating may occur;

2 An endocrine disorder which manifests itself clinically by cessation of menstruation (amenorrhoea) in females;

3 A morbid fear of becoming fat which may be fully expressed by the subject or may be more explicit in her behaviour. To safeguard herself against what she calls 'losing control' — meaning not being able to stop eating — she strives to remain abnormally thin.

Thus the central feature of anorexia nervosa is an abnormally low body weight, maintained by an attitudinal and behavioural response that has been likened to a 'weight phobia' (Crisp, 1967). However, it is important to emphasise that although to the outside world the person suffering from anorexia appears rigidly overcontrolled, she will invariably see herself as being totally out of control. It is generally accepted, therefore, that the drive for thinness that is so characteristic of anorexia nervosa is secondary to concerns about being out of control (Bruch, 1973) or fears about the consequences of achieving a mature body shape (Crisp, 1970).

Another striking feature of anorexia nervosa concerns the observation that people with this condition typically exhibit a distortion of their body image, to the extent that even when they are very thin, they often claim to feel fat and bloated (Bruch, 1962). There is evidence that this is representative of a more general difficulty with thinking and perceptual processes, because they also tend to misperceive their affective (emotional) and visceral (bodily) sensations (Bruch, 1978), an area that will be covered in more detail later in this chapter.

Amenorrhoea is a feature that is required for a diagnosis of anorexia nervosa (Russell, 1970) and seems primarily to be a consequence of the weight loss because in 70 per cent of cases periods cease shortly after dieting commences (Fries, 1977; Hurd, *et al.*, 1977). Many of the other phenomena ascribed to the anorexic syndrome also appear to be direct consequence of starvation, because they can be found in all starving people, irrespective of the cause of the starvation (Casper and Davis, 1977). We know this as a result of a series of studies, known as 'the Minnesota studies', in which psychologically normal men were placed on semi-starvation diets for six months in order to investigate some of the likely consequences of being detained as a prisoner of war (Keys, *et al.*, 1950). These studies revealed that in common with their anorexic counterparts, the men experienced an intense preoccupation with food, they tended to approach eating with various rituals and great secrecy, and they also showed other strange food habits, such as combining odd mixtures of food. Bulimic, the rapid consumption of a large amount of food in a short period of time (see later), occurred in four of these subjects (Schiele and Brozek, 1948) and a few of the men were observed to steal small items that they were able to afford, which again has parallels with the behaviour of some anorexics with bulimia features, or some individuals who suffer from bulimia nervosa (Russell, 1979). This suggests that once an individual has embarked on an anorexic regime, irrespective of the underlying reasons that first led to the development of anorexia nervosa, the consequent starvation will itself produce characteristic features that will intensify and strengthen the anorectic behaviour. Specifically, the person will become locked in a vicious circle where fears about being in control lead to a restriction of food intake, which eventually in itself will result in a preoccupation with food and eating that escalates the fear about control issues, thereby leading to an exacerbation of dietary restriction.

Prolonged caloric restriction also leads to the emergence of symptoms such as irritability, poor concentration, anxiety, depression, apathy, lability of mood and fatigue (Garfinkel and Garner, 1982). Sleep disturbance, in the form of reduced time spent sleeping and early morning wakening, are common in anorexia nervosa (Crisp, Stonehill and Fenton, 1971). Disturbances in sleep and mood have also been related more generally to undernutrition (Crisp, 1980). However, it is very characteristic of individuals with anorexia nervosa to deny the adverse consequences of the disorder, such as the weight loss, feelings of hunger, and mood swings. This is done with a conviction and tenacity that can appear totally baffling to the observer: despite clear evidence to the contrary, the person with anorexia will often steadfastly deny that there is anything wrong.

There are several physical signs of starvation, the most striking of which is the weight loss. The extent of weight loss is variable but can be greater than 50 per cent of the matched population mean weight. Other physical signs of the disorder include dry, cracking skin, thinning hair on the scalp, brittle nails, lanugo hair (fine, downy hair growth over the body, especially over the back and face) and coldness in the extremities of the body. There are marked hormonal disturbances, including low levels of testosterone, follicle stimulating hormone, and luteinising hormone (for a comprehensive review of this area, see Garfinkel and Garner, 1982, pp. 58–99).

Bulimia Nervosa

Historical Overview

It has been known for many years that some individuals with anorexia nervosa show bulimia features, that is, have periods in which they binge eat, vomit voluntarily, or abuse laxatives and purgatives. Although recent evidence suggests that bulimic first emerged as a syndrome around 1940, with the early cases of bingeing and vomiting evolving in connection with anorexia nervosa (Casper, 1983), it was only named and identified as a distinct disorder from anorexia nervosa by Russell in 1979. In this study, he identified patients with bulimic symptoms, some of whom could not be classified as anoretic in terms of weight loss, and furthermore had no previous history of anorexia nervosa. These individuals typically alternated periods of food restriction with periods when they binged, that is, rapidly consumed a large quantity of food over a short period of time. Following a binge they would usually make themselves vomit or abuse laxatives or other purgatives, ostensibly to avoid the consequences (in terms of weight gain) of ingesting such an enormous number of calories, and also to alleviate the physical discomfort that is experienced as a result of bingeing. Russell also demonstrated that there was a clear overlap between patients with bulimia nervosa and the bulimic subgroup of anorexia nervosa patients.

Russell's viewpoint has been endorsed by other researchers (Casper, *et al.*, 1980; Garfinkel *et al.*, 1980) and it is now known that people with anorexia and people with bulimia can be differentiated on a number of demographic features. For example, when compared to individuals with anorexia nervosa, people with bulimia nervosa tend to be older (Casper, *et al.*, 1980) and are less likely to come from middle- or upper-class backgrounds (Lacey, 1983). There is also evidence that individuals with bulimia nervosa are more likely to have been overweight in the past (Russell, 1979; Fairburn and Cooper, 1983) and to engage in self-destructive or anti-social impulsive behaviours, such as shop-lifting, abusing drugs, or deliberate self-harm (Russell, 1979; Casper *et al.*, 1980; Pyle *et al.*, 1981; Abraham and Beaumont, 1982). Although it is difficult to draw any definite conclusions, evidence suggests that bulimia nervosa is a more intractable condition to treat compared with anorexia nervosa, and that those who suffer from bulimia have a poorer prognosis (Russell, 1979).

What is Bulimia Nervosa?

Russell's (1979) diagnostic criteria for bulimia nervosa are as follows:

1 the patients suffer from powerful and intractable urges to overeat;
2 they seek to avoid the 'fattening' effects of food by inducing vomiting or abusing purgatives or both;
3 they have a morbid fear of becoming fat.

Unlike their anorexic peers, individuals with bulimia nervosa are not necessarily thin and may be of normal weight, or even overweight and are more likely to have been significantly overweight in the past (Russell, 1979; Fairburn and Cooper, 1983). High carbohydrate, easily ingested food usually constitutes 'binge' food, with bulimic individuals reporting consuming energy contents between three and twenty-seven times the recommended daily energy allowance on a 'bad day' (Abraham and Beaumont, 1982).

Following a binge most sufferers induce vomiting, take large quantities of laxatives, or both. There are various physical complications associated with vomiting, including loss of electrolytes, an increased risk of developing urinary infections and renal failure, and increased susceptibility to epileptic seizures (Russell, 1979).

Depressive symptoms are a common feature in patients with bulimia nervosa (Russell, 1979; Pyle, *et al.*, 1981) and there is also evidence that they experience considerable lability of mood (Fairburn, 1980; Johnson and Larson,

1982). It is not unusual for sufferers to contemplate suicide after bingeing, or to actually make suicide attempts (Abraham and Beaumont, 1982). As noted previously, bulimic features (both in individuals with anorexia nervosa and bulimia nervosa) have been observed to be associated with poor impulse control and with a variety of impulsive, self-destructive, and anti-social behaviours, such as drug abuse, self-mutilation and stealing. In contrast to individuals with anorexia nervosa, denial is not usually a feature of bulimia nervosa and sufferers are generally well aware that they have a serious problem and require help (American Psychiatric Association, 1980).

Pica

Pica (from the Latin word meaning 'magpie') has been documented as far back as the sixteenth century (Parry-Jones, 1991). It is the desire to eat, or the eating of, substances usually considered to be inedible. The ingested substances may be plaster, dirt, carpet fibres, etc. Pica is a normal developmental feature of infants which usually declines by the age of two years (Bicknell, 1975). It has also been commonly observed among pregnant women who may have cravings for substances such as chalk or coal.

The biological explanation is that it is a behavioural sign of iron deficiency or general malnourishment. This may explain many cases, but psychological research indicates that other factors may be relevant. Millican, *et al.* (1956) looked at pica in older children and identified three main contributing factors:

1 Organic brain damage in the child;
2 Disturbance in the mother-child relationship;
3 Socioeconomic factors such as poor housing.

They later pointed out the importance of separation from one parent as an additional causal factor.

Obesity

What is Obesity?

'Obesity' is a difficult construct to define and assess for a number of reasons. First, the preferred body shape varies across culture and time, and therefore the values attributed to being overweight differ markedly. Thus Judith Rodin has noted that in Restoration England obesity was deemed to be a desirable attribute whilst in Ancient Crete a thin body image was prized (Rodin, 1983). In contemporary western society there is evidence that the ideal female shape has become thinner over the past few decades. For example, Garner, *et al.*

(1980) found that the average weight for age and height of Playboy Magazine centrefolds decreased significantly over a twenty year period.

A further complicating factor in the accurate assessment of obesity concerns the difficulty inherent in actually measuring this state. Most studies simply measure height and weight, a problematic method which only provides a crude indication of the body's fat content (Royal College of Physicians, 1983) and fails to take into account individual differences in overall physical size, shape, build or metabolism. For example, people who are fit and athletic and therefore have a muscular physique may weigh above the average for their age and height although they are not fat. At this point it is worth noting that irrespective of the assessment method that is employed, the limits of 'normality' (i.e., where should the boundary between 'normal' and 'obese' be placed) need to be defined. At present we define overweight and obesity in adults by reference to life insurance company standards that present the association between weight range and mortality rate (DHSS/MRC, 1976). Using this method 'overweight' is typically defined as individuals who weigh 110 to 119 per cent of standard weight, which is the weight range associated with the lowest mortality rate for each height category in an insured population. Obesity is generally defined as a body weight in excess of 120 per cent of the standard weight (i.e., if the optimum weight, in terms of longevity, for a particular age and height band was 10 stones, an individual would have to weigh 12 stones or more to be classified as 'obese').

When one considers the health risks associated with obesity, there is considerable evidence that this condition is associated with increased morbidity in a number of areas. For example, obesity plays a role in the development of coronary heart disease (Garrow, 1981), high blood pressure (DHSS/MRC, 1976), diabetes (Bray, 1979), gallbladder disease (Rimm, *et al.*, 1975) and certain types of cancer (Lew and Garfinkel, 1979).

As well as an increased risk to physical well being, it is well known that being overweight or obese has adverse consequences for the psychological health of the individual, especially for females. People who are overweight tend to be stigmatised and discriminated against, certainly in western cultures. Staffieri (1967) found that children as young as four or five years of age begin to produce unfavourable stereotyped responses towards endomorphic (obese) silhouettes. Richardson (1961) found that children aged ten and eleven shown drawings of children with various physical disabilities (e.g., sitting in a wheelchair) together with drawings of a 'normal' and an obese child, almost invariably saw the obese child as the least desirable.

Unfortunately, obese people are not only subjected to prejudicial attitudes but at times find themselves on the receiving end of overt discrimination. For example, Canning and Mayer (1966) suggested being obese adversely influenced whether high school students were accepted into the college of their choice. In recent years feminist writers and therapists have focused on the issues of obesity and compulsive eating (e.g., Orbach, 1983; Lawrence, 1987) and on the impact of 'the tyranny of slenderness' (Chernin, 1981) on women. These issues will be addressed in more detail when feminist models of eating disorders are outlined later in this chapter.

Who Develops Eating Disorders?

Anorexia nervosa typically affects young, well educated middle-class females. For example, a study of schoolgirls conducted in the United Kingdom in 1976 found that it was present in its severe form in one in a hundred girls in the sixteen to eighteen age range in the independent sector of education, with a figure of one in three hundred in the state education system (Crisp, *et al.*, 1976). However, because this study concerned itself solely with very severe cases of anorexia nervosa, and only with secondary school-age girls, these figures may represent an underestimation of the problem. It is important to emphasise here that eating disorders occur on a continuum — many young women, although not fulfilling the diagnostic criteria for anorexia or bulimia, nevertheless experience considerable difficulty in this area, and can be thought of as 'sub-clinical' cases. Some researchers have reported that the disorder appears to be becoming more equally distributed through all social classes (Garfinkel and Garner, 1982), although others report more equivocal findings (Jones, *et al.*, 1980). Most studies report an age range of between 12 and 25 years for developing anorexia (Garfinkel and Garner, 1982). In contrast, individuals showing bulimia features tend to be older. Russell (1979), for example, presented a mean age of onset for bulimia of 21.2 years, range 13–37.

Research suggests that bulimia nervosa has a higher prevalence rate than anorexia nervosa and that binge eating occurs frequently amongst women (Hawkins and Clement, 1980; Wardle, 1980). One study that looked at American college students found that 19 per cent of the females reported experiencing all the major symptoms of bulimia (Halmi *et al.*, 1981). In the United Kingdom a community study of bulimia nervosa was conducted in which 20.9 per cent of women reported bingeing, 2.9 per cent reported using vomiting as a means of weight control, and there was a prevalence rate of 1.9 per cent fulfilling diagnostic criteria for bulimia nervosa (Fairburn and Cooper, 1983). There is also evidence that women who develop bulimia nervosa are less likely to come from middle- or upper-class backgrounds, when compared with women who develop anorexia nervosa (e.g., Lacey, 1983).

One of the most striking demographic features of anorexia nervosa concerns the fact that the vast majority of sufferers, approximately 90–95 per cent of reported cases, are female (Bemis, 1978; Jones, *et al.*, 1980). This observation supports the contention that cultural factors are extremely significant in the aetiology (development) of anorexia, a viewpoint that will be discussed in greater depth at a later point. However, there is some evidence that male anorexics are more likely to be found in the chronic group and to have a poorer prognosis than females in general (Crisp *et al.*, 1977). The same researchers have also stated their belief that males are more likely to develop the bulimia form of the disorder, a hypothesis given some support by Halmi, *et al.*'s (1981) finding that 5 per cent of a sample of male college students reported experiencing all the major symptoms of bulimia. However, in clinical practice male patients with bulimia nervosa have been found to represent less than 5 per cent of total reported cases (Russell, 1979). It is also worth noting that male anorexics do not show the typical social class skewing that females do (Crisp and Toms, 1972; Marshall, 1978).

Until recently, reliable information concerning the proportion of British children and adults who are overweight was somewhat lacking. However, results are now available from two major surveys which examined the prevalence of overweight in children (Stark, *et al.*, 1981) and in adults (Office of Population Censuses and Surveys, 1981). In the Stark, *et al.* (1981) study, a nationally representative cohort of over 5,000 children, born in a particular week in 1946, had their weights and heights measured at age 6, 7, 11, 14, 20 and 26 years. This demonstrated that the prevalence of obese children (i.e., weighing more than 120 per cent of the standard figure) was relatively low (for example, 1.4 per cent of boys and 2.1 per cent of girls at age six). However, here was a trend for weight to increase with age such that by their mid-twenties, 31 per cent of men and 27 per cent of women were substantially overweight (more than 110 per cent of standard weight), whilst 12.3 per cent of men and 11.3 per cent of women were obese. The second study (Office of Population Censuses and Surveys, 1981) assessed a number of factors, including the heights and weights of all adults between 16–64 years of age in a sample of 5,000 households drawn from a random sample of 100 Local Authority districts. The findings revealed that across all age groups, an average of 39 per cent of men and 32 per cent of women were overweight, with 6 per cent of men and 8 per cent of women being classified as obese.

Obesity is also associated with social class. For example, men and women from upper socio-economic groups living in both London and New York are less likely to be obese. There is also a tendency for people who move up the social scale to lose their obesity. The association between being slender and higher social class has been observed even in children (Whitelaw, 1971).

What is the Outcome in Eating Disorders?

Reported mortality figures for anorexia nervosa range from 0–24 per cent (Williams, 1958; Farquharson and Hyland, 1966), with an average of about 9 per cent. However, studies that follow up anorexic patients for several years have found a higher death rate than this. Theander (1983) observed a total mortality rate of 17 per cent and a more recent study by Ratnasuriya, *et al.* (1991) reported a twenty year follow up study of forty-one patients with anorexia nervosa that demonstrated a mortality rate of 15 per cent from causes related to the eating disorder. At least 15 per cent of this sample had developed bulimia nervosa. Only 30 per cent had what was considered to be a good general outcome, with 32.5 per cent rated as having an intermediate outcome, and 20 per cent (not including those who had died) having a poor (chronically ill) outcome.

Theander (1970) reported that for fifty-eight of his patients, 47 per cent were anoretic for a duration of less than three years, 31 per cent for 3–5 years, and 22 per cent for greater than five years. Although recovery in terms of weight gain and stabilisation has been observed to occur in more than 50 per cent of patients, concerns with weight and a fear of fatness remain common, as do dietary restriction and feelings of anxiety when eating with others (Morgan and Russell, 1975; Hsu, *et al.*, 1979).

There has been little systematic work done on outcome in bulimia, although when reading the literature one gets the impression that the natural history of the disorder is such that the prognosis is poor. Russell, for example, has said that 'bulimia nervosa is more resistant to treatment, physical complications are more frequent and dangerous, and the risk of suicide is considerable' (Russell, 1979, p. 448). In this sample of patients, 37 per cent had attempted suicide with 17 per cent making serious attempts, and 3.3 per cent succeeding. Abraham, *et al.* (1983) found that following a treatment intervention comprised of counselling and supportive psychotherapy, 29–42 per cent of their patients could be considered 'cured' on follow-up, with the variable of commencement of binge eating before 16 years being indicative of good outcome.

It is almost a certainty that most readers of this chapter will know people who wish to lose weight and therefore diet, as it has been reported that at any one time a staggering 65 per cent of British women and 30 per cent of British men are trying to lose weight (Marketing, 1980). However, the chances are that few of them will succeed in reducing their weight on a permanent basis, as illustrated by the observation that overweight and obesity are continuing problems in Britain, despite the widespread efforts that are made to diet. Although it is relatively easy for people to achieve short-term weight loss, longer term follow-up studies have shown that the majority of people regain weight over time (Stunkard and Penick, 1979; O'Neil, *et al.*, 1980). Indeed, there is a growing body of opinion that holds that far from improving matters, the restriction of food intake may lead to the development of binge eating and actually make people fatter (Wardle and Beinart, 1981; Cannon and Einzig, 1983; Orbach, 1979).

Psychological Models of Eating Disorders

Behavioural Models

Behavioural approaches are concerned with assessing, and where appropriate changing, a person's behaviour or performance directly, with little or no reference to dispositional or mentalistic processes (see Chapter 1). Thus behavioural models do not infer the existence of any underlying causes of psychological problems, but hold that it is maladaptive behaviour patterns, acquired through traumatic or inappropriate learning that constitute the 'problem' that needs to be changed. Behavioural change is achieved by manipulating the environmental factors that maintain the problem behaviour by, for example, modifying the pleasurable or painful consequences of behaviour. Thus, in eating disorders, analysis will focus on how positive and negative reinforcers maintain the learned problem behaviour, namely avoidance of food in the case of anorexia, bingeing and vomiting in the case of bulimia, and overeating/eating high caloric foods in the case of obesity.

Techniques derived from behavioural theories have been demonstrated to have a role to play in alleviating some of the maladaptive behaviours associated with eating disorders. Operant conditioning procedures have been shown to be effective in promoting weight gain in anorexia nervosa, with negative reinforcers such as bed rest and isolation, and positive reinforcers such as increased social and physical activities contingent on food intake or weight gain, being employed (for example, Garfinkel, *et al.*, 1973; Halmi, *et al.*, 1975). Rosen and Leitenberg (1982) reported that exposure to food and vomiting response prevention led to the complete cessation of vomiting and bingeing in a single subject, and that this improvement was maintained at ten month follow-up. The behavioural treatment of obesity typically aims to teach people how to recognise the factors which maintain their eating habits and then how to devise methods to overcome these difficulties and establish new patterns of behaviour (Stuart, 1967). Thus the home or work environment can be modified to minimise stimuli that can lead to inappropriate eating. For example, high calorie foods such as cakes and confectionary can be eliminated from the home. The eating pattern itself can be modified by, for example, encouraging the person to eat only at specific times in a particular room in the house.

However, behavioural models can be criticised for failing to address the underlying difficulties that eating disorders are symptomatic of, for example, depression, issues about sexuality and relationships, and fears about not being in control of one's life. Attempting to treat serious eating problems such as anorexia nervosa solely by using behavioural techniques could, in our opinion, be extremely dangerous, because it will strengthen the fears that the sufferer has of not being in control of her life and could well result in an exacerbation of disordered eating patterns, as well as the subjective experience of feeling depressed, helpless, and having low self-esteem. Although the judicious and sensitive application of behavioural techniques may be of some use in dealing with the symptomatic aspects, such as food refusal and weight loss, of anorexia nervosa other intervention strategies need to be employed to tackle the underlying problems.

Cognitive Models

Cognitive models stress the vital role of cognition in mediating behaviour and focus on the relationship between maladaptive thinking patterns and psychological problems (see Chapter 1). Cognitive models of anorexia nervosa have focused on three major areas: disordered sensations of satiety and hunger, errors in thinking (conceptual distortions), and perceptual distortions, namely body image disturbance.

It is generally acknowledged that anorexics have difficulty in monitoring and reporting on their emotional and physical states, and that descriptions of their inner states may show inaccuracies. Furthermore, the anorexic's perceptions may be unduly influenced by external factors. For example, when food was directly introduced into their stomachs, anorexic subjects were found to be less accurate than normal controls in perceiving the quantity that they were given (Coddington and Bruch, 1970). They also display delayed gastric emptying when compared with controls (Dubois, *et al.*, 1979), and have been shown to fail to develop an aversion to sweet tastes, unlike normal controls (Garfinkel, *et al.*, 1978). Although these findings suggest an internal deficit in the mechanisms for regulating food/carbohydrate intake, Garfinkel (1974) reported that anorexic patients' feelings of fullness following a meal persist longer if they believe they have eaten a high calorie meal, suggesting that cognitive factors influence their satiety experience. Thus it is possible that cognitive factors mediating intake may be sufficiently prominent that they prevail over the internal, physiologically-mediated regulatory mechanisms.

Bruch (1977) has drawn attention to the disturbances in thinking that occur in anorexia nervosa and has emphasised the importance of relabelling misconceptions and errors in the anorexic's thinking during psychotherapy. Drawing on the work of Beck (1976) on depression and anxiety disorders, Garner and Bemis (1982) have developed a cognitive model of anorexia nervosa focusing on conceptual processes leading to faulty thinking. Their categories of aberrant conceptual processes, based on those proposed by Beck (1976), include selective abstraction (e.g., 'I am special if I am thin'), over-generalisation (e.g., 'I was not happy at my normal weight, so I know that gaining weight won't make me feel better'), magnification (e.g., 'gaining five pounds would push me over the brink'), dichotomous or all-or-none reasoning (e.g., 'if I gain one pound, I'll gain a hundred pounds'), personalisation and self-reference (e.g., 'I am embarrassed when other people see me eat'), and superstituous thinking (e.g., 'I can't enjoy anything because it will be taken away'). Garner and Bemis have detailed the basic assumptions, or principles, that underlie and organise the irrational ideas of the anorexic patient, for example, that weight, shape or thinness can serve as the sole or predominant basis for inferring personal value or self-worth, that complete self-control is necessary or even desirable, and that absolute certainty is necessary in making decisions. Thus when adopting a cognitive model, a major task of therapy would be to help the patient to develop more realistic, functional ways of organising her internal world.

The body image disturbance that is often a feature of anorexia nervosa can manifest itself in the form of being unable to assess one's size accurately (i.e., seeing oneself as fat and bloated, even when severely emaciated) or in holding disturbed attitudes towards one's body (generally either loathing the body, or, more rarely, overvaluing it). These two forms of body image disturbance can operate together in some cases.

Cognitive models have also provided an extremely useful framework within which to examine the phenomenon of binge eating. One of the most influential and well-researched theories of binge eating, Restraint Theory, suggests that thoughts and beliefs mediate bingeing, and that dietary restraint plays a causal role in relation to binge eating. There is insufficient space in this chapter to go into details about this area, but for the interested reader, the following papers are recommended: Wardle and Beinart, 1981; Herman and Polivy, 1984.

Feminist Models

Feminist models address themselves to the question of why the vast majority of individuals suffering from eating disorders are female and relate the development and maintenance of eating disorders to psychological and social factors relating to the position of women in society. Boskind-Lodahl (1976) has interpreted the anorexic's symptoms as a reflection of contemporary women's striving to please others and validate their self-worth from external sources, often by controlling their appearance. She believes that these women have never questioned their assumptions that wifehood, motherhood, and intimacy with men are the fundamental components of femininity. She also draws attention to the ascetic dimension of fasting, and the false sense of 'power', 'goodness' and 'control' that this provides, and suggests that in seeking to control the bulimic behaviour, fasting represents a struggle against a part of the self.

Marilyn Lawrence (1979, 1984) has also placed great emphasis on the asceticsm of fasting and suggests that the desire of the anorectic to engage in a battle with her body and to subdue and take control of it, is the result of an underlying sense of lack of control in other areas of life. She points out that anorexia typically develops at or around adolescence and is associated with young women 'feeling caught up in a struggle for autonomy with which they felt unable to cope' (Lawrence, 1979, p. 49). She hypothesises that adolescence, which demands increased autonomy and independence from the individual, is especially problematic for young women. Girls are brought up to be 'good' (i.e., passive and compliant) which makes it more difficult for females to negotiate the transition to independence. There has also been an historical association between sickliness and 'femininity' (Ehrenreich and English, 1978). In contrast, a certain degree of resistance and rebellion is regarded as healthy in boys, which makes for a smoother passage to independence. It also leads to the development of true self-esteem based on the individual having a sense of genuine self-worth. In contrast, because passivity, compliance and acquiescence to the needs of others are attributes which are encouraged in girls, the development of their self-esteem tends to be based on pleasing other people and meeting the needs of others. Thus it is more difficult for girls to develop a sense of fundamental self-value and to take their own needs seriously.

This approach therefore suggests that for the anorexic, anorexia nervosa represents the solution (albeit a maladapative one) to a problem that she finds impossible to deal with in any other way at the time, with the symptoms of anorexia functioning as a protective outer shell that hides and protects the real, needy person inside. Lawrence also emphasises the theme of symbolic nurturing through feeding which appears recurrently throughout women's lives. The relationship that women have with food is frequently extremely ambivalent. For example, the role of being the provider of food for one's family is one which is often associated with feelings of guilt. If you give your children what they like to eat, the chances are that it is not good for them, whereas, if you provide healthy food, they will probably complain that they are being deprived and demand chips and confectionary! Ambivalence also pervades the area of women as eaters, because food is a source of pleasure that is 'not allowed' for those who have the primary responsibility for providing it.

Other feminist writers have also focused on the role of women as providers and nurturers and how this occurs at the expense of their own physical and emotional needs, to the extent that many women do not even recognise their needs (e.g., Orbach, 1979; Eichenbaum and Orbach, 1984). For example, it is not uncommon for women to feed their families before they themselves eat, irrespective of how hungry they are themselves, and as any woman who has cared for a very young baby will attest, one's need for essentials such as food, sleep, companionship and time and space for oneself becomes totally subsumed under the demands and needs of the infant. Relationships with adults are not immune to this effect, such that many women allow the needs and wishes of their partners to take precedence over their own, apparently without question.

This perspective views eating disorders as defensive, protecting the person concerned from having to acknowledge or address the conflict between her own unmet needs and those of other people. Thus using this approach, (and grossly simplifying matters) anorexia nervosa can be seen as a total denial of neediness: the behaviour, values and professed beliefs of the individual with anorexia proclaim that she is without needs or desires, whether they be for food, warmth, relationships, sex, etc. The person who develops bulimia as a means of dealing with the issue of conflicting needs presents a much more ambivalent picture. Although the bulimic woman can take in food, which is symbolic of nurturance in general, she cannot retain it, and furthermore, often takes in 'bad' food. Other areas of her life will also have this quality of ambivalence. For example, she may crave to have close relationships but feel overwhelmed when this becomes a possibility, and therefore withdraw. Some bulimic women can sustain relationships, but only with partners who are unsatisfying and incapable of meeting her real needs, just like 'binge' food. Compulsive eating represents an attempt to meet emotional needs inappropriately, by using food. For example, as detailed by Orbach (1979) eating can provide an inappropriate means of dealing with feelings such as anxiety, boredom and anger.

Psychodynamic Models

Psychodynamic approaches stress the importance of internal, unconscious thoughts and hidden feelings in generating psychopathology. These approaches attempt to assess, and where appropriate change, a person's psychological make-up by dealing as directly as possible with thoughts, feelings and desires. These models look at the internal world and the role of early relationships with others in forming that world. For the internal world of the adolescent, for example, psychodynamic models propose that when an individual is faced with painful, conflicting feelings (for example, the desire to become more independent conflicting with anxiety about becoming more separate from parents) or real external threat, defence mechanisms are summoned to protect the individual's sense of herself or her ego. Defence mechanisms are unconscious strategies (see Chapter 1) that offer some degree of protection from feeling bad. Using this model, one can conceptualise the aberrant behaviours associated with eating disorders as defensive, and therefore as protecting the person from painful feelings. For example, to simplify matters grossly, the total denial of needs that one sees in anorexia nervosa (e.g., the need for food, warmth, friendships, etc.) can be seen to protect the person from the realisation of how needy and vulnerable she feels. Bulimia and vomiting often enable the sufferer to dispose of bad feelings that she finds overwhelming or frightening (e.g., if she feels angry with someone close to her, bingeing and then being sick will make these feelings disappear as if by magic). Compulsive eating can represent an attempt to meet needs inappropriately by using food. Thus these behaviours can be viewed as protective, which helps to account for the fact that many people with eating disorders are extremely reluctant to give them up, and even where they wish to do so, find this very difficult.

In providing a model for the formation of the internal world, contemporary psychodynamic formulations of eating disorders have focussed on object relations, that is the internal or cognitive representations of very early relationships between mother and baby, and how this relates to later difficulties. Such theories would argue that as object relations are established early on in development and are unconscious they can remain unchanged, adversely affecting adult functioning.

Bruch (1978) for example, has suggested that infants who later develop anorexia nervosa are extremely well cared for, but that this is done according to the mother's decisions and feelings, not according to the child's demands. Thus a mother may respond to her crying infant by always feeding her, rather than trying to discern whether her distress is attributable to needs other than hunger, such as needing to be changed, cuddled and comforted, or provided with more or less warmth. The child thus fails to learn to differentiate between hunger and other sources of discomfort, and grows up unable to discriminate between different bodily sensations and without having a sense of control over them. The subsequent lack of autonomy and difficulties with decision making that manifest themselves are praised by parents and teachers as 'special goodness', when in effect, the young person is never testing her own ideas and capacities. For Bruch, anorexia nervosa develops when such individuals feel at a disadvantage, and represents a struggle for self-mastery and a self-respecting identity that is maladaptively pursued through control over one's body. It also represents an attempt to escape from the overdemanding role that the family, which may have extremely high achievement expectations, sets.

Social-Cultural Models

The fact that anorexia nervosa occurs with a particular age, sex, and social class distribution, as well as its apparent increased incidence, suggests that sociocultural factors may play an important role in the development of the disorder. Sociocultural models therefore examine how sociocultural factors precipitate the disorder in those who are vulnerable or predisposed to developing it.

Several authors have stressed the important role that culture plays in the preferred or 'ideal' appearance of women. For example, one can find examples throughout history of potentially unhealthy customs that derived from the expectation that women should conform to an idealised appearance, such as footbinding in China (Lyons and Petrucelli, 1978), and the wearing of corsets in nineteenth century Europe (Vincent, 1979). As Garfinkel and Garner (1982) point out, particular illnesses have also been romanticised at times, and the characteristic look associated with them has become desirable. For example, the 'look' associated with tuberculosis was glamourised in the nineteenth century and the tubercular appearance was thought to be a sign of a romantic personality (Sontag, 1978). Garner and Garfinkel suggest that thinness and anorexia nervosa have likewise been glamourised in the twentieth century.

Garner (Garner and Garfinkel, 1980; Garner *et al.*, 1983) suggests that the current, and relatively recent, cultural emphasis on thinness in women represents an important social and cultural trend in the development of anorexia nervosa. They draw attention to how the conflict between the trend towards a smaller ideal shape, together with increases in actual body weights of females, can account for the pervasiveness of dieting among women (Huenemann, *et al.*, 1966; Dwyer, *et al.*, 1969; Jakobovits, *et al.*, 1977). Furthermore, there is indirect evidence that increased cultural pressure to diet and be slim facilitates the development of anorexia nervosa in individuals who must focus increased attention on a slim body (in this case, professional models and ballet students), particularly if they are in a competitive environment (Garner and Garfinkel, 1980). Other authors have focused on the changing role of women in society and social change generally, and how this relates to both the current 'epidemic' of anorexia and bulimia, and the patterning of symptoms such as vomiting and hyperactivity. Brumberg (1988), for example, has pointed out that bulimia could only emerge as a prevalent syndrome in modern, industrial-capitalist societies; lack of privacy and basic plumbing and sanitary amenities would have made it extremely difficult for young women to adopt bulimic behaviour patterns in the 1800s, and a plentiful supply of pre-processed food is also necessary to live a bulimic lifestyle. Bingeing would be difficult, if not impossible, if one had to prepare 'binge' foods, such as bread and cakes, from scratch.

Family Models

Family theories of eating disorders assume that the family of the patient has a role in causing or maintaining the disorder. There are many schools of family therapy (see Chapter 8), but the basic model behind them is the same: the eating disorder in the patient is a symptom of underlying family disturbance.

Minuchin (1978) noted several cases in his own practice where adolescent patients showed considerable improvement in their eating problems when treated as in-patients in hospital, but relapsed soon after returning home. He proposed that relationships and processes in the family (the family 'dynamics') in some way caused the patient to become ill again. A corollary of this proposal was that the patient's illness served an important function in the family and was necessary for the family's continued ability to function as a unit.

Attempts have been made to define the characteristics of families who have an anorexic member. For example, linked with the high incidence of the disorder in middle-class families, it has been suggested that the parents have very high performance expectations of their children and that this causes the children great stress. Another suggestion is that in such families, open rebellion is not permitted for the adolescent children and so their teenage reaction against parental values will have to be covertly rather than openly expressed.

Minuchin's clinical observations led him to develop a theory based on the functioning of the whole family. His 'structural' theory describes the family structure which reflects healthy family relationships (see Chapter 8). In anorexic families he found a different structure. He described them as 'enmeshed', that is, overinvolved with each other so that individuals in the family are too close to one another and the excessive togetherness leads to a lack of privacy. Members become unduly concerned about each other's welfare and they intrude on each other's thoughts and feelings. An additional feature of the families is the very high value they place on harmony. Open conflict is avoided and so underlying conflicts do not get addressed and dealt with.

Other family approaches present alternative descriptions. For example, Selvini-Palazzoli's (1974) description is of families with disturbed patterns of communication. Although contradiction is common in the family, there is little acknowledgment of conflict. The unspoken disagreements lead to covert coalitions and the child becomes a secret ally to both mother and father. The parents compete, for example, for a sense of moral superiority in who has made greater sacrifices for the sake of the family.

Both these theories emphasise how children reared in such families may have particular difficulty in becoming autonomous during adolescence. Although the theories present a model for understanding why someone in the family becomes ill, family theories generally do not explain why the illness which develops should be an eating disorder, nor why one child rather than another should become ill.

Carrying out research on families is extremely problematic; definitions of what constitutes normal family functioning and definitions of dimensions of family functioning are extremely difficult to derive. The family background and experiences of the researchers will colour their interpretation of any available definition. These points mean that more 'objective' measures are attempted, but then the problem arises that if you measure simple, observable features of the family, how can you then infer anything about complex interrelationships and interactions within the family?

Research on families has provided some support for the theories. Bruch (1978) found that parents often suffered depression, and marital problems came out into the open when the anorexic child recovered. Kalucy, *et al.* (1977) found an unusual interest in food, weight and shape in families of anorexic patients. Problems of dependency and insecurity were also common. Obesity was unusually common in the mothers, especially when the daughter suffered bulimic symptoms. A high incidence of alcoholism has been reported in the families, especially among the fathers. Martin (1983) found that anorexic families conformed to Minuchin's description of being enmeshed, but also found variation between families in the study. This variability has been repeatedly restated by other authors.

Integration

Garfinkel and Garner (1982) emphasised that eating disorders are multi-determined. That is, there is no single cause but a number of factors that operate together. Those factors are the ones we have identified in this chapter, and they are relevant both to what triggers the disorder in the first place, and what then maintains it.

Cultural factors provide the setting in which norms and ideals exist and change over time. Those ideals which relate to body shape may be present with different intensities in different cultures and many authors have linked the intense pressure on young women to be thin in contemporary western societies with the increase in incidence of anorexia nervosa and bulimia nervosa in the past thirty years. The feminist approaches link closely with this in looking at how women's position in society promotes the development of unhealthy eating patterns. These considerations, however, do not explain why different people react to the prevailing cultural pressures in different ways.

If a girl or young woman in such a culture also grows up in a family where tension is not expressed and conformity is valued, the pressure to behave and appear certain ways is further raised. Eating problems in one family member can lead to battles in the family (overt or covert) over who is in control of the eating. The issue of control is particularly live during adolescence, when the young person faces the developmental task of separating from her parents and developing her own autonomy. This task is typically acted out by rebelling against parental values and adopting those of the peer group. The adolescent can then reach her own compromise between the two sets of values to arrive at her own way of seeing things. In families which cannot tolerate the rebellion or the autonomy of the young person, the process may become blocked, and if the block is severe, battles over autonomy may become pathological (e.g., if they are always over food) and lead to the development of eating problems.

Apart from external factors, there are features of the individual which influence whether or not she will develop eating problems. Her very early relationships influence how she experiences things in later life. If food is provided whenever she is upset, the child will come to link eating with alleviation of not only hunger but also loneliness or other discomfort. It will then hold an inflated place in her life. Alternatively, if the child experiences withdrawal of love and affection by her mother whenever she does not perform mother's wishes, she may come to work hard at pleasing her mother in order to keep her love. Conforming to what the mother wants includes, in most families, issues around accepting food prepared by the mother. In both of these examples, feeding and emotional satisfaction or deprivation are linked. This link then influences how the individual thinks and behaves over food.

Given this complicated backdrop of pressures and influences, external events may bring things to a head. Stress, either acute or long-term, which lowers the self-worth and sense of self-control of a young girl may lead to something of a crisis. If her response to these feelings is to diet in order to enhance her self image, or to eat increasing amounts for comfort or other satisfaction, food and dieting then become bound up with the problems. The dieting may be experienced as successful or compelling to continue if partly successful, and may increasingly take over. Similarly, overeating may be experienced as satisfying in some way. The person may find that it offers many secondary gains, added to which chronic and severe dieting, or chronic overeating, will lead to physiological changes in her body. The complex cycle of underlying problems and eating related symptoms is then established.

Many factors in the individual, family, and culture may play a role in eating disorders. Exact causal mechanisms are not known, but the disorders are syndromes that are the result of an interaction of a number of forces. These forces predispose the individual to develop an eating disorder, precipitate its emergence and maintain it once it has started. For any individual, the circumstances contributing will interact in a complex way.

Research has not been done on why other vulnerable individuals, such as sisters of patients, do not develop the disorder. It is clear that many people have the individual, family, and cultural characteristics we have described, and these lead to the development of a full blown eating disorder within the context of stressors which initiate dieting, weight loss and the pursuit of thinness. Eating disorders are not discrete identifiable illnesses, but people show degrees of eating related pathology, the extremes of which are called anorexia nervosa, bulimia nervosa or obesity.

Recommended Reading

CRISP, A.H. (1980) *Anorexia Nervosa: Let Me Be*, London, UK: Academic Press.

This presents the view that anorexia nervosa represents a psychobiological regression, and includes many references to research, while remaining readable.

GARFINKEL, P.E. and GARNER, D.M. (1982) *Anorexia Nervosa: A Multidimensional Perspective*, New York, NY: Brunner Mazel.

A useful reference book which covers the main factors which contribute to eating problems; it is the closest to a textbook of anorexia nervosa.

LAWRENCE, M. (1984) *The Anorexic Experience*, London, UK: The Women's Press.

An excellent short book that will be of interest to a wide audience. As well as providing information for those who wish to find out more about anorexia nervosa, women suffering from this condition and their families will find this book extremely helpful.

MacLeod, S. (1981) *The Art of Starvation*, London, UK: Virago.

An extremely thoughtful first hand account of the experience of suffering from anorexia nervosa that was MIND book of the year.

References

Abraham, S.F. and Beaumont, P.J.V. (1982) 'How patients describe bulimia or binge eating', *Psychological Medicine*, **12**, pp. 625–35.

Abraham, S.F., Mira, M. and Llewellyn-Jones, D. (1983) 'Bulimia: A study of outcome', *International Journal of Eating Disorders*, **2**, pp. 174–80.

American Psychiatric Association (1980) *Diagnostic and Statistical Manual of Mental Disorders*, Washington, DC.

Beck, A.T. (1976) *Cognitive Therapy and the Emotional Disorders*, New York, NY: International Universities Press.

Bemis, K.M. (1978) 'Current approaches to the etiology and treatment of anorexia nervosa', *Psychological Bulletin*, **85**, pp. 593–617.

Bicknell, D.J. (1975) *Pica*, London, UK: Butterworths.

Boskind-Lodahl (1976) 'Cinderella's Stepsisters: A feminist perspective on anorexia nervosa and bulimia', *SIGNS: Journal of Women in Culture and Society*, **2**, pp. 342–56.

Bray, G.A. (Ed.) (1979) 'Obesity in America', proceedings of the 2nd Fogarty International Centre Conference on Obesity, No. 79, Washington, DC: US DHEW.

Bruch, H. (1962) 'Perceptual and conceptual disturbances in anorexia nervosa', *Psychosomatic Medicine*, **24**, pp. 187–94.

Bruch, H. (1973) *Eating Disorders*, New York, NY: Basic Books.

Bruch, H. (1977) 'Psychological antecedents of anorexia nervosa', in Vigersky, R. (Ed.) *Anorexia Nervosa*, New York, NY: Raven Press.

Bruch, H. (1978) *The Golden Cage: The Enigma of Anorexia Nervosa*, Cambridge, MA: Harvard University Press.

Brumberg, J.J. (1988) *Fasting Girls: The Emergence of Anorexia Nervosa as a Modern Disease*, Cambridge, MA: Harvard University Press.

Canning, H. and Mayer, J. (1966) 'Obesity: Its possible effect on college acceptance', *New England Journal of Medicine*, **275**, pp. 1172–74.

Cannon, G. and Einzig, H. (1983) *Dieting Makes You Fat*, London, UK: Century.

Casper, R.C. (1983) 'On the emergence of bulimia nervosa as a syndrome' *International Journal of Eating Disorders*, **2**, pp. 3–16.

Casper, R.C. and Davis, J.M. (1977) 'On the course of anorexia nervosa', *American Journal of Psychiatry*, **134**, pp. 974–78.

Casper, R.C., Eckert, E.D., Halmi, K.A., Goldberg, S.C. and Davis, J.M. (1980) 'Bulimia: its incidence and clinical importance in patients with anorexia nervosa', *Archives of General Psychiatry*, **37**, pp. 1030–35.

Chernin, K. (1981) *Womansize: The Tyranny of Slenderness*, New York, NY: Harper and Row.

Coddington, R.D. and Bruch, H. (1970) 'Gastric perceptivity in normal, obese and schizophrenic subjects', *Psychosomatics*, **11**, pp. 571–79.

Crisp, A.H. (1967) 'The possible significance of some behavioural correlates of weight and carbohydrate intake', *Journal of Psychosomatic Research*, **11**, pp. 117–31.

CRISP, A.H. (1970) 'Premorbid factors in adult disorders of weight with particular reference to primary anorexia nervosa (weight phobia). A literature review', *Journal of Psychosomatic Research*, **14**, pp. 1–22.

CRISP, A.H. (1980) 'Sleep, activity, nutrition and mood', *British Journal of Psychiatry*, **137**, pp. 1–7.

CRISP, A.H. and TOMS, D.A. (1972) 'Primary anorexia nervosa or weight phobia in the male. Report on 13 cases', *British Medical Journal*, **1**, pp. 334–38.

CRISP, A.H., PALMER, R.L. and KALUCY, R.S. (1976) 'How common is anorexia nervosa? A prevalence study', *British Journal of Psychiatry*, **218**, pp. 549–54.

CRISP, A.H., STONEHILL, E. and FENTON, G.W. (1971) 'The relationship between sleep, nutrition, and mood. A study of patients with anorexia nervosa', *Postgraduate Medical Journal*, **47**, pp. 207–13.

CRISP, A.H., KALUCY, R.S., LACEY, J.H. and HARDING, B. (1977) 'The long-term prognosis in anorexia nervosa: some factors predictive of outcome', in VIGERSKY, R. (Ed.), *Anorexia Nervosa*, New York, NY: Raven Press.

DHSS/MRC (1976) *Report on Research on Obesity*, Compiler W.P.T. James, London, UK: HMSO.

DUBOIS, A., GROSS, H.A., EBERT, M.H. and CASTELL, D.O. (1979) 'Altered gastric emptying and secretion in primary anorexia nervosa', *Gastroenterology*, **77**, pp. 319–23.

DWYER, J.T., FELDMAN, J.J., SELTZER, C.C. and MAYER, J. (1969) 'Body image in adolescents: attitudes toward weight and perception of appearance' *Journal of Nutritional Education*, **1**, pp. 14–19.

EHRENREICH, B. and ENGLISH, D. (1978) *For Her Own Good: 150 Years of the Experts' Advice to Women*, New York, NY: Pluto Press.

EICHENBAUM, L. and ORBACH, S. (1984) *What do Women Want?* London, UK: Fontana.

FAIRBURN, C.G. (1980) 'Self-induced vomiting', *Journal of Psychosomatic Research*, **24**, pp. 193–97.

FAIRBURN, C.G. and COOPER, P.J. (1983) 'The epidemiology of bulimia nervosa', *International Journal of Eating Disorders*, **2**, pp. 61–7.

FARQUHARSON, R.F. and HYLAND, H.H. (1966) 'Anorexia Nervosa: the course of 15 patients treated from 20 to 30 years previously', *Canadian Medical Association Journal*, **94**, pp. 411–19.

FRIES, H. (1977) 'Studies on secondary amenorrhoea, anorectic behavior, and body image perception: Importance for the early recognition of anorexia nervosa', in VIGERSKY, R. (Ed.), *Anorexia Nervosa*, New York, NY: Raven Press.

GARFINKEL, P.E. (1974) 'Perception of hunger and satiety in anorexia nervosa', *Psychological Medicine*, **4**, pp. 309–15.

GARFINKEL, P.E. and GARNER, D.M. (1982) *Anorexia Nervosa: A Multidimensional Perspective*, New York, NY: Brunner Mazel.

GARFINKEL, P.E., KLINE, S.A. and STANCER, H.C. (1973) 'Treatment of anorexia nervosa using operant conditioning techniques' *Journal of Nervous and Mental Disease*, **157**, pp. 428–33.

GARFINKEL, P.E., MOLDOFSKY, H. and GARNER, D.M. (1980) 'The Heterogeneity of Anorexia Nervosa: Bulimia as a distinct subgroup', *Archives General Psychiatry*, **37**, pp. 1036–40.

GARFINKEL, P.E., MOLDOFSKY, H., GARNER, D.M., STANCER, H.C. and COSCINA, D.V. (1978) 'Body awareness in anorexia nervosa: Disturbance in body image and satiety', *Psychosomatic Medicine*, **40**, pp. 487–98.

GARNER, D.M. and BEMIS, K. (1982) 'A cognitive-behavioral approach to anorexia nervosa', *Cognitive Therapy and Research*, **6**, pp. 1–27.

GARNER, D.M. and GARFINKEL, P.E. (1980) 'Socio-cultural factors in the development of anorexia nervosa', *Psychological Medicine*, **10**, pp. 647–56.

GARNER, D.M., GARFINKEL, P.E. and OLMSTEAD, M.P. (1983) 'An overview of sociocultural factors in the development of anorexia nervosa', in DARBY, P.L. *et al.* (Eds), *Anorexia Nervosa: Recent Developments in Research*, New York, NY: Alan R. Liss.

GARROW, J.S. (1981) 'Obesity and Energy Balance', in DAWSON, A.M., COMPSTON, N. and BESSER, G.M., *Recent Advances in Medicine*, No. 18, pp. 75–92. London, UK: Churchill Livingstone.

HALMI, K.A., FALK, J.R. and SCHWARTZ, E. (1981) 'Binge eating and vomiting: a summary of a college population', *Psychological Medicine*, **11**, pp. 697–706.

HALMI, K.A., POWERS, P. and CUNNINGHAM, S. (1975) 'Treatment of anorexia nervosa with behavior modification', *Archives of General Psychiatry*, **32**, pp. 92–6.

HAWKINS, R.C. and CLEMENT, P.F. (1980) 'Development and construct validation of a self-report measure of binge eating', *Addictive Behaviours*, **5**, pp. 219–26.

HERMAN, C.P. and POLIVY, J. (1984) 'A boundary model for the regulation of eating', in STUNKARD, A.J. and STELLAR, E. (Eds) *Eating and Its Disorders*, New York, NY: Raven, pp. 141–56.

HSU, L.K.G., CRISP, A.H. and HARDING, B. (1979) 'Outcome of anorexia nervosa', *Lancet*, **1**, pp. 61–5.

HUENEMANN, R.L., SHAPIRO, L.R., HAMPTON, M.C., MITCHELL, B.W. and BEHNKE, R.A. (1966) 'A longitudinal study of gross body composition and body conformation and their association with food and activity in a teenage population: Views of teenage subjects on body conformation, food, and activity', *American Journal of Clinical Nutrition*, **18**, pp. 325–38.

HURD, H.P., PALUMBO, P.J. and GHARIB, H. (1977) 'Hypothalamic-endocrine dysfunction in anorexia nervosa', *Mayo Clinic Proceedings*, **52**, pp. 711–16.

JAKOBOVITS, C., HALSTEAD, P., KELLEY, L., ROE, D.A. and YOUNG, C.M. (1977) 'Eating habits and nutrient intakes of college women over a thirty-year period', *Journal of the American Dietetic Association*, **71**, pp. 405–11.

JOHNSON, C. and LARSON, R. (1982) 'Bulimia: An analysis of mood and behaviour', *Psychosomatic Medicine*, **44**, pp. 341–51.

JONES, D.J., FOX, M.M., BABIGAN, H.M. and HUTTON, H.E. (1980) 'Epidemiology of anorexia nervosa in Monroe County, New York: 1960–1976', *Psychosomatic Medicine*, **42**, pp. 551–58.

KALUCY, R.S., CRISP, A.H. and HARDING, B. (1977) 'A study of 56 families with Anorexia Nervosa', *British Journal of Medical Psychology*, **50**, pp. 381–95.

KEYS, A., BROZEK, J., HENSCHEL, A., MICKELSEN, O. and TAYLOR, H.L. (1950) *The Biology of Human Starvation* 2 (vols). Minneapolis, MN: University of Minnesota Press.

LACEY, J.H. (1983) 'The bulimia syndrome at normal body weight. Reflections on pathogenesis and clinical features', *International Journal of Eating Disorders*, **2**, pp. 59–62.

LAWRENCE, M. (1979) 'Anorexia nervosa: The control paradox', *Women's Studies International Quarterly*, **2**, pp. 93–101.

LAWRENCE, M. (1984) *The Anorexic Experience*, London, UK: The Women's Press.

LAWRENCE, M. (Ed.) (1987) *Fed Up and Hungry: Women, Oppression and Food*, London, UK: The Women's Press.

LEW, E.A. and GARFINKEL, L. (1979) 'Variations in mortality by weight among 750,000 men and women', *Journal Chronic Diseases*, **32**, p. 563.

LYONS, A.S. and PETRUCELLI, R.J. (1978) *Medicine: An Illustrated History*, New York, NY: Harry N. Abrams.

MARKETING (1980) 'Slimming foods face new curbs', **3**, No. 4, pp. 20–1.

MARSHALL, M.H. (1978) 'Anorexia nervosa: Dietary treatment and re-establishment of body weight in 20 cases studied on a metabolic unit', *Journal of Human Nutrition*, **32**, pp. 349–57.

MARTIN, F. (1983) 'Subgroups in anorexia nervosa' in DARBY, P.L., *et al.* (Eds), *Anorexia Nervosa: Recent Developments in Research*, New York, NY: Allan Liss.

MILLICAN, F.K., LOURIE, R.S. and LAYMAN, E.M. (1956) Emotional factors in the aetiology and treatment of lead poisoning. *American Journal of Disorder of Childhood*, **91**, pp. 144–50.

MINUCHIN, S. (1978) *The Psychosomatic Family*, in MINUCHIN, S., ROSMAN, B.L. and BAKER, L. (Eds), *Psychosomatic Families*, Cambridge, MA: Harvard University Press.

MORGAN, H.G. and RUSSELL, G.F.M. (1975) 'Value of family background and clinical features as predictors of long-term outcome in anorexia nervosa: Four year follow-up study of 41 patients', *Psychological Medicine*, **5**, pp. 355–71.

OFFICE OF POPULATION CENSUSES AND SURVEYS (1981) *OPCS Monitor*, ref. SS 81/1.

O'NEIL, P.M., CURREY, H.S., SEXANER, J.D., RIDDLE, F.E. and MOLONY-SINNOTT, V. (1980) 'Persistence at three-year follow up of male-female differences in weight loss', in *Alimentazione Nutrizione Metabolismo, Abstracts of the Third International Congress on Obesity*, **1**, p. 333.

ORBACH, S. (1979) *Fat is a Feminist Issue*, London, UK: Hamlyn.

PARRY-JONES, B. (1991) 'Historical terminology of eating disorders' *Psychological Medicine*, **21**, pp. 21–8.

PYLE, R.L., MITCHELL, J.E. and ECKERT, E.D. (1981) 'Bulimia: A report of 34 cases', *Journal of Clinical Psychiatry*, **42**, pp. 60–4.

RATNASURIYA, R.H., EISLER, I., SZMUKLER, G.I. and RUSSELL, G.F.M. (1991) 'Anorexia nervosa: Outcome and prognostic factors after 20 years', *British Journal of Psychiatry*, **158**, pp. 495–502.

RICHARDSON, S.N. (1961) 'Cultural uniformity and reaction to physical disability', *American Sociology Review*, **26**, pp. 241–47.

RIMM, A.A., WERNER, L.H., VAN YSERLOO, B. and BERNSTEIN, R.A. (1975) 'Relationship of obesity and disease in 73,532 weight-conscious women', *Public Health Report*, **90**, p. 44.

RODIN, J. (1983) *Controlling Your Weight*. London, UK: Century.

ROSEN, J.C. and LEITENBERG, H. (1982) 'Bulimia nervosa: Treatment with exposure and response prevention', *Behaviour Therapy*, **13**, pp. 117–24.

ROYAL COLLEGE OF PHYSICIANS (1983) 'Obesity: A report of the Royal College of Physicians', reprinted from the *Journal of the Royal College of Physicians*, **17**, No. 1, January, 1983.

RUSSELL, G.F.M. (1970) 'Anorexia nervosa: Its identity as an illness and its treatment', in PRICE, J.H. (Ed.), *Modern Trends In Psychological Medicine*, **2**, London, UK: Butterworths.

RUSSELL, G.F.M. (1979) 'Bulimia Nervosa: An ominous variant of anorexia nervosa', *Psychological Medicine*, **9**, pp. 429–48.

SCHIELE, B.C. and BROZEK, J. (1948) '"Experimental Neurosis" resulting from semi-starvation in man', *Psychosomatic Medicine*, **10**, pp. 31–50.

SELVINI-PALAZZOLI, M. (1974) *Self-Starvation*, London, UK: Chaucer.

SONTAG, S. (1978) *Illness as Metaphor*, New York, NY: Farrar, Straus and Giroux.

STAFFIERI, J.R. (1967) 'A study of social stereotypes of body image in children', *Journal of Personality and Social Psychology*, **7**, pp. 101–4.

STARK, O., ATKINS, E., WOLFF, O.H. and DOUGLAS, J.W.B. (1981) 'Longitudinal study of obesity in the National Survey of Health and Development', *British Medical Journal*, **283**, p. 13.

STUNKARD, A.J. and PENICK, S.B. (1979) 'Behavior modification in the treatment of obesity: the problem of maintaining weight loss', *Archives of General Psychiatry*, **36**, p. 801.

STUART, R.B. (1967) 'Behavioural control of overeating', *Behaviour, Research and Therapy*, **5**, p. 357.

THEANDER, S. (1970) 'Anorexia nervosa: A psychiatric investigation of 94 female patients', *Acta Psychiatrica Scandinavica*, suppl. p. 214.

THEANDER, S. (1983) 'Long-term prognosis of anorexia nervosa: A preliminary report' in DARBY, P.L. *et al.* (Eds), *Anorexia Nervosa: Recent Developments in Research.* New York, NY: Alan R. Liss, Inc.

VINCENT, L.M. (1979) *Competing with the Sylph: Dancers and the Pursuit of the Ideal Body Form*, New York, NY: Andrews and McMeel.

WARDLE, J. (1980) 'Dietary restraint and binge eating', *Behavioural Analysis and Modification*, **4**, pp. 201–9.

WARDLE, J. and BEINART, H. (1981) 'Binge eating: A theoretical review', *British Journal of Clinical Psychology*, **20**, pp. 97–109.

WHITELAW, A.G.L. (1971) 'The association of social class and sibling number with skinfold thickness in London schoolboys', *Human Biology*, **43**, p. 414.

WILLIAMS, E. (1958) 'Anorexia nervosa: A somatic disorder', *British Medical Journal*, **2**, pp. 190–95.

Chapter 6

Obsessive-Compulsive Disorder

Padmal de Silva

Introduction

Obsessive-compulsive disorder is one of the conditions traditionally considered as a neurotic disorder. In psychiatric classificatory systems, it is listed among anxiety disorders; the others in this category include phobias, generalized anxiety disorder and post-traumatic stress disorder. The literature on obsessive-compulsive disorder is extensive, and excellent clinical accounts and experimental reports are available. The features of the disorder are well recognized, and are in many ways fascinating.

Essentially, obsessive-compulsive disorder is characterized by *obsessions* (unwanted, intrusive and repetitive thoughts, images or impulses) and/or *compulsions* (purposeful, stereotyped behaviours carried out with a sense of compulsion). For a person to be diagnosed as suffering from this condition, he would have either obsessions, or compulsions, or both. It is, however, not the mere presence of these that makes someone a candidate for this diagnosis; most people have obsessions and/or compulsions. Many people have fleeting unwanted thoughts that intrude into their consciousness. Studies have shown that over 75 per cent of normal adults experience these. Equally, many have various compulsive behaviours such as checking light switches or door handles more than once. It is when the obsessions and/or compulsions are so intensive or pervasive that one is distressed by them, or one's life and functioning are affected, that one is considered to be suffering from obsessive-compulsive disorder in the clinical sense. This highlights an important point: obsessive-compulsive problems are not qualitatively different from normal behaviour. They are within the spectrum of normal behaviour, and become a problem only when excessive.

A brief word is necessary here about obsessional personality or character. The obsessional personality is generally considered as characterized by orderliness, meticulousness, parsimony, neatness and perfectionism. Some consider obsessive-compulsive disorder to be necessarily related to obsessional personality (e.g., Reed, 1985). However, clinical data show that many obsessive-compulsive patients do not have a premorbid obsessional personality (Lewis, 1965). Equally, a large majority of individuals with an obsessional personality do not develop the disorder at all (Pollak, 1979).

Historical Aspects

The nature and features of the disorder were described in detail by early authors such as Janet (1903), Freud (1895) and Jaspers (1923). Esquirol in 1838 and Westphal in 1878 had earlier given several descriptions identifying obsessions and compulsions. Historically, the phenomenon had been described or alluded to in much earlier times, though not recognized as a clinical entity. Shakespeare's description of Lady Macbeth's handwashing rituals is well known and much quoted. John Bunyan, the author of *Pilgrim's Progress*, suffered considerably from obsessional thoughts of a blasphemous nature, by his own account. A similar example from a different part of the world is that of the Japanese Zen Buddhist master Hakuin (1685–1768 A.D.), who is described as having had severe obsessional problems as a young man (Kishimoto, 1985). A very early Buddhist text describes a monk in the Buddha's time (563–483 B.C.), who repeatedly engaged in ritualistically sweeping the monastery, an activity that took priority over everything else.

It is clear, then, that obsessive-compulsive problems are not a new phenomenon. Nor are they confined to the industrialized west. In fact many descriptions of the disorder have come from such distant countries as Hong Kong, India, Israel and Sri Lanka. The basic features are the same in all of these places.

Nature of Obsessive-Compulsive Disorder

It will be useful, at this stage, to give an account of the nature of obsessive-compulsive problems. This is best done in two ways: first, by looking closely at the phenomenology, and second, by describing the main clinical presentations.

Phenomenology

The major aspects of the disorder are obsessions and compulsions. As noted earlier, an obsession is an unwanted, intrusive cognition which is repetitive, persistent and generally resisted. It can take the form of a thought, an image or an impulse, and is often a combination of two or all three of these. Some clinical examples are given below:

- Thought that he was polluted by germs (male, 26 years)
- Thought, plus visual image, that he may have knocked someone down (male, 29 years)
- Image of her parents lying dead (female, 23 years)
- Impulse, with associated doubting thought, to shout obscenities during a church service (female, 19 years)

Compulsions are repetitive and seemingly purposeful behaviours that are performed in a stereotyped way or according to certain rules. The compulsion is carried out because of a strong subjectively felt urge to do so, although the person often tries to resist this urge. Unlike the obsession, which is essentially a passive experience (it happens to the person), a compulsion is an active experience; the person does it, despite not wanting to. Given below are some clinical examples:

- Repeated and extensive washing of hands, to get rid of 'dirt and germs' (female, 32 years)
- Checking gas and electrical switches, door handles, etc. three times each time he went past them (male, 28 years)
- Touching the four walls clockwise, every time he entered a room (male, 24 years)

The above are all motor compulsions, involving overt behaviour. Some compulsions are covert — that is, cognitive or mental, as illustrated by these clinical examples:

- Imagining sequence of photographs of family members (male, 38 years)
- Saying certain phrases silently four times (female, 26 years)
- Counting backwards from twenty-one (male, 21 years)

In most cases an obsession leads to a compulsion, although obsessions without an associated compulsion are not rare. Less frequent are compulsions without a preceding obsession. The relationship between the obsession and the compulsion is perhaps best understood in the context of all the key elements which may be involved in an obsessive-compulsive experience. These are presented in Figure 6.1 (see p. 116).

This scheme will fit many obsessive-compulsive episodes. This is not to say that all the elements given in the table are found in every single obsessional experience; nor is there always an invariant sequence of them, although most would follow the order given under A (i to vi). A patient's main problem may be the recurrent intrusion (A-ii) of the thought and associated visual image that he may have killed someone. This thought might be triggered (A-i) by the hearing or reading of news of murders and other violent acts (external trigger) and, less frequently, whenever he remembers a dead relation (internal trigger). The cognition is hard to dismiss and results in a strong feeling of discomfort, or even anxiety (A-iii). Associated with this may be a sharply felt urge (A-iv) to look at his hands. More often than not he will yield to this urge and so indulge in this compulsive behaviour (A-v). The compulsion may well follow a set pattern with his looking first at the left hand and then at the right with the whole sequence being followed three times. Completion of the compulsion markedly reduces the feeling of discomfort (A-vi). This marks the end of the obsessive-compulsive episode and the victim may then be relatively free of this experience for several hours until the whole thing becomes triggered off once more.

Figure 6.1: Elements of an obsessive-compulsive sequence. *The Figure illustrates two possible sequences, one in which an obsession is followed by a compulsion, and a second in which a compulsion occurs without a preceding obsession. The elements are labelled A(i), A(ii), etc., in order to illustrate the similarities and differences between the sequences. (See text for further examples.)*

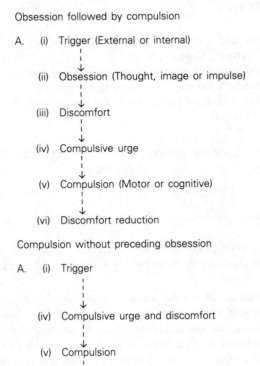

Obsession followed by compulsion

A. (i) Trigger (External or internal)
     ↓
(ii) Obsession (Thought, image or impulse)
     ↓
(iii) Discomfort
     ↓
(iv) Compulsive urge
     ↓
(v) Compulsion (Motor or cognitive)
     ↓
(vi) Discomfort reduction

Compulsion without preceding obsession

A. (i) Trigger
     ↓
(iv) Compulsive urge and discomfort
     ↓
(v) Compulsion
     ↓
(vi) Discomfort reduction

In other examples, a trigger may lead to an intrusive image, and to discomfort, with a compulsive urge which is translated into cognitive compulsive behaviour. A women complained of being assailed by images (A-ii) of asymmetrical patterns or objects. In her case the compulsive behaviour (A-v) was to imagine or visualize the offending patterns or objects in a perfect symmetrical form. Doing so brought relief (A-vi). Other instances may only involve the distressing intrusive cognition without any compulsive act or urge. A young woman had intrusive and recurrent thoughts and images of her wedding (A-ii). The cognitions particularly centred on the flower arrangements at the reception which she felt were not right. These thoughts assailed her repetitively, they were hard to dismiss and caused distress (A-iii). She had no associated compulsive behaviour, either overt or covert. As also shown in Figure 6.1, a small number of cases have a compulsive urge with resultant compulsive behaviour with no preceding obsession. An example is the case of a young woman who always had to look at the four corners (A-v) of any room she entered. Entering a room was the trigger (A-i) for this urge (A-iv), but there was no intrusive cognition (obsession). Finally, there are a small number of cases where the carrying out of the compulsive behaviour does not bring about a reduction of the discomfort/anxiety and may even increase it.

This account and examples do not illustrate a number of factors which may be present in a good number of cases. Fears of disaster are common and can be manifest at the occurrence of the obsession (A-ii), or even upon exposure to the trigger (A-i). They contribute to the discomfort felt by the person (A-iii) and thus to the strength of the compulsive urge (A-iv). Many patients resort to reassurance seeking which they usually receive from their family members. Often an obsessional thought (A-ii) in the form of a doubt (e.g., 'Did I do it correctly?', or 'Was it done the right way?') leads to this externally elicited form of relief. Avoidance is found in many cases where there is a clear external trigger to set off the whole experience. Thus a woman who gets the thought that she might attack her own children with knives or other sharp objects (A-ii) and mainly in the presence of such items (A-i), may avoid knives, scissors, etc. when she is on her own. Patients who have obsessions about contamination by dirt or germs, usually leading to extensive cleaning and washing rituals if exposed to stimuli that they believe are contaminating, tend to avoid such situations as far as possible. In extreme cases a patient may have only a small safe area in the home where he/she can move about freely. A patient may not wash in the morning because this behaviour requires a long, complicated ritual. Another may go to bed in his day clothes to avoid prolonged and exhausting compulsions involved in changing.

It has already been mentioned that both the obsession and the compulsion may be resisted by the sufferer. In his much quoted paper, Sir Aubrey Lewis (1936) argued that an essential feature of obsessive-compulsive disorder was the strong resistance that the patient had. More recent studies (e.g., Rachman and Hodgson, 1980; Stern and Cobb, 1978) have shown that, whilst resistance is very common, it is not found invariably. It is possible that in the early stages a patient may resist his obsessions and/or compulsive urges strenuously, but after repeated failures over a period of time may begin to show much less resistance. There are chronic obsessive-compulsive patients where resistance to symptoms is quite low (Rasmussen and Tsuang, 1986).

Two other terms used to describe aspects of obsessive-compulsive disorders need to be mentioned. A *ritual* in the present context is a compulsive behaviour, either overt or covert, which has a rigid set pattern or sequence of steps with a clear-cut beginning and end. An example is a checking ritual where a system of checks is carried out in an invariant sequence. Most compulsive behaviours have a ritualistic quality to them. A *rumination* is a train of thoughts, usually unproductive and prolonged, on a particular topic. A young man had complicated and time-consuming ruminations on the question 'Am I genetically flawed?' He would ruminate on this for long periods, going over various considerations and arguments and contemplating what superficially appeared as evidence. A rumination has no satisfactory conclusion, nor is there a set sequence of steps with a clear-cut end point, so it is different from a cognitive ritual. Not surprisingly, ruminations are hard to classify as either obsessions or compulsions. The decisive issue is whether they come as an intrusive experience, in which case they would fall into the category of obsessions, or whether there is a compulsive urge to think through a topic, in which case they would be compulsions. Clinically, it seems to be the case that most ruminations are compulsions and that they are usually preceded by an obsession. To illustrate this, the intrusive cognition 'Am I mad?' or 'Am I going mad?' would lead to the compulsive urge to think through the subject. The muddled 'thinking through' that follows is the rumination.

The content of obsessions and compulsions are characterized by a few common themes. Contamination and dirt, disease and illness, violence and aggression, death, and moral or religious topics are among them. Other themes include order, numbers, symmetry and sequence. Sexually related themes are also found. Sometimes the content of an obsession may be apparently senseless or totally trivial. A middle-aged man, for example, complained of the repeated thought 'these boys when they were young'.

Clinical Presentations

There are several major clinical presentations of obsessive-compulsive disorder. A person may have more than one problem at a given time and/or may have had different obsessions and/or compulsions over a period of time. Notwithstanding this, there is usually a clear and predominant clinical picture when someone presents for help. These clinical presentations are described below:

Contamination/washing/cleaning problems. These patients have fear of contamination or pollution as their main obsessional concern, and usually have extensive cleaning or washing rituals. They are the largest sub-group of obsessive-compulsive patients. Their cleaning is usually quite excessive and may include the use of soap and detergents in large quantities. There can also be extensive avoidance.

Checking. Those with this problem check various things, such as gas taps, electric switches, doors, etc. The aim of their checking is to ensure that no room is left for any harm to come, either to themselves or to others. Sometimes they fear that major disasters will happen if they do not carry out their checking rituals. Checkers have an exaggerated sense of responsibility, and feel that they have to act to ensure safety. These are the second largest sub-group.

Other overt rituals. Many patients have other extensive ritualistic behaviours, usually including doing certain things in a highly stereotyped way and in a predetermined sequence. Repetition of the behaviour a certain number of times may be a feature, as indeed it can be with washers and checkers. These overt rituals include touching, arranging, looking, hoarding and many other behaviours.

Obsessions without associated overt compulsive behaviour. A significant minority of patients with obsessive-compulsive disorder do not display overt compulsive behaviour. However, only some of this group are free of compulsions. Many do have compulsions, but their compulsions are cognitive or mental.

Primary obsessional slowness. This is a relatively recently described condition, and those presenting with this clinical picture are small in number. In these most behaviour, especially self-care behaviour, is exceedingly slow. Each step is meticulously carried out, and in a set sequence. The slowness is not secondary to other compulsions such as checking or washing, or to mental rituals. The slowness of some of these patients with regard to their self-care and grooming behaviour is amazing. A man in his fifties got up at five each morning, but was not able to get ready to leave his home until well after ten. Obviously, primary obsessional slowness can handicap someone's functioning considerably.

Some Basic Facts

Prevalence

Obsessive-compulsive disorder was considered to be quite rare until recently. The commonly accepted estimate for its prevalence in the general population was 0.05 per cent. The recent National Epidemiology Catchment Area surveys in the United States suggest a much higher rate (e.g., Robins, Helzer and Wiessman, 1984). In Baltimore, for example, a life-time prevalence of 3 per cent was found. This is a very high figure, considering earlier low estimates. In other areas, somewhat lower but still relatively high rates were found. As many obsessive-compulsives tend to be secretive about their problems and often successfully conceal their disorder for many years, the high figures unearthed by thorough and systematic epidemiological studies are perhaps not surprising.

Sex

There is no clear preponderance of males or females among clinical obsessive-compulsive patients. There are, however, clear sex differences in some of the subgroups of these patients. Among washers/cleaners, there is a preponderance of women. Primary obsessional slowness is largely a male phenomenon.

Onset and Course

The onset of obsessive-compulsive disorder is usually in adolescence or early adulthood. Onset after the age of forty-five is rare. Most cases emerge by the age of thirty. Recent data on childhood obsessive-compulsive disorder suggest that the age of onset in some cases can be quite early, even before the age of five. Such early onset is more common in boys than in girls. In general, males have earlier onset than females.

The course of the disorder is a fluctuating one. Periods of severe problems may be followed by relatively symptom-free periods. In almost a half of all cases, however, there is a steadily worsening course. It is well established that stressful experiences make the obsessive-compulsive disorder worse, and can precipitate relapse. It is also known that depression is commonly associated with this disorder, and the problems tend to get exacerbated with significantly low mood.

Theoretical Approaches

There are many theories and models aimed at explaining obsessive-compulsive disorder. For the most part, the tendency has been to assume that the disorder represents a unitary phenomenon, with each theoretical model being offered to account for a diversity of symptoms and presentations. More recent reviews (e.g., de Silva, 1986; Rachman, 1982; Sturgis, 1984) suggest that such a unitary view may be mistaken. Apart from the fact that obsessions and compulsions are distinct phenomena, there are also differences between subgroups of patients with compulsive rituals. Rachman and Hodgson (1980) and Foa and her team (Foa, Steketee, Turner and Fischer, 1980; Steketee, Foa and Grayson, 1982), amongst others, have documented important differences between those whose main compulsions are checking behaviours and those whose main problem consists of washing and cleaning rituals. It is important to recognize this diversity in proffering and evaluating theories for explaining these disorders. It must also be noted that the accounts offered for the aetiology of the disorders may not be adequate to account for the maintenance, and vice versa.

The Psychoanalytic Approach

Historically, the oldest and best-known theoretical account of obsessive-compulsive disorder is the psychoanalytic one. Freud's writings on obsessive-compulsive problems display different and changing views over time (e.g., 1895, 1913). What is loosely described as the psychoanalytic view is in fact a version of these as developed by later writers such as Fenichel (1945). Repressed memories, desires and conflicts are held to be the source of neurotic anxiety which manifests itself as various symptoms. Fixation at a particular stage of psychosexual development, caused by various factors during the formative years, determines the nature of the manifest problem when the neurosis appears in later life. Obsessive-compulsive disorder is assumed to be linked to the anal-sadistic stage of development in which toilet training is a major feature and with which anger and aggression are also associated. Those who do not successfully negotiate this phase of development are vulnerable to obsessive-compulsive problems in later years.

The Learning Approach

The behavioural/learning view has been more widely held and discussed in recent years. It derives from Mowrer's two-factor theory of learning (1939, 1960). Certain stimuli and situations may acquire anxiety-producing properties by a process of classical conditioning. On later occasions, the anxiety (conditioned emotional response) which results from exposure to the conditioned stimulus is terminated by an escape or avoidance response. This produces anxiety relief, thus reinforcing the response. This is a case of instrumental conditioning. Extending these views to obsessive-compulsive behaviour, it is assumed that the compulsive acts are performed in response to anxiety generated by certain stimuli, which may include the individual's own obsessions, and are strengthened as a result of the anxiety reduction that follows (Dollard and Miller, 1950). The model is essentially one of learned anxiety reduction.

Rachman and Hodgson (1980) have suggested that in these patients the critical negative emotion should be considered as discomfort rather than anxiety since in many cases patients report feelings other than those of anxiety. The view is then that discomfort reduction is the crucial element in the maintenance of obsessive-compulsive behaviour.

There is much evidence in support of this position. The studies of Rachman and his associates carried out in London in the 1970s provide appreciable corroboration (Hodgson and Rachman, 1972; Rachman, de Silva and Roper, 1976; Rachman and Hodgson, 1980). In these experiments it was found that both checkers and cleaners show heightened anxiety/discomfort when exposed to certain situations and/or stimuli (cues) which normally generated their ritualistic behaviours. For example, a cleaner made to touch an item which he believed to be contaminated would typically report a marked heightening of anxiety or discomfort. When the compulsive behaviour, e.g., hand-washing, was carried out there was considerable reduction in discomfort. Associated with the discomfort, and following the same course, was the compulsive urge subjectively felt by the patient. In a small number of cases, the execution of the compulsive behaviour actually led to an increase in discomfort. Nevertheless, despite the exceptions, the model appears to be robust.

Further evidence supporting the model comes from two sources. First, Likierman and Rachman (1980) showed that repeated trials of exposure to cues in the same patient led to progressively lower levels of both discomfort and felt compulsive urge, and to progressively quicker dissipation of these under conditions of response prevention (i.e., the patient not being allowed to carry out his compulsive behaviour). This shows that there is a cumulative effect in repeated exposure to discomfort cues or, in other words, a habituation process. This fits well into the discomfort reduction model. If the compulsive behaviours were maintained by the reduction of anxiety/discomfort achieved by carrying out the behaviour, then the prevention of these behaviours in the presence of the relevant cues should have certain effects. With repeated exposures the urge to engage in the compulsive behaviours, and the behaviours themselves, should gradually reduce. This is exactly what the Likierman and

Rachman (1980) experiment demonstrated. The second line of supporting evidence comes from the numerous treatment studies of obsessive-compulsive patients using the exposure and response prevention paradigm in which the patient's desire to engage in the compulsive behaviour is provoked, but he is persuaded not to carry it out. This is done in the context of a trusting thera- peutic relationship. The success of this approach is well established and fits in well with the discomfort reduction model. These studies are summarized in detail elsewhere (e.g., Marks, 1981; Rachman and Hodgson, 1980).

The discomfort reduction aspect of this approach is thus supported by both experimental and treatment studies. On the other hand, the theory is on less sure grounds with regard to the aetiology of the disorder. Why is it that only certain types of stimuli tend to lead to these behaviours, as shown by de Silva, Rachman and Seligman (1977)? Why is it that many patients do not have a traumatic (conditioning) experience as the starting point for their problem behaviours? The criticisms of the Mowrer two-factor theory as a model for neurosis are well known and need not be repeated here (see Chapter 1 and Chapter 3). Dollard and Miller (1950) proposed that certain behaviour patterns which previously led to anxiety reduction, such as hand-washing or checking, become exaggerated and take the form of compulsions. For example, washing in childhood is often associated with avoidance of, or escape from, parental criticism. However, how and why some behaviours turn into adult compul- sions, or why only some individuals are subject to them, is not explained. Further, the learning model does not offer much help in understanding obsessions that are not accompanied by compulsive behaviours. Finally the elaborate, repetitive, and even bizarre nature of compulsive behaviour which is best seen as active avoidance, unlike the passive avoidance found in phobias (see Gray, 1982; Rachman and Hodgson, 1980), needs to be explained more fully than the conditioning theory would allow.

Some writers have examined the animal-learning literature as a possible source of understanding of obsessive-compulsive disorders. In a key paper, Teasdale (1974) suggested that compulsive behaviours may be considered as avoidance behaviours which are under poor stimulus control. They are remin- iscent of the unnecessarily high frequency of responses shown by animals in experiments using the Sidman avoidance paradigm, where electric shocks are given to promote avoidance learning, but the delivery of the shock is unsignalled (Sidman, 1955). Compulsive rituals can also be seen as not having good feedback or safety-signal properties and hence their inefficiently high rate of occurrence (Rachman and Hodgson, 1980; Teasdale, 1974). For example, a patient will not know easily whether the germs he is trying to wash off have been effectively removed since there is no safety signal or feedback to indicate that this has happened. The same applies to many checking rituals intended to ward off future disasters.

Another aspect of the avoidance literature which has been cited as poss- ibly relevant comes from the findings of Fonberg (1956), as cited by Wolpe (1958) (p. 65). In this study, she first trained dogs to make a response (e.g., leg-lifting) to avoid an aversive stimulus. They were then subjected to a second conditioning procedure aimed at inducing an experimental 'neurosis' by making the required discrimination increasingly difficult. As the animals' behaviour became more and more 'neurotic' it was observed that they began to show the previously learned avoidance response (leg-lifting) at a high frequency, although no more discriminative stimuli for this particular response were presented. What seemed to be happening was that a response learned to avoid aversive stimulation re-emerged in a different setting when anxiety was induced in a different way. The relevance of this to the present topic is that it appears to provide a parallel for the wide variety of situations in which compulsive behaviours are performed by the patient. For example, a patient may engage in repetitive hand washing behaviour when under stress, although the hands are not in any way dirty or contaminated.

Thus there are several findings from animal avoidance learning which have been considered as possibly relevant to the understanding of obsessive-compulsive disorders. None of these provides a full, or even closely approximate, analogy. However, they throw some light on the possible ways in which obsessive-compulsive behaviours may be acquired, why they occur in different settings, why some of them appear unrelated to the situation in which they are manifest, and why they are strongly persistent.

Cognitive Deficit Approaches

It has been suggested that obsessive-compulsive patients have a major difficulty in decision making which may explain their symptoms (e.g., Beech and Liddell, 1974; Milner, Beech and Walker, 1971). Reed (1976; 1985) has also emphasized this aspect of obsessive-compulsive problems. There is some evidence of this (Volans, 1976), but it is not clear that it can be taken as an explanation of obsessive-compulsive phenomena. Emmelkamp (1982) has argued that the decision-making difficulty could equally well be a consequence of the symptoms. The proper evaluation of decision-making difficulties in these disorders must await further investigation.

Adopting a somewhat different approach, Carr (1974) has argued that obsessive-compulsive patients make very high subjective estimates of the probability of aversive outcomes. Compulsive behaviours develop to reduce the threat of these outcomes. The behaviours lead to the relief of anxiety and reduce the subjective threat. Further arguments along these lines are presented by McFall and Wollersheim (1979).

A more general cognitive theory has been offered by Reed (1985). According to a summarization by Reed, the main problem is 'that the obsessional finds difficulty in the spontaneous structuring of experience and attempts to compensate for this by imposing artificial, rigidly defined boundaries, category limits, and time markers. The rigidity and specificity of definition themselves lead to further uncertainty as to the ' "appropriate" allocation of category items, schematization, completion times, etc.' (Reed, 1985, p. 220). Reed attempts to explain all the major phenomena of the disorder in terms of this central concept. For example, checking may be seen as a failure in 'terminating response' coupled with uncertainty. Rituals are an example of the imposition of artificial structure geared to the arbitrary definition of tasks and situations. A study by Persons and Foa (1984) provides some independent evidence of certain features of the thought patterns of ritualizers consistent with Reed's views. Ritualizers appeared to use 'complex concepts', i.e., concepts that are excessively complex and over-specific. There are further data on the possible role of cognitive deficits in obsessive-compulsive problems. Sher, Mann, Frost and Otto (1983) found that non-clinical compulsive checkers had poorer memories for prior actions than non-checkers. They were also found to underestimate their ability to distinguish memories of real and imagined events ('reality monitoring'). Both these factors were considered to contribute to checking rituals. A subsequent study by Sher and Frost (1984) confirmed the previous findings and also showed that compulsive checkers had a particular memory deficit for meaningfully linked sequences. Despite this work, it is not yet possible to make a proper evaluation of Reed's position or of any other cognitive-deficit model. The postulated central deficit assumes too much uniformity in the phenomena. Both clinical and other data show too great a diversity. Such models also fail to take into account the selective nature of the content of obsessive-compulsive problems.

The Explanation of Obsessions — Emotional Processing

It is necessary at this point to discuss obsessions briefly. Many of the theoretical models address themselves to the origins and maintenance of compulsions, especially overt rituals. In theory they could apply equally well to cognitive rituals. If cognitive compulsive behaviour reduces discomfort, then it is likely that it will be manifest to avoid impending discomfort. But what of the obsessions, the intrusive cognition that in some cases occurs on its own and in others leads to a compulsion? In both these instances what is primarily needed is an explanation as to why the cognition occurs in the first place. This relatively neglected aspect of obsessive-compulsive disorder has only recently received systematic study. Following Rachman's (1971) view that such experiences may not be uncommon in the normal population, research has confirmed that normal people do have similar unwanted intrusive cognitions, or 'normal obsessions' (Parkinson and Rachman, 1980; Rachman and de Silva 1978). The amount of disturbance that they cause seems to determine how difficult they are to control (Rachman, 1982). The discomfort they generate may lead to anxiety reducing compulsions. It appears that their genesis may be related to stress, both naturally occurring and artificially induced. Studies by Horowitz have shown that experimentally delivered traumatic input causes intrusions of related cognitions later on (e.g., Horowitz, 1975). Similar intrusions are found in those undergoing uncontrived stress experiences (Rachman and Parkinson, 1981). These common, normal experiences seem to be short-lived and removal of the stress dramatically reduces them. On the other hand, unresolved stress may cause them to become chronic. This would be especially so in cases where the initial stress is not clear-cut or where there are multiple stresses. Further, Sutherland, Newman and Rachman (1982) have shown experimentally that induced dysphoria helps to evoke unwanted intrusive cognitions and also makes these difficult to remove. In the light of present knowledge, perhaps the best explanation for the persistence of obsessions, and of how normal intrusions become more chronic and achieve clinically significant levels of severity, lies with the broad concept of emotional processing as proposed by Rachman (1980). Elements of stressful material which have not been successfully processed emotionally, may appear in an intrusive way from time to time and cause distress. This can, and indeed does, happen to most people. The individual is more vulnerable to these when mood is low and when affected by fresh stresses. In those who are predisposed in certain ways (whether genetic, due to early social experiences, or whatever), such experiences are likely to become more persistent, more intense, more distressing, and more difficult to control. While in some cases the intrusion directly reflects the stress, in others it may do so only indirectly or in a fragmented form. In numerous cases where the obsession is associated with a compulsion, the explanation of the compulsion is still plausible along the lines of discomfort reduction.

Biological Theory

The view that obsessive-compulsive disorder has a clear biological causation has been put forward by several authors in recent years. A few comments on this are in order.

The biological theory proposes that the disorder is caused by a biochemical imbalance in the brain. In particular, it is claimed that obsessive-compulsive disorder arises from an inadequate supply of serotonin. (Serotonin is a neurotransmitter — that is, a chemical substance which carries messages between cells in the brain. It is known that serotonin plays quite an important part in brain functioning.) This theory originally emerged from the finding that an anti-depressive drug, clomipramine, which blocks the natural loss of serotonin, can produce therapeutic effects in these patients. A useful discussion is available in Insel and Winslow (1990).

This theory has gained some support, but has also been criticized. Therapeutic effects of equal or greater magnitude than produced by clomipramine or similar drugs have been achieved through purely psychological treatment methods — when the serotonin level is ignored. There is no evidence that people suffering from obsessive-compulsive disorder have serotonin levels that differ from those of people suffering from other comparable psychological disorders, especially other anxiety disorders, or levels that differ from people free of any such disorder. Further, there is no relationship between the amount of clomipramine absorbed and the degree of therapeutic change. Even with high doses of the drug, and hence high levels of serotonin, relatively few patients are free of obsessive-compulsive symptoms. Some patients simply do not improve, even with high doses of serotonin bolstering drugs such as clomipramine. It has also been found in recent research that the patient's initial response to clomipramine does not provide a good basis for predicting the longer term effects of this medication. Another criticism of the biological theory is that the attempt to decide the cause of a disorder from a therapeutic effect is risky. For example, the fact that aspirin relieves a headache tells us little about the cause of the headache, and it certainly does not tell us that the headache occurred because the person was short of aspirin. The fact that clomipramine often reduces obsessive-compulsive symptoms does not mean that the disorder was caused by a shortage of clomipramine, or of serotonin which clomipramine bolsters.

A great deal of research is being carried out at present on this issue. No doubt within a few years a good deal of new light will be shed by these studies on the biological theory. The evidence supporting the theory is at the moment not persuasive.

Concluding Comments

None of the theories outlined here offers a fully convincing and comprehensive account of obsessive-compulsive disorder. It is possible that different aspects of the disorder need different explanations. Several of the theoretical approaches proposed have some validity in explaining some aspects of the disorder, but do not provide a comprehensive account. It is likely that there is some biological predisposition that may be genetically transmitted. Personal experiences and social learning are also likely to be implicated. The role of the stressful experiences in triggering and worsening obsessive-compulsive disorder is well known. Stresses that are not satisfactorily emotionally processed and absorbed may well be the major cause of obsessions. Compulsions may be seen as anxiety reducing behaviours which have been well established and ritualized. Their maintenance can be understood as the result of their efficacy in anxiety reduction. In other words, anxiety reduction may be said to reinforce the compulsive behaviour and thus perpetuate it. In this specific sense, the learning theory approach appears to have clear support. Whether there is a causal role for cognitive deficits or style is at present doubtful.

Our present understanding of obsessive-compulsive disorder is incomplete. There is no doubt that it will continue to generate much empirical research. Such research is likely to enhance our understanding of this fascinating disorder, and to help develop testable theoretical accounts.

Recommended Reading

JENIKE, M.A., BAER, L. and MINICHIELLO, W.E. (Eds) (1990) *Obsessive-Compulsive Disorders: Theory and Management, 2nd Edition.* Chicago, IL: Year Book Medical Publishers.

This edited volume gives useful up-to-date information on many aspects of the problems and discusses important theoretical issues.

RACHMAN, S.J. and HODGSON, R.J. (1980) *Obsessions and Compulsions*, Englewood Cliffs, NJ: Prentice-Hall.

This book provides a description and discussion of the field of obsessive-compulsive disorder. It describes what is known about obsessions and compulsions, gives an account of the authors' research, and comments on theoretical issues. Still the best single text on the subject.

BARLOW, D. (1988) *Anxiety and Its Disorders*, New York, NY: Guilford Press.

A comprehensive book on the whole range of anxiety disorders, with a particularly useful chapter on obsessive-compulsive disorder.

TURNER, S.M. and BEIDEL, D.C. (1988) *Treating Obsessive-Compulsive Disorder*, New York, NY: Pergamon.

This brief text gives an excellent, concise, account of treatment.

References

BEECH, H.R. and LIDDELL, A. (1974) 'Decision-making, mood states and ritualistic behaviour among obsessional patients', in BEECH, H.R. (Ed.) *Obsessional States*, London, UK: Methuen.

CARR, A. (1974) 'Compulsive neurosis: a review of the literature', *Psychological Bulletin* **81**, pp. 331–18.

DE SILVA, P. (1986) 'Obsessional-compulsive imagery', *Behaviour Research and Therapy* **24**, 333–50.

DE SILVA, P., RACHMAN, S.J. and SELIGMAN, M.E.P. (1977) 'Prepared phobias and obsessions: therapeutic outcome', *Behaviour Research and Therapy*, **15**, pp. 65–78.

DOLLARD, J. and MILLER, N.E. (1950) *Personality and Psychotherapy: An Analysis in Terms of Learning, Thinking and Culture*; New York, NY: McGraw-Hill.

EMMELKAMP, P.M.G. (1982) *Phobic and Obsessive-Compulsive Disorders*, New York, NY: Plenum.

FENICHEL, O. (1945) *The Psychoanalytic Theory of Neurosis*, New York, NY: Norton.

FOA, E.B., STEKETEE, G., TURNER and R.M. FISCHER, S.C. (1980) Effects of imaginal exposure to feared disasters in obsessive-compulsive checkers', *Behaviour Research and Therapy* **18**, pp. 449–55.

FREUD, S. (1895) 'Obsessions and phobias', in STRACHEY, J. (Ed.) *Standard Edition of the Complete Psychological Works of Sigmund Freud*, London, UK: Hogarth, **3**, pp. 45–61.

FREUD, S. (1913) 'The disposition to obsessional neurosis', in STRACHEY, J. (Ed.) *Standard Edition of the Complete Psychological Work of Sigmund Freud*, London, UK: Hogarth, **12**, pp. 317–26.

GRAY, J.A. (1982) *The Neuropsychology of Anxiety*, Oxford, UK: Clarendon.

HODGSON, R.J. and RACHMAN, S.J. (1972) 'The effects of contamination and washing in obsessional patients', *Behaviour Research and Therapy*, **10**, pp. 11–17.

HOROWITZ, M. (1975) 'Intrusive and repetitive thoughts after experimental stress', *Archives of General Psychiatry*, **32**, pp. 145–63.

INSEL, T.R. and WINSLOW, J.T. (1990) 'Neurobiology of obsessive-compulsive disorder', in JENIKE, M.A., BAER, L. and MINICHIELLO, W.E. (Eds) *Obsessive-Compulsive Disorder: Theory and Management*, Chicago, IL: Yearbook Medical Publishers.

JANET, P. (1903) *Les Obsessions et la Psychasthenie*, Paris, FR: Alcan.

JASPERS, K. (1923) *General Psychopathology* (translated by HOENIG, J. and HAMILTON, M.W. 1963), Chicago, IL: University of Chicago Press.

KISHIMOTO, K. (1985) 'Self-awakening psychotherapy for neurosis: attacking unimportance to oriental thought, especially Buddhist thought', *Psychologia,* **28**, pp. 90–100.

LEWIS, A. (1936) 'Problems of obsessional illness', *Proceedings of the Royal Society of Medicine,* **29**, pp. 325–36.

LEWIS, A. (1965) 'A note on personality and obsessional illness', *Psychiatia et Neurologia,* **150**, pp. 299–305.

LIKIERMAN, H. and RACHMAN, S.J. (1980) 'Spontaneous decay of compulsive urges: cumulative effects', *Behaviour Research and Therapy,* **18**, 387–94.

McFALL, M.G. and WOLLERSHEIM, J.P. (1979) 'Obsessive-compulsive neurosis: a cognitive-behavioural formulation and approach to treatment', *Cognitive Therapy and Research,* **3**, pp. 333–48.

MARKS, I.M. (1981) *Cure and Care of Neuroses,* New York, NY: Wiley.

MILNER, A.D., BEECH, H.R. and WALKER, V.J. (1971) 'Decision processes and obsessional behaviour', *British Journal of Social and Clinical Psychology,* **10**, pp. 88–9.

MOWRER, O.H. (1939) 'A stimulus-response theory of anxiety', *Psychological Review,* **46**, pp. 553–65.

MOWRER, O.H. (1960) *Learning Theory and Behaviour,* New York, NY: Wiley.

PARKINSON, L. and RACHMAN, S.J. (1980) 'Are intrusive thoughts subject to habituation?', *Behaviour Research and Therapy,* **18**, pp. 409–18.

PERSONS, J.B. and FOA, E.B. (1984) 'Processing of fearful and neutral information by obsessive-compulsives', *Behaviour Research and Therapy,* **22**, pp. 159–65.

POLLAK, J.M. (1979) 'Obsessive-compulsive personality: A review', *Psychological Bulletin,* **86**, pp. 225–41.

RACHMAN, S.J. (1971) 'Obsessional ruminations', *Behaviour Research and Therapy,* **9**, pp. 229–35.

RACHMAN, S.J. (1980) 'Emotional processing', *Behaviour Research and Therapy,* **18**, pp. 51–60.

RACHMAN, S.J. (1982) 'Obsessional-compulsive disorders', in BELLACK, A.S. HERSEN, M. and KAZDIN, A.E. (Eds) *International Handbook of Behaviour Modification and Therapy,* New York, NY: Plenum.

RACHMAN, S.J. and DE SILVA, P. (1978) 'Abnormal and normal obsessions', *Behaviour Research and Therapy,* **16**, pp. 233–48.

RACHMAN, S.J. and HODGSON, R.J. (1980) *Obsessions and Compulsions,* Englewood Cliffs, NJ: Prentice Hall.

RACHMAN, S.J. and PARKINSON, L. (1981) 'Unwanted intrusive cognitions', *Advances in Behaviour Research and Therapy,* **3**, pp. 89–123.

RACHMAN, S.J., DE SILVA, P. and ROPER, G. (1976) 'The spontaneous decay of compulsive urges', *Behaviour Research and Therapy,* **14**, pp. 445–53.

RASMUSSEN, S.A. and TSUANG, M.T. (1986) 'Clinical characteristics and family history in DSM-III obsessive-compulsive disorders', *American Journal of Psychiatry,* **143**, pp. 317–22.

REED, G.F. (1976) 'Indecisiveness in obsessional-compulsive disorder', *British Journal of Social and Clinical Psychology,* **15**, pp. 443–45.

REED, G.F. (1985) *Obsessional Experience and Compulsive Behaviour,* London, UK: Academic Press.

ROBINS, L.N., HELZER, J.L. and WEISSMAN, M.M. (1984) 'Life time prevalence of specific psychiatric disorder in three sites', *Archives of General Psychiatry,* **41**, pp. 949–58.

SHER, K.J., MANN, B., FROST, R.O. and OTTO, R. (1983) 'Cognitive deficits in compulsive checkers: an exploratory study', *Behaviour Research and Therapy*, **21**, pp. 357–63.

SHER, K.J. and FROST, R.O. (1984) 'Cognitive dysfunction in compulsive checkers: further explorations', *Behaviour Research and Therapy*, **22**, pp. 493–502.

SIDMAN, M. (1955) 'Some properties of warning stimulus in avoidance behaviour', *Journal of Comparative and Physiological Psychology*, **48**, pp. 444–50.

STEKETEE, G., FOA, E.B. and GRAYSON, J.B. (1982) 'Recent advances in the behavioural treatment of obsessive-compulsives', *Archives of General Psychiatry*, **39**, pp. 1365–71.

STERN, R.S. and COBB, J.P. (1978) 'Phenomenology of obsessive-compulsive neurosis', *British Journal of Psychiatry*, **132**, pp. 233–39.

STURGIS, E. (1984) 'Obsessional and compulsive disorder', in ADAMS, H.E. and SUTKER, P.B. (Eds) *Comprehensive Handbook of Psychopathology*, New York, NY: Plenum.

SUTHERLAND, G. NEWMAN, B. and RACHMAN, S.J. (1982) 'Experimental investigations of the relation between mood and intrusive unwanted cognitions', *British Journal of Medical Psychology*, **55**, pp. 127–38.

TEASDALE, J. (1974) 'Learning models of obsessional-compulsive disorders', in BEECH, H.R. (Ed.) *Obsessional States*. London, UK: Methuen.

VOLANS, P.J. (1976) 'Styles of decision-making and probability appraisal in selected obsessional and phobic patients', *British Journal of Social and Clinical Psychology*, **15**, pp. 430–50.

WOLPE, J.R. (1958) *Psychotherapy by Reciprocal Inhibition*. Stanford, CA: University of Stanford Press.

Chapter 7

Couple and Sexual Problems

Greg Dring and Breda Kingston

This chapter is concerned with relationship problems experienced by people living with one another in a partnership such as marriage. It is about the problem which arises when one or both partners experience unhappiness about the relationship in general, and the problem of one or both partners experiencing unhappiness about the sexual relationship in particular. Although most thinking about such problems has arisen from thinking about heterosexual relationships, similar principals apply to the treatment of problems in homosexual relationships.

Difficulties within couples' relationships may be significant for other problems, such as problems experienced by their children. This issue will not be discussed but is discussed in chapter 8 on Family Therapy.

There is an increasing tendency in society for couples to live together without marrying. Because of this we have chosen not to use the terms 'marital problems' or 'marital therapy', instead we use the terms 'couple problems' and 'couple therapy'.

The Nature of the Problem

Unhappiness in relationships gives rise to a number of patterns of behaviour. In some couples there are arguments and fights, while others drift apart with little expression of dissatisfaction or emotion, at least to one another. In some instances one partner will declare dissatisfaction with the relationship while the other seeks to disqualify this by arguing that the dissatisfaction arises from reasons which are invalid or imaginary. Another important pattern emerges where one partner has formed a romantic and/or sexual attachment to a third party.

Individuals Experience of Relationship Problems

Whatever the pattern of relationship problems in a couple it is likely that common factors of experience emerge. Some of these concern the experience of the relationship, while others are experiences of the self. As far as the experience of the relationship is concerned, common factors are: loss of satisfactory mutual exchanges; loss of trust in the partner's benevolent intentions; and the experience of inability to negotiate solutions with the partner. These factors give rise to or maintain a negative frame of reference of each partner to the other.

The situation gives rise to a number of threats to each partner's sense of self. For each partner there will be a threat to self-esteem arising from his or her own fear of inadequacy or unworthiness in the relationship, or from experience of the partner's accusations in this respect. Such a threat to self-esteem, whether or not it is acknowledged, is likely to be a determinant of behaviour. In addition, unhappiness in relationships carries with it an explicit or implicit threat of the ending of the relationship. For each partner this carries with it the possibility of loneliness, and the fear of losing the nurturance the other has provided. Many people may fear the breakdown of a relationship because they see it as involving a loss of face. It certainly contains other threatening possibilities such as a break in the continuity of relationships, for example with children, and the danger of a decline in material well-being. A number of psychological approaches to the treatment of such problems have been developed.

Behavioural Marital Therapy

This approach arises from the development within psychology of the learning based models of human behaviour (see Chapter 1). Behavioural marital therapy draws mainly on operant theory and social learning theory. It is the underlying assumption of this approach that partnerships are based on reciprocal positive reinforcement (Stuart, 1969). That is to say, each partner must behave in ways that reinforce the behaviour of the other. To use the terminology of behavioural theory one would say that each dispenses social reinforcement to the other. In the successful partnership each will work to maximise mutual rewards while minimising individual costs. In the unsuccessful or distressed marriage each partner rewards the other at a low rate and so each becomes unattractive to the other. Partners in such marriages will work to minimise their costs in the relationship with little expectation of reward. Jacobsen and Margolin (1979) argue that each responds on the basis of past experience with his or her partner. The impact of a partner's behaviour as a reinforcer is influenced by the recipient's appraisals and attributions. For example, one partner's affectional statements might be positively reinforcing, but they might become ineffective or negative if that partner had just been found to be involved in an affair. Because of the past experience of reciprocal positive reward in the relationship each will be able to tolerate delay before reward is received. They suggest that this gives rise to an operational definition of 'trust' in a relationship. The time interval that can be tolerated in a relationship between positive reinforcement can be seen as indicative of the state of the 'trust' in the relationship. People who cannot tolerate delay for long are likely to experience the relationship as distressed. Another way of looking at it would be that the unhappy relationship has become one that depends on negative reinforcement instead of positive reinforcement.

In addition, partners in unhappy marriages are seen as having skills deficits in a number of areas. They are seen as not competent in establishing relationships based on positive reciprocal reward, not competent in problem solving and lacking appropriate communication skills.

Assessment. The maladaptive behaviour of the couple is the central concern of the behavioural marital therapist. She or he begins therapy by meeting the couple with a view to beginning to make an assessment and to build in the couple a positive expectation of the therapy. In a first interview a history of the relationship is taken. Problems are not fully investigated at that early stage. Instead the couple are asked before the next meeting to complete questionaires reporting the pleasing and displeasing behaviours produced by their partners. They indicate how they would like to change and how they would like their partner to change in the relationship. In a subsequent session the therapist sets the couple a communication task, using material drawn from their questionaire responses, and assesses their communication skills by direct observation.

Increasing positive behaviour exchanges. In the next stage the couple are not encouraged to address their complaints about one another and the relationship, but to begin to increase the number of already existing behaviours that please the partner. Great emphasis is placed on specific behavioural description at all stages. Alternatively, they may be asked to increase the frequency of mutually satisfactory activities. Sometimes a written contract is made between the partners governing how they will behave towards one another at this stage. As Jacobsen and Margolin (1979) say 'The spouses first learn to identify important relationship behaviours by monitoring their own behaviour and its relationship to the partner's daily satisfaction. An increase in significant relationship behaviours is then engineered with the expectation that marital satisfaction will also increase. The overall strategy addresses both the erosion of relationship reinforcement and spouses' abdication of control over their relationship.'

Communication training. The couple receive training in communication and problem-solving skills relevant to the behavioural exchange model. Couples are taught these skills through a systematic programme of training, utilising techniques such as instruction, feedback and behavioural rehearsal. They are taught to pinpoint target behaviours and to utilise behavioural management techniques such as shaping. They learn to base their control techniques in the relationship on positive rather than negative reinforcement and to change in the direction of more desirable behaviour through direct negotiation. In addition, the couple are taught listening skills, and to relate positively to one another by validating the legitimacy of each person's feelings and by positive expressions of affection and praise. At this stage the therapist's role is to teach, model and give feedback to each partner on the development of communication skills.

Problem solving training.   Problem solving is the process of negotiating about complaints about the behaviour of one or both partners in the relationship. At first couples are encouraged to discuss problems at set times rather than continuously, with an agenda in order to concentrate on specific issues, and with a collaborative attitude. Communication skills are seen as crucial to successful problem solving. Emphasis is given to the idea that solutions should include mutuality and compromise, with each partner changing some aspect of his or her behaviour. Behaviour change agreements are made in specific terms and spelt out in writing.

Contingency contracting.   Finally, couples are encouraged to develop quid pro quo contracts. These are written agreements in which each partner agrees to change his or her behaviour in exchange for changes made by the other.

Generalisation.   Behavioural marital therapists are concerned not to create a situation in which couples can resolve problems only in the consulting room. In order to encourage the generalisation of changes to everyday life, homework tasks are used at an early stage. For the same reason the therapist, though very active early in treatment, fades out his or her involvement in later sessions. Couples who are able to maintain their negotiation and positive behaviour changes when the therapist is less involved are those most likely to benefit from this approach.

Psychotherapeutic Approaches to the Couple

From the point of view of many psychotherapeutic models, problems arising in relationships reflect underlying intrapsychic causes. Such conflicts arise in their turn from childhood experiences. These experiences give rise to internal conflicts. Such conflicts arising in the distant past are acted out in current relationships. Unconscious intrapsychic conflicts are seen as determining the choice of partner. In this way they set the scene for the conflicts which will be experienced in the relationship. Emotional conflicts arising from childhood are reactivated in the context of the intimate relationship of the couple.

Dicks (1967) drew on object-relations theory in developing an approach to conflicts between partners. He viewed marital conflicts as arising from a number of causes. He saw some as arising from social and cultural norms or from discrepant expectations about the relationship. He saw others as reflecting unconscious problems having to do with the person's perception of self in relation to the other. It was this third level of unconscious problems which he explained in terms of *object-relations theory*. From this point of view the defences of each partner depend on maintaining a certain view of the other. Conflict arises between the partners when one or both of them behave in ways which are incompatible with the internalised image maintained by the other.

Psychotherapeutic Approaches to the Treatment of the Couple

Psychoanalytic views. A central concept in the psychoanalytic explanation of therapeutic change is the idea of *transference* (see Chapter 1). It is supposed that emotional conflicts arising from early life experiences manifest themselves in the relationship in the form of a distortion of the relationship. The psychoanalyst's task is to observe this distortion and interpret it to the patient. It is through this process, the development of the transference and its interpretation by the analyst that the patient develops insight, that is to say the patient develops an understanding of the emotional conflicts and the way in which they distort his or her current relationships. For this reason individual therapy of one or both partners would be seen as the appropriate treatment for unhappy relationships. Today such a view seems old fashioned. An alternative psychoanalytic view has been advanced which sees transference as being manifested primarily between the partners in the relationship. Some psycho-analytic therapists argue that in working with a couple a therapist may directly confront misperceptions and help spouses to acknowledge positive aspects of their partners' behaviour.

Other psychotherapeutic views. Seen from a non-psychoanalytic perspective couples therapy does not need to be explained in terms of transference. Ables and Brandsma (1977) describe an approach in which the therapist establishes a working alliance with both spouses. It is important to establish a safe, non-judgemental environment. The therapist proceeds from the point of view that each partner is entitled to his or her feelings. Non-judgemental explora-tion of the feelings of each partner helps to reduce the mutual defensiveness within the relationship. In this way it is hoped that a more trusting, under-standing and intimate relationship will ultimately be achieved.

Systems Approaches to Couples Problems

Theoretical approaches to family therapy based on general systems theory have clear implications for the treatment of couples problems and sexual problems. These approaches are discussed in Chapter 8 on Family Problems. What follows is a description of the implication of this theoretical position for under-standing and treating the problems of couples.

Theoretical Implications

Couples do not exist in isolation. The relationship of a couple exists within a network or system of other relationships. Of these, the relationships they have with their families of origin, especially parents and parents-in-law, and with their children, are the most significant. Problems within the couple relationship reflect problems in its relationship with the wider system. Change in the couple's relationship will require change in the relationship with other parts of the system.

Families are rule bound systems. Families are seen as organised by unspoken rules. These rules govern the way family members behave, and the ways in which they can see themselves and one another.

Couple formation and the family life cycle. When a new couple is formed each partner comes to it with rules derived from his or her family of origin. These rules will be, to a greater or lesser degree, different from those of the other partner. The formation of the new relationship involves a collision of these rules and the working out of a synthesis governing the behaviour of the new couple, and in due course, of the family they create. This process of synthesising the rules will be active at the beginning of the relationship and will be reactivated when the couple face new challenges which have a bearing on their relationship, such as transitions (see Chapters 2 and 8).

System stability, rigidity, autonomy and individuation. Because systems are rule-governed they provide a degree of stability and predictability in the behaviour of family members. However, a family system in which behaviour is too rigidly defined will have difficulty in adjusting to necessary change. Therefore individuals from families with rules which are too rigidly defined are likely to experience difficulty working out a rule system acceptable to both partners. Structural family therapists use the term *autonomy* to describe the state of an individual's differentiation from his or her family or origin. The process by which this is achieved is called *individuation.* In so far as a person's behaviour is rigidly controlled by the rules of the family of origin, he or she has failed to achieve autonomy. This is so even if the person consciously objects to or rejects the rules. For example, in Minuchin (1978) the anorexic teenager is seen to refuse to eat because this is the only area in which she can establish control of her own behaviour. That is, it is a rejection of the family of origin's over-controlling rules. But in so far as it is rigidly organised in relation to those rules, it indicates a lack of autonomy. The process of individuation is one in which the teenager negotiates for more freedom of action, and, achieving this, relaxes her rigidly organised rejection of food. In the creation of a new couple the extent to which each individual has achieved autonomy will determine the flexibility each can demonstrate in generating the rules of the new relationship as a couple.

Behaviour and meaning are two sides of the same coin. The ways in which family members see one another, their frames of reference about their families' lives, are sustained and confirmed by the interactions which they see and experience, while the interactions, in turn, are organised and sustained by the frames of reference. Therefore no precedence is given to the cognitive or the behavioural. Change must take place in both if it is to be sustained.

Circular causality; punctuation. Causality is seen as circular. Hence Christine may think that Jack is a person who withdraws and ignores her, so that she has to do all the work in the relationship and ends up nagging him; while Jack sees Christine as a critical, nagging woman and it is therefore right for him to keep his distance from her. These are linear perceptions, and a circular description of the same situation might be 'The more that Christine pursues and criticises Jack, the more he withdraws and rejects her, and the more he withdraws and rejects her the more she pursues and criticises him.' Descriptions of circular patterns have to start with the behaviour of one person or another. This one starts with Christine. Choosing the starting point is called *punctuating* the statement. Now if we punctuate the same statement the other way, it reads 'The more Jack withdraws and rejects Christine the more she pursues and criticises him and the more that Christine pursues and criticises Jack, the more he withdraws and rejects her.'

Family structure. Families contain boundaries, sub-systems, hierarchy, alliances and coalitions (Minuchin, 1974). Sub-systems are functional units within the family. The sub-system that functions to deal with the relationship issues within a family is traditionally known as the *marital sub-system*. The sub-system through which they mediate problems to do with the children is called the *parental sub-system*. If, in a situation of distress about the relationship, one partner forms a coalition with a child against the other partner, this represents a failure to maintain an effective boundary between the marital and parental sub-systems. Boundaries are sets of rules governing behaviour in the family which serve to protect the integrity of sub-systems and individuals in the family from inappropriate interference by other sub-systems and individuals.

Symmetry/Complementarity/Balance and Hierarchy. The concepts of symmetry, complementarity and balance refer to the weight that is given to each partner's point of view in the relationship. If one partner makes a statement and the other rejects it and states the opposite point of view this is a *symmetrical transaction*. If one partner makes a statement and the other accepts it this is a *complementary transaction*. A relationship in which each partner is able to express a point of view, and this is sometimes accepted and sometimes rejected by the other, is a *balanced relationship*. Balance, in this sense, is a necessary basis for negotiation. Couples who are distressed about their relationships are often stuck in chronic symmetrical or complementary patterns.

Unlike the concepts of symmetry, complementarity and balance the concept of *hierarchy* is about control. If a parent directs a child to do something, and he or she does it, then this is the evidence of a parental hierarchy, which if the direction given was age-appropriate, would be seen as a desirable thing. To illustrate the difference between these concepts let us suppose that Mr and Mrs Black have an 18-year-old son, Colin, who has left home after a confrontation with his father about money stolen by the son from his father. Mr Black says to Mrs Black that Colin was wrong to steal the money and she agrees, that he must not be allowed to come to the house, and she agrees, that he must repay the money, and she agrees and that he must on no account be given money by either of them, and she agrees. This is a complementary transaction. Next Colin comes to the back door of the house while his father is out, and his mother gives him money, but does not tell her husband. This illustrates that there is not a hierarchical relationship between husband and wife, even though the complementary quality of their earlier transaction might have led us to expect one. This is just as well, since it would not be seen as age-appropriate for a husband and wife to be in a hierarchical relationship with one another. A family therapist would see it as appropriate to create a more balanced relationship between Mr and Mrs Black, in order that they negotiate a more functional relationship with Colin. This example strays across the boundary between family and couple therapy. Perhaps this illustrates why it is difficult for systems-based approaches to see couples in isolation, or to see the boundary around the 'marital sub-system' as so rigidly defined that therapists can ignore other relationships in their efforts to help couples distressed by difficulties in their relationship with one another.

Drawing on this theoretical framework it is possible to work on couples' problems using a wide range of techniques. Such approaches are described in Chapter 8. Crowe and Ridley (1990) describe the application of some of these techniques to couples' problems, including sexual problems.

Sexual Problems

The focus in this section of this chapter is on sexual problems that arise between couples. The problems described can be thought of as problems of sexual dysfunction. It is important to differentiate between sexual dysfunction and sexual variation (previously referred to as deviation or perversion). In sexual dysfunction, there is some impairment of and dissatisfaction with the actual sexual response. In sexual variation, the actual sexual response may be unimpaired, but the object of desire or the method of obtaining sexual satisfaction is a variation of the norm. This could include experiencing sexual excitement only in relation to inanimate objects or animals or through sadistic or masochistic acts. Whilst some of the behaviour that can be described as sexual variation may be dangerous, degrading and damaging to a partner and lead to major problems between couples, the emphasis here is on problems of sexual dysfunction. Recommended reading in the area of sexual variation is given at the end of this chapter.

What will be discussed here will be sexual dysfunction between heterosexual couples. This reflects the fact that there is little or no work as yet described in the area of sexual dysfunction between homosexual couples. The relative absence of information about couple work of any kind with gay and lesbian couples is addressed by Ussher (1991). She suggests that 'many of the services at present available for families and couples could easily accommodate gay and lesbian clients given appropriate training and sensitive marketing of the service to the homosexual community' (Ussher, 1991). It is likely that this could apply also to services which are specifically for sexual dysfunction.

The work of Masters and Johnson in the 1960s and 1970s is generally regarded as a landmark in the field of sexual behaviour and sexual problems, and it was following their work in the United States that sexual problem clinics were established in the United Kingdom. The first phase of their work was a study of the sexual responses of men and women; this is published in their book *Human Sexual Response* (1966). The four-stage model as described by Masters and Johnson continues to be used in current literature when describing male and female patterns of sexual response and this is outlined later in this chapter. The second phase of their work was on specific sexual problems and treatment as reported in *Human Sexual Inadequacy* (1970); this has formed the basis of much of the classification of and therapy for sexual problems.

Extent of Problems of Sexual Dysfunction

For several reasons, it is difficult to get accurate estimates of the prevalence of sexual problems. There is no universally accepted method of classification, nor are there established norms for sexual behaviour. Indeed, it is not desirable that there should be. A level of sexual activity with which one couple might be happy might be regarded as a problem by another couple. The validity of the responses given to questions about sexual behaviour is another potential problem in estimating prevalence. For most people, it is a private area about which they are likely to be reticent. Others may assume that there are agreed standards from which they do not wish to appear to deviate.

Apart from the inherent difficulties in asking questions about sexual behaviour, there are other methodological problems in most of the population surveys carried out to date. The earliest and most extensive of these was done by Kinsey, *et al.* in the 1940s. A great deal of information was gathered from interviewing more than 6,000 men and almost 6,000 women, but the sample was biased in the direction of those in higher education and therefore not representative of the population as a whole. Some of their main findings for men were that erectile problems increased with age with prevalence rates of 0.8 per cent at age thirty rising by the age of seventy to 27 per cent (Hawton, 1985). In their survey of women, they found that 30 per cent were not orgasmic when first married but only 10 per cent were not orgasmic when married for ten years (Kaplan, 1974). A 12 per cent rate of orgasmic dysfunction is the figure given in the Hite report (Hite, 1976). This is based on the responses of 3,000 women, but again, the sample was a biased one, relying mainly on responses to newspaper advertisements.

Hawton (1985) summarises both general population surveys and clinical population surveys and concludes that the most common problem reported by women is impaired interest in sex; premature ejaculation is the problem most reported by men. Whatever the findings from general population surveys, it is the case that, once established, psychosexual problem clinics are inundated with referrals and usually have long waiting lists. This is sometimes used as an indicator of high levels of psychosexual problems in the community. However, the question of the appropriateness of these referrals needs to be kept in mind. It is possible that because of a relative absence of other resources, people are referred inappropriately to a psychosexual problem clinic. Catalan, Hawton and Day (1990) reported on a study of 200 couples referred to such a clinic.

They found that one third had significant marital and relationship problems and that more than 30 per cent were suffering from psychiatric disorder, albeit mild to moderate. Thirty-three per cent of males and 18 per cent of females were suffering from physical problems likely to contribute to the sexual dysfunction. They emphasise the need for very careful assessment to attempt to clarify which is the primary and which the secondary problem and to avoid the inappropriateness of offering sex therapy if the sexual problem is secondary to a marital, physical or psychiatric problem.

Sexual Response

In thinking about the kinds of sexual problems for which people seek help, it is helpful to have in mind the physiological pattern of sexual response. Masters and Johnson's four-stage model will be used to describe this. Sexual problems can and do occur in any of the four stages described for both men and women. The four successive stages into which Masters and Johnson divided the sexual response are: excitement, plateau, orgasm and resolution.

Excitement. This phase is characterised by the onset of erotic feelings and the development of sexual arousal in response to some stimulation either in fantasy or reality. The principal physiological changes which accompany this phase are vaginal lubrication in women and penile erection in men. Vaginal lubrication is accompanied by the beginnings of expansion and distension of the inner two-thirds of the vagina, and this prepares it to accommodate the penis. The clitoris swells during the excitement phase.

Plateau phase. This is a more intense and heightened state of sexual tension accompanied by a levelling off of arousal. During the plateau phase both vaginal and penile changes are at their peak. For men, the penis is filled and distended with blood to the limits of its capacity, the erection is firm and the shaft of the penis is extended to its maximum size. It is worth noting that the increase in size of a small penis is often proportionately greater than that of a larger penis, and that the size of the erect penis is not a crucial factor in sexual satisfaction for women — a myth which has caused much anxiety to many men.

For women, vaginal distension continues during the plateau phase with a swelling of the outer third of the vagina which leads to a narrowing of the entrance to the vagina. This swelling is referred to by Masters and Johnson as the *orgasmic platform*. The clitoris retracts into the clitoral hood.

Orgasm. A sense of *orgasmic inevitability* or *ejaculatory inevitability* for men pre-ceeds orgasm. For women, orgasm consists of rhythmic contractions of muscles around the vagina and the swollen tissues of the orgasmic platform. The number of contractions may vary from between five to fifteen and are of .8 second duration each. These contractions can occur without a woman's awareness. Freud's distinction between clitoral and vaginal orgasm and his attribution of greater maturity to women who experienced vaginal orgasm was a very long-lived myth. Masters and Johnson (1966) were able to show that there is but one kind of female orgasm and that clitoral stimulation either direct or indirect is always involved in female orgasm. They described the clitoris as the 'transmitter and conductor' of erotic sensation.

For men, orgasm occurs when sexual excitement reaches a point beyond which ejaculation is inevitable. Following the sense of ejaculatory inevitability, semen is emitted into the urethra and the second phase is the expulsion of seminal fluid out of the penis. The rhythmic contractions of the prostate gland, perineal muscles and the shaft of the penis give rise to the expulsion of the seminal fluid and the experience of orgasm.

Resolution. During this period the sex organs gradually return to their pre-excitement state. For men, there is a rapid initial loss of erection followed by a slower detumescence. Men have what is called a refractory period during which further ejaculation is not possible. This time period varies from minutes to hours and increases with age. Women do not have a refractory period.

Causes of Sexual Problems

Usually, there is more than one factor contributing to the development and maintenance of sexual problems. The factors involved can be either physical or psychological. The emphasis in this chapter is on psychological factors, but an excellent summary of physical causes is given by Hawton (1985) in his book *Sex Therapy: A Practical Guide.* This covers the effects on sexuality of physical illnesses such as diabetes and cardiovascular diseases, and the effects of prescribed drugs such as anti-depressants or major tranquillizers. Good information and counselling, when necessary, are an important part of a physician's role with patients when either their illness or the prescribed treatment is likely to give rise to sexual problems. Psychological factors leading to sexual problems can be both long-term and short-term. They may be specific to a particular relationship or situation or they may represent more enduring aspects of the individual. Attitudes to sexuality which are developed during formative years play a major part in the aetiology of sexual problems. For some people, their childhood environment will have induced guilt and shame about sex, which may last into adulthood and leave them inhibited in their sexual behaviour. For others, an absence of sex education leaves them uninformed, anxious and lacking in confidence and reluctant as adults to seek the information they need. Hawton (1985) advocates the use of an educational session for all couples in the course of therapy to ensure that people will have accurate information. It provides an opportunity to dispel myths that either partner may believe. Specific sexual problems are frequently reported when describing the long-term effects of childhood sexual abuse. Jehu (1988) in his work with fifty-one women who had been sexually abused in childhood found that 94 per cent of them complained of psychosexual problems. The most frequently reported were phobias of and aversion to sexual activity.

Whilst some causes of sexual problems can be seen to arise in childhood experiences, others can be attributed to more recent events. Traumatic experiences in adult life can trigger sexual problems. Burgess and Holmstrom (1980) looked at changes in sexual behaviour following the experience of rape in a sample of eighty-one women. In looking at changes in frequency, symptoms such as flashbacks, discomfort with sex, aversion and non-orgasmic responses, they found that 74 per cent of the women felt fully recovered by follow-up at six years, and that 50 per cent of these felt recovered within months, but 26 per cent did not feel recovered by the six-year-follow up.

Childbirth is frequently a precipitant of sexual problems. Problems can arise either from a difficult experience with giving birth, or follow on from a poorly repaired episiotomy. (An episiotomy is a cut frequently made to facilitate childbirth.) Particular couple problems may arise in relation to sex and childbirth. Some men may have difficulty relating to their partner both as a mother to the baby and as a sexual partner. Some women lose interest in sex during the months following childbirth. This can arise because of being centred primarily on the baby and on meeting the baby's needs; many women feel too exhausted during this time to be interested in sex.

Once sexual problems arise, they can be maintained by many factors. Performance anxiety and anticipation of failure are frequent responses to erectile failure. This will serve to inhibit the sexual response, consequently the problem of erectile dysfunction is maintained. Some sexual problems such as orgasmic dysfunction in women or erectile failure in men are maintained by insufficient stimulation and in particular by restricted foreplay. Failure to communicate about sexual problems is a common factor in the maintenance of problems.

Problems of Sexual Dysfunction

The main problems with which women present are:

- vaginismus
- dyspareunia
- orgasmic dysfunction

The main problems with which men present are:

- premature ejaculation
- retarded ejaculation
- erectile dysfunction

Both men and women present with what can be called impaired interest in sex.

Vaginismus. Vaginismus is a condition which makes penetration of the vagina impossible. Vaginismus is due to an involuntary spasm of the muscles surrounding the vaginal entrance which occurs whenever an attempt is made to introduce anything into the vagina. Attempts at penetration are painful, but there is no anatomical abnormality. A phobic avoidance of vaginal penetration usually follows as a secondary reaction to vaginismus. Vaginismus is a conditioned response arising from the association of pain or fear with attempts at vaginal penetration.

Causes. Any physical pathology which makes intercourse painful could lead to vaginismus through the association of pain with intercourse. These could include a poorly repaired episiotomy, a rigid hymen or pelvic inflammatory disease.

Psychological causes could include fear and guilt associated with sexual activity and psychological effects of rape or childhood sexual abuse.

Orgasmic dysfunction. Orgasmic dysfunction simply means failure to reach orgasm. This can be situational when, for example, a woman may be orgasmic through masturbation, but not intercourse or with one partner but not with another. Anorgasmic women are not necessarily inhibited in earlier stages of sexual excitement and can reach the plateau phase but not beyond that to orgasm.

Causes of orgasmic dysfunction include:

- fear of losing control and fear of the intensity of the feelings
- insufficient or insensitive stimulation
- fear of asserting independence
- ambivalence about the relationship
- guilt about sexuality

Premature ejaculation. Premature ejaculation is a condition in which a man has inadequate voluntary control over his ejaculatory reflex, so that once sexually aroused, he ejaculates very quickly. Premature ejaculation can be transient and associated with early sexual experiences and can cease to be a problem with greater maturity. It can arise from stressful conditions associated with the initial sexual experience and any anxiety which distracts from clear perception of sensation. Kaplan (1974) describes it as being attributable to a failure of being aware of the sensations which are premonetary to orgasm, which prevents regulatory power of higher nervous influence.

Retarded ejaculation. Retarded ejaculation is sometimes referred to as ejaculatory incompetence. In this condition, ejaculation is selectively impaired with no erectile problem. A man is unable to ejaculate even though he feels aroused and desires orgasmic release. It can be situational or it can be total. Some men may be able to ejaculate when masturbating alone but not during sexual activity with a partner. Retarded ejaculation rarely has a physical basis and is associated with conscious or unconscious anxieties about letting go.

Erectile dysfunction. Erectile dysfunction is technically a failure of the erectile reflex mechanism to pump sufficient blood into the cavernous sinuses of the penis to render it firm and erect. The erectile and ejaculatory reflexes can function independently and some men with erectile failure are able to ejaculate. Erectile dysfunction can be partial or complete.

Primary erectile failure (i.e., in men who have never had a satisfactory erection) can have a physical basis. Physical causes can include diabetes, alcohol abuse, neurological diseases and some medications. Secondary erectile dysfunction (i.e., in men who have previously had erections) can be situational.

Psychological causes of erectile dysfunction include depression, performance anxiety, fear, guilt and shame about sex, fear of failure and any factor that causes anxiety and inhibits spontaneity.

Impaired sexual interest. Impaired sexual interest or disorder of sexual desire, the term used by Helen Kaplan (Kaplan, 1979) is a frequently occurring sexual problem for both men and women. Here, potentially arousing situations are not sought and may actively be avoided, and there is an absence of sexual fantasy. It is a much more general problem than simply an absence of attraction or loss of attraction towards a particular partner. If stimulation is permitted, the sexual response 'works', but the quality of the experience is usually not very satisfying for the person with a low level of desire.

This problem can be secondary to some other problem, such as depression, and may remit if the depression is successfully treated. It can also arise in the context of some mild or transient couple problems; the individual's sexual interest may return to its previous level if these can be resolved. Impaired sexual interest is frequently a more serious problem than the other sexual dysfunctions. It can be a manifestation of serious problems, such as a fear of intimacy, or a long-standing hostility towards members of the opposite sex, in general, which is acted out in relation to a particular partner.

Therapy for Sexual Problems

Much of the sex therapy practised in this country contains elements of the Masters and Johnson approach. This is primarily a behavioural approach to helping with sexual problems. A very careful assessment of the causes and nature of the sexual dysfunction needs to be carried out before embarking on a particular course of therapy. The importance of establishing whether the sexual problem is primary or secondary has already been stated. When it is clearly secondary to depression or physical illness, for example, the primary problems would need to be treated. In a study referred to earlier, Catalan, *et al.* (1990) found that one third of the couples referred to the psychosexual problems clinic had significant marital or relationship problems and recommended that when sexual problems were secondary to such serious relationship problems sex therapy would be inappropriate. The distinction between sexual problems which are secondary to relationship problems and those which are not is not always easy to make, and there is often a complex interaction between the two. Where there are serious couple problems, the problems of sexual dysfunction are unlikely to respond to a relatively straightforward behavioural approach directed at the sexual problems. However, when couples are resistant to acknowledging the seriousness of their problems, sex therapy can be a useful starting point. It can serve as part of a continuing assessment, may help couples to realise the extent of their problems, and it may be what enables them to get involved in therapy about their relationship.

A Behavioural Approach

Counselling and an educational element are used in conjunction with a behavioural approach to sexual problems, but specific task assignment is a key component of the therapy. Having identified the factors which contribute to and maintain the problems, a series of graded tasks is used through which it is hoped the couple can build or re-establish a satisfactory sexual relationship.

In a behavioural approach to sexual problems, anxiety is seen as a major contributory and maintaining factor and much of the intervention is directed at reducing this anxiety. The first instructions given to a couple are to forego sexual intercourse and orgasm for a period of time and instead to engage in what Masters and Johnson referred to as *sensate focus*. The couple are instructed to pleasure each other in a non-demanding way and to avoid touching genital areas. The aim is for the couple to allow themselves to experience pleasure on being touched and touching without the expectation that it will lead on to further sexual activity which has become associated with disappointment, frustration and a sense of failure. Crown and D'Ardenne describe sensate focus as 'an attempt to alter the balance between sexual performance anxiety and sexual arousal in favour of the latter' (Crown and D'Ardenne, 1982, p. 70).

Following this early phase of the therapy, and when both partners feel at ease with each other in this situation, a series of graded tasks is devised for the particular problem with which they present. For some problems of sexual dysfunction, these tasks are highly specific, for example, in the therapy of premature ejaculation. It will be recalled that premature ejaculation is a condition in which a man has inadequate voluntary control over his ejaculatory reflex and an absence of awareness of the sensations which are premonetary to orgasm so that once aroused he ejaculates very quickly. The aim of the therapy is to increase this awareness and thus bring about greater control. A method called the 'squeeze technique' is one that is used. The instructions given to the woman are that when her partner has an erection she should squeeze his penis between her forefingers and thumb just below the glans and to press hard until he loses a good part of the erection. This is repeated several times, and intercourse is not attempted until the man has gained greater control over his ejaculatory response.

In the treatment of vaginismus, a specific behavioural technique called *in vivo* desensitisation is used. The aim is to desensitise or decondition the response of vaginismus which has arisen from the association of pain or fear with attempts at vaginal penetration. A series of graduated dilators is used, the smallest of these being extremely fine. A dilator is inserted gently into the vagina and only when the previous size has been well tolerated is the next size introduced. This procedure may be carried out over several weeks. When she is ready, the woman moves on to allowing her husband to penetrate her with his erect penis. He is instructed to do this in a non-demanding way and initially, without thrusting. Treatment of vaginismus is now frequently carried out using fingers, either the woman's own or her partner's, instead of dilators. The woman is taught relaxation as part of this treatment. Clearly, *in vivo* desensitisation for vaginismus, as with other problems, requires the co-operation and a high degree of motivation from the woman involved.

In vivo desensitisation is used also in the treatment of retarded ejaculation. It is more often the case than not that there is some situation in which a man can ejaculate. The failure to ejaculate is most common either with a partner or specifically intravaginally, and this is understood as a phobic response to these situations. In the treatment of retarded ejaculation, the ejaculatory capacity that exists is built upon. The man is instructed to masturbate in whatever situation is optimal for him. A series of graded tasks is worked out for him and his partner with the aim of bringing the successful experience of ejaculating closer to the situation of intercourse with his partner. In the later stages of the programme, the man is stimulated close to ejaculation by his partner and enters her vagina when ejaculation is impending. He then moves on to entering the vagina at earlier stages of stimulation. Ejaculation which has resulted from stimulation by a partner is regarded as a landmark in the treatment of retarded ejaculation. Whilst in the treatment of premature ejaculation, the man is encouraged to become more aware of his sexual response so that he can gain greater control, a man with retarded ejaculation needs to have less control and is encouraged to use methods to distract him from awareness of his sexual response.

Inadequate stimulation is often a contributory factor to problems of orgasmic dysfunction and erectile failure and in working with these problems, ways of increasing the amount of stimulation are incorporated into the treatment programme.

Psychodynamic Approaches

It will be clear from the above account that a behavioural approach requires a high degree of co-operation between the couple and a sympathetic approach to helping each other. For some couples, the hostility between them is too great to allow this. Kaplan (1979) distinguishes between milder sexual problems arising, for example, from uncomplicated performance anxiety or unrealistic expectations and more profound problems which are destructive adaptations to traumatic childhood experiences. For this latter group, she would not expect sex therapy on its own to be effective. Kaplan uses a psychodynamic approach to understanding human behaviour, and for couples whose sexual problems arise from profound anxieties, she advocates the integration of structured sex therapy with a psychotherapeutic exploration of resistances. Being asked to carry out specific tasks in relation to a sexual problem can make a couple's conflicts more accessible. These conflicts and the resistances to improving the sexual relationship would be worked on actively in the therapy sessions in addition to the more directive work of the sex therapy programme.

This approach is different from what would normally be expected within a psychodynamic way of working; being directive in this way is what distinguishes Kaplan's work from a psychodynamic approach to sexual problems as described by Rosen (1982). There is much common ground in relation to the areas which need to be assessed, such as the individual's maturity and capacity to form a relationship with a partner, the presence of resistances arising from internal conflicts, the extent to which unconscious aggression is interfering with the capacity to love. The intensity and length of therapy recommended would depend on the complexity of the individual's problems. Rosen considers that the involvement of the psychodynamic therapist in a planned programme of sexual tasks is incompatible with a central belief of psychodynamic therapy 'that the patient should be the prime mover in their own successful functioning' (Rosen, 1982, p. 87). The relationship between the patient and the therapist becomes central in the working through of conflicts and anxieties, which are re-experienced and re-enacted in the relationship. Feelings arising from earlier relationships are transferred onto the therapist. A directive role on the part of the therapist would interfere with the transference relationship and might prevent the resolution of conflicts. A sexual problem may be a manifestation of a particular pattern of relationship difficulties, for example, an individual with erectile problems who has problems in relation to authority figures. He might comply with carrying out the assigned tasks for fear of displeasing but in doing so fails to work on his underlying conflicts.

Whilst specific sexual problems and the distress they cause are acknowledged within a psychodynamic approach, they are not specifically targetted as in a behavioural approach. Personal autonomy and greater freedom from destructive anxieties and conflicts remain the aims of psychodynamic therapy with the expectation that sexual relationships will improve as a consequence. Satisfactory sexual relationships are seen to have more to do with how people feel about themselves and how they are in their relationships, rather than on what they do. The 'quality of the orgasm depends on the involvement of the self and the emotions in a meaningful way' (Rosen, 1982, p. 92).

· Groups run for women with orgasmic problems were first described by Barbach and Ayres (1980). These were developed for women without a regular sexual partner or with partners unwilling to attend or for women who did not want to tell their partners about the problem. Following a programme with educational aspects, support from group members and specific 'homework' tasks including masturbation alone, the aim was to achieve orgasm with a partner, though not necessarily through intercourse. Several self-help manuals such as Delvin's (1976) *Book of Love*, and Heiman, *et al.*'s (1976) *Becoming Orgasmic: A Sexual Growth Programme for Women*, are available. These are often used in conjunction with therapy, but for some couples may be of sufficient benefit on their own.

There have been feminist criticisms of sex therapy on the grounds that it is too male centred, conveys the message that there is a right kind of sexual experience to have, and pays insufficient attention to female sexual experience (Seidler-Feller, 1985).

Effectiveness of Sex Therapy

Outcome studies of sex therapy are mainly from behavioural approaches and are of the short-term outcome. Satisfactory outcome rates of 66 per cent are reported (Crown and D'Ardenne, 1982). There is variation in relation to different problems, with higher rates of successful outcome for vaginismus, premature ejaculation and erectile dysfunction. The need to do more research to establish which parts of the intervention contribute to successful outcome is emphasised by Crown and D'Ardenne (1982). Information about the quality of the general relationship between a couple, the extent of individual disturbance, and the duration and severity of the sexual problems need to be taken into account in relation to outcome.

Careful initial assessment is of paramount importance in the area of sexual problems. The presenting sexual problem alone may contribute relatively little to determining the most appropriate intervention, and several other factors need to be taken into account. Brief and structured sex therapy is likely to be most appropriate when the problems can be attributed to inadequate information or are the result of anxiety about sexual performance at a relatively superficial level and arise in the context of a basically good relationship and in individuals who are not very disturbed. When there are more complex factors surrounding the sexual problem, other or additional forms of intervention need to be considered.

Recommended Reading

Couples Problems and Therapy

ABLES, B.S. and BRANDSMA, J.M. (1977) *Therapy for Couples*, San Francisco, CA: Jossey-Bass.

A useful description of an eclectic psychotherapeutic approach to couples' problems.

CROWE, M. and RIDLEY, J. (1990) *Therapy with Couples*, Oxford, UK: Blackwell Scientific Publications.

Describes both behavioural and systems based approaches and includes discussion of when each of these approaches is most appropriate.

JACOBSON, N.S. and MARGOLIN, G. (1979) *Marital Therapy*, New York, NY: Bruner/Mazel.

A practical basic text describing a behavioural approach.

Sexual Problems

HAWTON, K.E. (1985) *Sex Therapy: A Practical Guide*, Oxford, UK: Oxford University Press.

A clearly written, comprehensive guide to the management of sexual problems.

Sexual Variation

BANCROFT, J. (1983) *Human Sexuality and its Problems*, Edinburgh, UK: Churchill, Livingstone.

CHALKLEY, A.J. (1987) 'Problems related to sexual variations — investigations', in *Handbook of Adult Mental Health Psychology* LINDSAY, S.J. and POWELL, G.E. (Eds) Aldershot, UK: Gower.

References

ABLES, B.S. and BRANDSMA, J.M. (1977) *Therapy for Couples*, San Francisco, CA: Jossey-Bass.

BARBACH, L.G. and AYRES, T. (1980) 'Group process for women with orgasmic difficulties', in *Women and Mental Health*, HOWELL, E. and BAYES, M. (Eds) New York, NY: Basic Books Inc.

BURGESS, A.W. and HOLSTROM, L.L. (1980) 'Rape: 'Sexual disruption and recovery', in *Women and Mental Health*, HOWELL, E. and BAYES, M. (Eds) New York, NY: Basic Books Inc.

CATALAN, J., HAWTON, K.E. and DAY, A. (1990) 'Couples referred to a sexual dysfunction clinic: Psychological and physical morbidity', *British Journal of Psychiatry*, **156**, pp. 61–7.

CROWE, M. and RIDLEY, J. (1990) *Therapy with Couples*, Oxford, UK: Blackwell Scientific Publications.

CROWN, S. and D'ARDENNE, P. (1982) 'Controversies, methods, results: Symposium on sexual dysfunction', *British Journal of Psychiatry*, **140**, pp. 70–7.

DELVIN, D. (1974) *The Book of Love*, London, UK: New English Library.

DICKS, H.V. (1967) *Marital Tensions*, London, UK: Routledge and Kegan Paul.

HAWTON, K.E. (1985) *Sex Therapy: A Practical Guide*, Oxford, UK: Oxford University Press.

HEIMAN, J., LoPICCOLO, L. and LoPICCOLO, J. (1976) *Becoming Orgasmic: A Sexual Growth Program for Women*, Englewood Cliffs, NJ: Prentice-Hall, Inc.

HITE, S. (1976) *The Hite Report*, New York, NY: Macmillian.

JACOBSON, N.S. and MARGOLIN, G. (1979) *Marital Therapy*, New York, NY: Bruner/Mazel.

JEHU, D. (1988) *Beyond Sexual Abuse: Therapy with Women who were Childhood Victims*, Chichester, UK: Wiley and Sons.

KAPLAN, H.S. (1974) *The New Sex Therapy*, London, UK: Bailliere Tindall.

KAPLAN, H.S. (1979) *Disorders of Sexual Desire*, London, UK: Balliere Tindall.

MASTERS, W.H. and JOHNSON, V.E. (1966) *Human Sexual Response*, Boston, MA: Little Brown.

MASTERS, W.H. and JOHNSON, V.E. (1970) *Human Sexual Inadequacy*, Boston, UK: Little Brown.

MINUCHIN, S. (1974) *Families and Family Therapy*, London, UK: Tavistock.

MINUCHIN, S., et al. (1978) *Psychosomatic Families*, Cambridge, MA: Harvard University Press.

ROSEN, I. (1982) 'The psychoanalytical approach: Symposium on sexual dysfunction', *British Journal of Psychiatry*, **140**, pp. 85–93.

SEIDLER-FELLER, D. (1985) 'A feminist critique of sex therapy', in *Handbook of Feminist Therapy* ROSEWATER, L.B. and WALKER, L.E.A. (Eds) New York, NY: Springer.

STUART, R.B. (1969) 'Operant interpersonal treatment for marital discord', *Journal of Consulting and Clinical Psychology*, **33**, pp. 675–82

USSHER, J. (1991) 'Family and couples therapy with gay and lesbian clients: acknowledging the forgotten minority', *Journal of Family Therapy*, **13**, pp. 131–48.

Chapter 8

Family Problems

Karen Partridge

Introduction

From Problems to Relationships

The term *family problems* can be seen as encompassing a multitude of ills. Problems presented as family problems may include the full range and diversity of symptoms presented in clinical practice from anxiety and bedwetting to sexual abuse, anorexia and schizophrenia. This raises the question of what makes a problem a family problem and what distinguishes it from an individual or marital problem. In fact, any presenting problem can be seen as a family problem if one chooses to view it in relational terms, that is, if a problem is seen as a communication which affects and organizes relationships. This means that there can be no specific definition of what constitutes a family problem without asking the question of who chooses to describe a particular behaviour or series of behaviours as a problem and what their relationship is to those they describe as having the family problem. So the problem is in the eye of the observer.

The observer may be a family member observing his or her own behaviour or that of other family members. Since relatively few clients present themselves for treatment explicitly requesting help for family problems, the observer is frequently someone outside the family unit such as a relative, neighbour or friend or a health care professional such as a GP or health visitor. There are a number of situations where an observer to the family unit is likely to describe the family as having family problems. First, when more than one member of a family appears to be very involved in the presenting problem. Second, when there are a number of different presenting problems affecting different family members. Third, when previous attempts at help have failed. Finally, a family may be described as having family problems or even as being a 'problem family' when a number of different therapeutic, legal or statutory agencies are involved with them, as for example, in the case of domestic violence or disclosure of sexual abuse.

These problems of definition mean that it is not possible to identify and categorize family problems according to the presenting problem, nor to talk about their prevalence and epidemiology as if they were a separate class of problems from any other presented in clinical practice. It is more meaningful to talk in terms of a family approach to problems. One is then able to talk about those problems most frequently addressed by using a family approach and those problems which have been found to be more effectively treated in this way.

Many clinicians might argue, that by taking family relationships into account when they approach a problem, they are taking a *family approach*. *Behavioural approaches* may, for example, include parents in implementing a behaviour programme for a child, while *psychodynamic approaches* may focus on an individual's relationships. However, the three main approaches that this chapter will outline take a step further than that which identifies them as family therapy approaches. They conceptualize the family system as the main target for treatment and see the individual who is labelled as having the problem as the designated patient, that is, the family 'elects' an individual to present the symptom on behalf of the system. This can be described as a *family systems approach*. The first model of family therapy to be outlined in this chapter is an example of a family systems approach.

The second and third approaches to be described take a further step from the family systems approach. These approaches remove the boundary from the group of persons described as a family to include the wider system. This may include friends, work relationships, the referring network, other helping agencies, and, in the case of the third approach to be outlined, will always include the therapist and the therapeutic agency of which he or she is a part.

The three approaches to be described represent the three most distinct and influential current developments in the field. The first approach is Salvador Minuchin's Structural Therapy. The second is the Brief Therapy Model of Steve de Shazer, and the third is the Milan Associates approach and post Milan developments arising out of the work of Gianfranco Cecchin and Luigi Boscolo. The chapter will not cover in detail the strategic approach to family therapy, which is most clearly articulated by Jay Haley (1963) and the Palo Alto Group on the West Coast of America, that is, Watzlawick, Weakland and Fisch (1974), since few currently practising family therapists now identify themselves purely with this approach. The work of those practioners who have not sought to be or have actively resisted being defined in a particular school, such as Milton Erikson, Carl Whitaker, and Virginia Satir will not be covered in this chapter. Their unique and charismatic style has made these approaches difficult to describe and to teach, although much can be learnt from them at an abstract, creative level. Compared to the systemic approaches discussed here, behavioural and psychodynamic approaches to family therapy have far less influence in the field. These approaches will not be outlined in detail but will be briefly compared and contrasted with the approaches presented here. The interested reader should refer to the work of the Adolescent Department at the Tavistock Clinic (Box, Copley, Magagna and Moustaki, 1981) and to the work of Ian Falloon (1988) for detailed accounts of the psychodynamic and behavioural family therapy approaches.

The Historical Context: from Symptom to System

Since the early 1960s when R.D. Laing (Laing and Esterson, 1964) first started looking at the family relationship, in particular the relationships that his schizophrenic patients had with their mothers, a quiet revolution has been taking place within the field known as family therapy. The revolution is tantamount to what Kuhn (1962) described as a paradigm shift. Prior to these developments any family work which did take place was usually conceived of from a psychodynamic perspective. Crucial to this shift, which began in the early 1970s, was the work of Gregory Bateson (1972) and Von Bertalanffy's General Systems Theory (1968). A number of key ideas can be seen as fundamental in the ensuing developments. First, Bateson's use of 'communication theory', in which he differentiated between different levels of meaning, for example between the verbal and nonverbal. Second, his use of the term 'context' which he saw as providing meaning to behaviour, and third the idea of 'punctuation'. Bateson described causality as a circular process, and it is a matter of punctuation where one chooses to draw the distinction between cause and effect. The shift from punctuating our experience in terms of cause and effect to describing the form and pattern of organization of behaviour is what is termed a cybernetic approach.

These ideas fitted closely with the shift towards general systems theory that was happening in science. Systems were seen as being structured by feedback, reaching a stable state as the opposing forces for change and stability create a balance for each other. Like a central heating system regulated by a thermostat, any change in one part of the system was seen as necessitating a corresponding change in every other part, that is, if you turn off a radiator without adjusting the thermostat all the other radiators will become hotter.

In observing a *system* Bateson described information as a 'difference' and 'difference' as a relationship. So family therapists became interested in mapping the differences in relationships between family members (Bateson, 1972). These ideas led to a development that further distinguishes family therapy from other approaches — the use of teamwork. Bateson noted that by observing from two different perspectives, a third dimension, depth, could be observed. Using this idea family therapists began to use a one-way screen with a therapy team behind the screen observing the therapist and family interaction.

These ideas were developed by the Palo Alto group on the West Coast of America and the Milan Associates in Italy. This era in family therapy is described as *first order cybernetics*, that is, the observer stands outside the system in order to describe its characteristics. Around the mid to late 70s a further change took place. Instead of emphasising the stability of systems, more emphasis was placed on their constantly evolving nature and the observer was seen to be part of the system rather than standing outside it. This is described as a *second order cybernetic approach*.

One of the implications of expanding the system to include the observer is that the proponents no longer describe themselves as family therapists but as systemic therapists or systemic consultants. Since the system is created by the observers, a therapist/consultant may decide to define the system as an individual, a couple, a family, a work group, an organization or any mixture of these. The shift from a first to second order cybernetic view also has implications for the way in which a symptom is viewed. For example, alongside the earlier view is the idea of symptom functionality, that is, the system leads to the production of the symptom as a solution to a problem. In contrast, the idea of Problem Determined Systems (Anderson, Goolishian and Windermand, 1986) describes problems creating systems around them rather than the other way round. Lynn Hoffman (1981) graphically uses the analogy of the golden goose in the fairy tale to describe this process. In the fairy tale everybody who touches the golden goose sticks to it until a whole chain of people are stuck together around the golden goose. In a problem determined system everybody who touches the problem 'sticks' until a system is created. This more dynamic view of systems is extremely helpful in working with multi-agency families or clients who have received a lot of previous help, because it allows one to consider the way in which the helping agency has become part of the system.

The most recent influence on family therapies is social constructivism (Hoffman, 1988). The most important idea is that reality is socially constructed. This means that there are as many versions of reality as there are observers to draw the distinction and we cannot 'know' reality independently of our perception of it (Von Foerster, 1981; Von Glaserfeld, 1984). The corollary of this stance is that there is no right way to be or to live, but that some constructions may be more useful than others. Social constructivism also places the emphasis on language, since stories about reality and, therefore, problems are created in language. Therapy becomes an attempt to create different stories hence different realities for people who present with problems. Here there is a divergence between family therapists working in this way with other therapists, including, for example, David Smail, Miller Mair, and the psychoanalyst Lacan, who are interested in narrative and the meaning of language.

To summarise, it seems that the wheel has come full circle in terms of working with individuals or whole families. From a focus on the individual there was a shift to a family perspective. For a period there was rigid adherence to working with the whole family, who were sometimes even turned away if all did not attend. With the advent of second order cybernetics the system was enlarged to include the observer, referring agents and other networks. Once again, it became possible to address the relationship between the client and the therapist, this time not in terms of transference, but in terms of 'fit', circularity and feedback. With this shift it became less important to see the whole system; much work is now carried out with parts of a system or with individuals.

To some extent the approaches that will be described in this chapter are presented in a developmental and historical sequence, but there has been much cross fertilization. Each of the three approaches to be described in some detail have made major contributions to the field that have been taken up and developed by the other schools, such that current practice in family therapy is becoming more blurred in its origins.

Structural Family Therapy

Structural family therapy is perhaps the most well known of all family therapy approaches. As its name suggests, it is interested in family structure. Salvador Minuchin's approach is best represented in *Families and Family Therapy* (Minuchin, 1974). Minuchin has a clear view of how a healthy family would appear in terms of a clear organization hierarchy and well defined permeable boundaries between subsystems as illustrated in Figure 8.1. For example, the parental subsystem should be hierarchically at a higher level than the sibling subsystem in terms of duties, rights and responsibilities. Boundaries ensure privacy, autonomy and individuality. The marital subsystem will have closed boundaries to protect the privacy of the marital couple, but the boundary will be permeable enough to allow children to move in and out of the parental subsystem. The marital and parental subsystems will be distinct. The sibling subsystem will have its own boundaries and will be organized hierarchically with children being given tasks and privileges appropriate to their age and sex. Individuals will also have clear boundaries in terms of respect for privacy and individuality. Finally, the boundary round the family system will also be respected, although this will depend to some extent on cultural, social and economic factors. According to these factors there may be great variety in the extent to which other family relationships and other agencies may be allowed into the family system.

Figure 8.1: Family organization

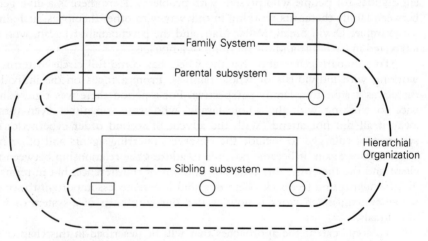

Key

--- Permeable boundary

☐ male

◯ female

Figure 8.2: Stages of family organization

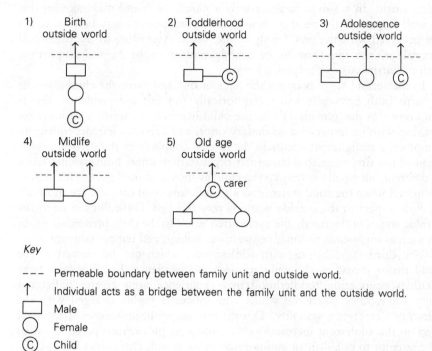

1) Birth
   outside world

2) Toddlerhood
   outside world

3) Adolescence
   outside world

4) Midlife
   outside world

5) Old age
   outside world

Key

--- Permeable boundary between family unit and outside world.

↑ Individual acts as a bridge between the family unit and the outside world.

☐ Male

○ Female

Ⓒ Child

The life span view of development has influenced all family therapy approaches, in particular the structural approach. Development is seen as continuing throughout the life cycle and can be marked by a series of normative transitions which characterise each life stage. This shifting scenario is known as the *family life cycle* which will be described in some detail because of its importance to the other models outlined.

At each transition point in the life of the family, relationships are renegotiated with subsequent shifts in alliances between family members as the family structure changes. The idea of the family life cycle embodies a central idea in therapeutic practice. That is, that there is a normative developmental sequence in relationships (see also Chapter 2). Problems are seen as likely to arise at points of transition if the family has difficulty adjusting its relationships to a new structure which is more appropriate to its stage of development. This means that many interventions in family therapy are seen as attempts to 'unblock' or 'unstick' obstacles which may have arisen in the normal developmental process.

There are many possible versions of the family life cycle. The example given here can be described as following four major structural changes in family organization as illustrated in Figure 8.2. At the first stage of the cycle, birth of a child, the mother is primarily occupied with the baby and the father can be seen as containing the mother/child dyad and acting as a bridge to the outside world. In a single parent family a parent or friend may take on this role with respect to the mother. If available, grandparents may become much more involved with the new family at this stage. According to the history of relationships, the involvement of grandparents may be helpful/supportive, unhelpful/intrusive or unhelpful/rejecting.

In the second stage between the ages of one and three the child takes its first steps both physically and metaphorically towards independence, this is often known as the 'terrible 2s'. As the child begins to establish a stronger relationship with its father or a secondary carer, and becomes less dependent on the mother, a realignment occurs in the marital couple from the vertical organization of the first stage to a triangular organization where both parents relate in a different but equal capacity to the child as shown in the figure. This shift is highlighted when the child starts school or full time child care and the mother's role with respect to the outside world is reestablished. Difficulties in negotiating these stages in the family life cycle often result in the child presenting problems such as night-time waking, bedwetting, soiling, and temper tantrums.

The third stage begins with adolescence, which can be viewed as the second major thrust of the child towards independence. Families who have difficulties negotiating toddlerhood may experience even greater difficulties during adolescence when the whole atmosphere is highly charged with the adolescent's emerging sexuality. During this stage the influence of the peer group on the adolescent increases as the child struggles against parental values in the attempt to establish an autonomous sense of self. Difficulties in negotiating this stage of the life cycle may result in behaviour problems in adolescence such as smoking, drinking, school refusal and at the severe end of the continuum anorexia/bulimia and emergence of schizophrenic symptoms.

The third stage of the cycle culminates in the young person leaving home and finding a partner. This establishes the adolescent as a young adult able to make his or her own relationships separate from the family of origin. This stage gives rise to what is often referred to as the 'empty nest syndrome' where the original marital couple are turned back on themselves after years of relating to a third party in the form of children or dependent parents. Difficulties in reestablishing themselves as a couple, as well as forging new roles with respect to the outside world, may result in referral for anxiety, agoraphobia, depression and sleep problems, as well as for sexual or marital problems.

Depending on the age of the parents the fourth stage, that of midlife may overlap with the previous one. Issues of midlife include the end of child-bearing years for women, and fears of waning attractiveness in both sexes. This is often coupled by the need to acknowledge that one has reached the peak in career terms and that the future holds old age and decline, although alternatively many women start a new career at this stage. This parental 'midlife crisis' is often exacerbated by the decline of grandparents who may become more dependent through illness and disability and by their eventual death.

The second half of life brings with it increased awareness of one's own mortality. This is highlighted with 'retirement', literally a retirement from the world, when issues around one's self worth and past achievements come to the fore with the realization that one is unlikely to further achieve in external terms. Difficulties in negotiating retirement are emphasised by a reversal in sex roles in the marital couple. Men frequently become more home loving and internally focused while women who may have been restricted by childcare or caring for dependent relatives may use their new found freedom and confidence to become efficient and busy members of the local community. If one's children produce grandchildren, a new link to the future can be made, perhaps giving a sense of immortality, otherwise issues of mortality and the finite nature of life may be more keenly felt. Family pets may take on an important role especially for childless couples.

Stage five brings old age, and with it a greater likelihood of illness, disability and greater dependence. This will require another realignment of relationships and may place different demands on sons and daughters, women being expected to take on more of a caring role with respect to elderly parents and relatives. Religion may increase in importance as a way of creating meaning for life and in cushioning the fears of one's own mortality.

In describing the life cycle, cultural context is a fundamental issue. The sequence described is essentially a white, middle-class, western pattern. Stages will be different and have different meanings associated with them within a different cultural context. This means that the life cycle must be considered in its cultural and political context, by reifying the life cycle as the way in which a family 'should' behave cultural, class and gender bias will be reinforced.

The genogram or 'family tree' is an essential tool in structural family therapy which is also used in other family therapy approaches. It can be described as a map of the family structure which includes major life changes including births, marriages, separations and deaths. It illustrates the stage of the life cycle that the family is currently negotiating and provides the therapist with useful ideas about the interactions that may be occurring around a problem. An example of a three generational genogram for the Smith family is illustrated in Figure 8.3 (p. 158). The Smith family were referred for family therapy by Stella's individual therapist. Stella presented the problem as her feeling of isolation and difficulty in dealing with her three children, Simon, James and Isobel. Her husband Ian is a freelance journalist very involved in his work. The genogram illustrates that Ian and Stella have been together for twelve years, they left South America to come to this country ten years ago. Ian is the eldest of four children, Stella the eldest of three children. All their relatives live in South America. Stella's father died four years ago and one year ago Ian's grandmother died. She was seen as having had a 'traumatic life' and had a great influence on the family. Similarly Stella's maternal grandmother was also seen as a very important figure in the family. The structural family therapist may construct a genogram with the family in one of the first sessions of therapy, as a way of 'joining' family members. Together with the family the therapist might then look for patterns between and within generations and use the genogram as a means of highlighting these patterns, for example the therapist might note the pattern of powerful and influential women on both sides of the family and two recent family deaths, which are related in time to Ian and Stella seeking individual therapy.

Karen Partridge

Figure 8.3: Genogram for Smith family

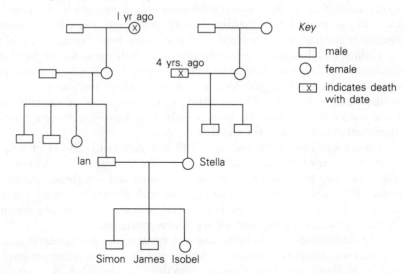

Given the view of normative family functioning proposed by the structural school the therapist's task is to note to what extent the presenting family adheres to this normative structure. If it does not, the aim of therapy is to create a new structure which is more appropriate for the life stage the family has reached, so development can continue in a normative way. The therapist does this by initially 'joining' or 'engaging' with all family members as she attempts to understand the family structure and the role of each family member within it. This is done by mapping the family terrain. The therapist notes important factors such as membership of *alliances* and *coalitions*. Alliances are overt close relationships between family members, while coalitions are covert and are normally directed against a third party. Membership and structure of subsystems and the location and permeability of boundaries are also included. Family organization is described as chaotic if there is no clear hierarchical structure or rigid if this is so fixed that there can be no flexibility, for example, if parents are so remote that children do not have full access to them. Relationships are described as *disengaged* if they are so distant that creative communication cannot occur or *enmeshed* if individuals have no personal space. Any of these polarities of organization may result in problems at points of transition, if the family lacks the flexibility to readily adapt its structure to the new life stage.

In mapping family structure the therapist takes on the role of an active intruder within it. Taking the example of the Smith family, the therapist might note from the genogram that the family is reaching the stage in the life cycle when the youngest child will soon start school. This means that the couple must renegotiate their relationship, and Stella must reestablish a role with respect to the outside world. The therapist might note that in this case the marital and parental subsystems are not distinct, and that a coalition against Ian exists between Stella and the two boys. Within the sibling subsystem there is no hierarchical organization, because all the children enjoy the same status and privileges irrespective of age.

The next phase of therapy involves the therapist challenging the family structure and the way that things are done using a variety of verbal and non-verbal techniques including *enactment* and *sculpting*. Enacting involves acting out patterns in the here and now. For example, the therapist might ask the Smith family children to 'go on the rampage' and for Ian and Stella to behave as they would normally. In sculpting the therapist asks the family to position themselves physically, to make a family sculpture, in terms of certain criteria, for example, who is closest to whom and most involved in the problem. The therapist may unbalance the family structure by changing seating arrangements or by siding with a member who has been scapegoated by other family members. For example, she might side with Ian, since he is being excluded from the family, or with Simon who is being labelled as being unpopular and difficult at school.

Thirdly, the therapist restructures the family by offering alternative ways of operating. Minuchin sees change as coming about by challenging the family's perception of reality, offering alternative ways of interacting and by bringing these about by providing a new experience within the family, which will reinforce new structures and relationships. She might, for example, instruct Ian and Stella in setting limits for the children and give them the experience of putting these into practice during the session by enacting a different scenario. The therapist will set clear goals for therapy and takes on an educative position in bringing these about.

A major deficiency in Minuchin's model of change is that although he describes the structure of families and their organization in great detail, his theory is not comprehensive enough to include the idea of 'resistance' or an explanation of the so-called paradoxical techniques which deal successfully with it, especially with those families which Minuchin would label as enmeshed. Nevertheless, the method is probably the most well researched of all family therapy models and has been shown to be particularly effective with psychosomatic problems in children (Minuchin, Rosman and Baker, 1978).

The Brief Therapy Model

The history of the brief therapy approach can be traced back to Milton Erickson (1963). He saw the key to *brief therapy* as utilizing what clients bring with them to help them meet their needs in such a way that they can make satisfactory lives for themselves. The Brief Therapy model proposed by Steve de Shazer, *et al.* (1986) developed alongside the strategic approach until 1972 and has since built on and extended these ideas, especially those put forward in Jay Haley's later work (1963) and Watzlawick, Weakland and Bodin's famous paper 'Brief Therapy: Focussed Problem Resolution' (Watzlawick, *et al.*, 1974). Whereas the strategic group focused on problems, the way in which they are maintained and how to solve them, De Shazer focuses on solutions; like the cheer leaders who warm up audiences in the United States, De Shazer sees himself as cheering on solutions. The approach is focused and goal directed. It is based on the idea if something works do more of it, if not do something different.

Like other models of family therapy the brief therapy model sees problems being developed and maintained in the context of human interactions. To emphasise that a problem is a particular distinction made by an observer, the brief therapy model refers to problems as 'complaints'. In order to construct solutions, it is important to understand as much as possible about the constraints of what is termed the complaint situation and the interactions involved, so that the solution will 'fit' the situation. Like a key in a lock, the idea is to fit sufficiently to turn the lock and to open up the possibilities for solutions. This means that some keys might be sufficient to operate a number of different locks. By using this model only a small change is necessary, no matter how complex and difficult the situation appears, since change in one part of the system leads to change in the system as a whole. This means that the brief therapy model will often work with a part of a system and frequently with an individual client. The aim of brief therapy, like structural family therapy, is to help clients to do something different by changing the way they interact with each other, or like the Milan Associates, to change the way that they interpret their situation or their beliefs so that a solution to their problems can be achieved. However, this model is not concerned with the structural organization of the family system and has no normative view of how a healthy family would function.

There are a number of unique terms in the brief therapy model which differentiate it from other models of family therapy. For example, De Shazer defines difficulties as 'the one damn thing after another of everyday life' (de Shazer, *et al.*, 1986, p. 210). These include such things as the car not starting, the tin opener not working, an argument now and again, etc. Clients often present these as problems. A complaint is a difficulty, plus a recurring, ineffective attempt to overcome it, and/or a difficulty, plus the perception on the part of the client that nothing is changing so 'one damn thing after another becomes the same damn thing over and over' (de Shazer, *et al.*, 1986, p. 210). Solutions are the behavioural and/or perceptual changes that the client and therapist construct to alter the difficulty or the ineffective way of trying to overcome it and/or the construction of an acceptable alternative perspective that allows the client to experience the situation differently.

The brief therapy model approach is very simple and very focused, as it is built around the idea that clients already know what to do to solve problems, they just do not know that they know. The brief therapist's role is to help them construct for themselves a new use for the knowledge that they already have. The approach is narrow, focused and goal directed and it is seen as achieving good results within its scope (de Shazer, *et al.*, 1986).

The Milan Associates and Post Milan Developments

The Milan approach, or systemic approach, as it is sometimes called refers to the work of four Italian psychiatrists and psychoanalysts, Palazzoli, Prata,

Boscolo and Cecchin. They were greatly influenced by Watzlawick, Beavin and Jackson (1967) from the Mental Research Institute, and their approach adheres closely to Bateson's (1972) systemic ideas. The approach was initially developed with families containing a designated anorexia or schizophrenic member, but it is now applied to a wide range of problems especially to those seen as chronic. This approach focuses on therapeutic technique to a greater extent than the others presented here. The most well known early publication is their book, *Paradox and Counterparadox* (Palazzoli, Boscolo, Cecchin and Prata, 1978) which outlines the method. At this point in their development they viewed systems as reaching a stable organization around a central point which might be a double bind or paradoxical injunction. For example, parents might give a son two mutually exclusive instructions simultaneously, one verbally and one non-verbally. Placed in this double bind and therefore being unable to act the son may respond by producing schizophrenic symptoms. The aim of therapy was to direct an intervention or 'counter paradox' (i.e., against paradox) towards this central point with the intention of changing the rules that organize the system and thereby eliminating the symptom.

The early Milan team laid great emphasis on the role of the therapy team to provide an overview or 'meta-perspective' on the client-therapist system; the therapist's role was at times relegated to a messenger of the team. The language used to describe the interactions between the team and therapist/family system in their early work is almost adversarial in nature. This may in part be due to the extremely difficult families, with anorexic and schizophrenic members, that they were treating. It also illustrates that although they were beginning to look at wider systems, in particular the role of the referring person in maintaining the problem, their view of systems remained more in line with a first order cybernetic paradigm. If fact, their early work has more in common with a strategic approach than with subsequent developments.

The Milan Associates proposed a five stage session which remains relatively unchanged in later developments. It is made up of a pre-session discussion, the session, an intersession break, delivery of an intervention and a post-session discussion. Three guiding principles — *hypothesizing, circularity* and *neutrality* (Palazzoli, *et al.*, 1980) — inform therapist activity throughout these stages. Hypothesising takes place primarily in the pre-session discussion where the therapist and team put together the information they have about the clients. The Milan approach advocates a telephone intake interview with the designated patient, in which factual information about the family structure and the presenting problem is gathered. On the basis of this information, and any communication from the referring person, a genogram will be constructed in the pre-session discussion. This together with all other information is used to hypothesise about the family and the presenting problem. A number of alternative possible hypotheses will be created. During hypothesising a wealth of ideas from other therapeutic approaches may be incorporated, including for example attachment theory, psychodynamic ideas and psychosocial transitions. The hypothesis which is chosen to guide the therapist should connect as many of the family members as possible. The hypothesis is systemic rather than linear in that it does not attempt to identify a cause-effect relationship but to punctuate a circular pattern. For example, on the basis of a telephone intake interview with the Smith family (see Figure 8.3, p. 158), the team's original *systemic hypothesis* was that the children were creating problems in order to pull professionals into the family to provide them with a new extended family; first Stella's individual therapist, next the children's school, then Ian's individual therapist and now, via this referral, a family therapist and team. Via therapy sessions and discussions Ian is pulled back into the family, so preventing Stella from being isolated, but at the same time this maintains some distance between Stella and Ian so the children create problems to pull them together, etc.

The second part of the session, the interview with the client, is carried out using *circular questioning*, which is the main tool of the Milan Associates. It illustrates the second guiding principle of circularity. Circular questioning makes connections between people, between events and between ideas. Circular questions encourage what is often termed 'gossiping in the presence of' by asking one family member about the relationship between another two. For example, 'When Simon decides not to do his homework, do Stella and Ian argue more or less?', 'If Stella were to feel competent in managing the children who would notice first, Ian or her therapist?' The Milan team also makes use of questions to track patterns of behaviour surrounding a problem, as in the brief therapy model, for example, 'When Isobel has a tantrum, what does Stella do?', 'Where are Simon and James?', 'Do they talk more to their father or less?', and 'Then what happens?', etc. In tracking behaviour patterns it is seen as important to continue questioning until a circular pattern emerges. So the family begins to shift from a linear to a circular view of the problem. The third type of questions used are ranking questions which highlight differences by asking questions such as 'Who notices first when Ian is feeling isolated? Then who?, Then who?' etc. until the whole family is ranked. Discrepancies between rankings by different family members are seen as contradictions to be explored.

Circular questions are the means by which the therapist tests out the team's hypothesis. If, in the series of questioning, the hypothesis clearly does not fit, the therapist takes a break in order to formulate a new guiding hypothesis with the team. The aim of the hypothesis is to guide the therapist to ask questions that make a difference. If the hypothesis is too far away from the family' own belief system about the problem, they will not accept the new ideas that emerge. Similarly if the hypothesis fits too well with the family's own ideas about the problem, there will be no 'news of difference'. So the hypothesis needs to be continually revised throughout the session on the basis of information generated by the questioning.

In asking circular questions and in managing the session as a whole the therapist needs to be actively aware of the third guiding principle, *neutrality*. By the end of the session all family members should feel equally engaged with the therapist. Unlike the structural therapist, who might make a strong alliance with a scapegoated family member, the Milan therapist promotes an equal alliance with each family member, illustrating that the Milan approach purports not to hold any view on how the family should be. The notion of neutrality extends beyond neutrality to persons to include neutrality to ideas and even to change itself. The concept emphasises that no one piece of information is any more important than any other, but that it is the process or pattern that is important. In fact, the concept of neutrality has drawn much criticism of the Milan team's work. The neutral therapist has been accused of being cool and detached, and it has been argued that since no one can ever be truly neutral the term masks implicit racism, sexism, etc. on the part of the therapist.

The message to the family in stage four of the session was originally referred to as the *intervention*, which was put together by the team in the intersession break. The Milan team became well known for their dramatic, largely strategic interventions which were often paradoxical in nature. Paradoxical interventions may include prescribing the symptom or prescribing 'no change'. Prescribing the symptom involves asking the client to carry out what has been described as the problem behaviour at a designated time and place, thus shifting the context of the problem behaviour from one in which the problem is seen as uncontrollable to one in which it is predicted and therefore controlled. Prescribing 'no change' within the context of therapy, which is about change, is similarly paradoxical. These elements were often included as a part of a ritual task. The most well known task of the early Milan team is the 'odd days, even days' ritual (Palazzoli, *et al.*, 1978), in which parents who were unable to control their children were told to take sole control of the children on alternative days. The other parent was instructed to observe and make notes on the difference it made. Ritual tasks act by introducing a third dimension, that of time, into the double bind so that the mutually exclusive injunctions are no longer happening concurrently. Traditionally the therapist delivered the message and left very promptly so that the family left with the message foremost in their minds. The team found that, in order for the repercussions from the intervention to filter throughout the system and for the system to reorganise itself, a month's gap between sessions was most beneficial. Milan style therapy has often been described as 'long short term therapy', since the number of sessions is unlikely to exceed twelve, but these may take place over a year or more in duration.

The last part of the session, the post-session discussion, involves the therapist and team hypothesizing about the effect of the intervention on the family. Any reaction, whether positive or negative, is treated as information about the system to inform future action by the therapy team. Contact from the family between sessions is treated similarly.

Although the traditional style messages are still frequently used it is this part of the session that has been changed the most in post-Milan developments. Typical components of the message might include positive connotation of the presenting problem, identification of common themes and identification of the double bind in which the family is caught. Since most post-Milan therapists see everything that the therapist does as an intervention, this part of the session is now usually seen as a summary to glue together the new links that have been made in the session.

After the publication of *Paradox and Counter-Paradox* (1978), the Milan team underwent a shift in their view of the system and they began to include themselves in the system as observers. Around this time the team split and the two women, Palazzoli and Prata, continued to pursue their research interests with anorexic and schizophrenic families. Meanwhile Boscolo and Cecchin have led what has been termed the post-Milan developments. Karl Tomm (1984) has acted as a spokesman for their approach.

The most exciting developments have come about via the influence of Chilean biologist Humberto Maturana (Maturana and Varela, 1980) and of social constructivism (Von Glaserfeld, 1984). This has led to a much more dynamic view of systems, as they are seen to be socially constructed in language by observers. In turn this has led to a more egalitarian co-evolutionary model of therapy, which is concerned with opening up possibilities and alternatives, rather than trying to change the system. This major revision also has implications for the therapy team which may take a more active role in the therapy, for example by Anderson's (1987) use of the 'reflecting team', in which the family is invited to listen while the team discuss their ideas. Therapists currently using these ideas include Peter Lang, Martin Little and John Burnham at Kensington Consultation Centre London, and the Charles Burns Clinic Birmingham, Michael White in Australia and Laura Fruggeri in Italy.

Evaluation and Critique

The number of studies reported in the literature evaluating family therapy approaches is sparse. This reflects the relatively recent popularity of the approach. The research literature raises some major epistemological issues in the evaluation of family therapy approaches. The main debate centres around the issue of using a positivistic research methodology to evaluate approaches which are based on a nonpositivistic paradigm. The two sides of the argument are articulated by those who have been termed 'old hatters' versus those who have been termed 'new wavers' (Gurman, 1983). The old hatters advocate the use of standard research procedures as currently the best available. The 'new wavers', on the other hand, argue that new means must be evolved to evaluate work which is based firmly within a second order cybernetic framework.

Probably the most comprehensive analysis of the literature to date was carried out by Gurman and Kniskern (1979) who surveyed over 200 studies. They tentatively concluded that overall 61 per cent of individual cases and 73 per cent family cases improved using a systemic family therapy approach, and that most studies found family therapy to be more effective than individual treatment, although this was not exclusively so. Individual schools are beginning to produce results, although at present, these remain limited in number and often based on clinical impression. On the basis of client self report as a way of evaluating the brief therapy model, de Shazer, *et al.* (1986) have concluded that their model can be effective within a short period of time and within a limited number of sessions. Out of 1,600 cases seen on average for six sessions, 72 per cent either met their goals for therapy or felt that significant change had occurred, such that they did not require further sessions.

The Milan team states that it finds improvement in 68 per cent of its cases (Tomm, 1984); since the Milan team sees families who may be regarded as some of the most difficult, this figure is particularly significant. Tomm (1984) also states that by using the Milan approach change occurred in fewer sessions, allowing the same number of staff to increase the number of cases seen by 25 per cent over a four year period after introducing this approach. A number of outcome studies are currently in progress; clearly much research still needs to be done.

The main criticisms of family therapy centre around the issue of power. The most clearly articulated is the feminist critique (MacKinnon, 1987). The feminist position sees family therapy as supporting patriarchal society in reifying the nuclear family as the 'right' way to live. It argues that the nuclear family subjugates women and requires their submission in order to maintain white male middle-class supremacy. This is institutionalized by society in governmental structure to which women have little access. Similarly, family therapy has been criticised as upholding middle-class, white western values and not addressing issues of race, sexual orientation, disability or aging, implicitly upholding societal structures and values which oppress members of these minority groups. Further criticisms of the approach are levelled against the position of power assumed by the therapy team. Family therapists have been accused of objectifying families and of being manipulative social engineers often using deceit to achieve their dubious aims.

Criticisms of family therapy tend not to differentiate between the different approaches; whilst many of the above criticisms might justifiably be levelled at approaches based on a first order cybernetic thinking, more recent approaches can theoretically encompass the issue of power. Most criticisms of family therapy are based on a view of power as a linear concept consisting of unilateral control over another person. Maturana (1980) describes this as the 'myth of power' and argues that one part of a system cannot have unilateral control over another part of a system. This more circular view, however, has further fueled feminist criticism, which views circular causality as blaming victims of incest/child abuse/wife battering and not addressing the issues of responsibility and the wider social context. With the move to constructivism a greater diversity of definitions of power have begun to emerge. Despite these moves MacKinnon argues that although systemic approaches can address the issue of power from a theoretical perspective, family therapy has remained constrained by the conservatism of its proponents and has not as yet adequately addressed the power question. It remains to be seen whether in the 1990s developments in the field will rise to the challenge.

Comparison and Integration

The aim of this section is to compare and contrast the three models of family therapy that have been described in this chapter together with behavioural and psychodynamic family therapy approaches. These approaches have not been addressed in detail because they represent a relatively minor influence in the field. *Behavioural family therapy* is best outlined by one of its major proponents, Ian Falloon (1988). As he states in his overview, behavioural family therapy is still in its infancy, but it has undergone major change since its inception twenty years ago. Growing out of the pioneering work of Patterson (1967), Liberman (1970) and Stuart (1969) the shift was made from focusing on the patient to complex behavioural analyses of the whole family environment. The aim of therapy was to restructure the reciprocal exchange of rewards in family relationships and to maximise exchanges of positive behaviour, often using written contracts between family members. In the 1970s a major transformation took place with the introduction of packages for parent retraining of deviant children (Falloon and Liberman, 1983), *Behavioural Marital Therapy* (Stuart, 1969; Liberman, 1970) and sex therapy which was made well known by the work of Masters and Johnson (1970). The most recent developments in the field have aimed at addressing limiting features of the approach. The most striking inclusions are consideration of the therapeutic alliance and of resistance, that is, those families who do not improve as readily or easily as one might expect, and approaches to reconstruct family members subjective experiences using cognitive strategies. As Falloon (1988) states, the approach is very much in its infancy and lacks a clear theoretical framework, but cross-fertilization between behavioural and systemic family therapy approaches is beginning to occur.

Psychodynamic family therapy is best represented by the work of the Adolescent Department at the Tavistock Clinic in London (Box, *et al.*, 1981). Its members share an interest in applying psychoanalytic principles to the understanding of groups and institutions and in particular to families. The approach is based on two particular developments, that of 'object relations' psychoanalytic practice derived from the work of Freud and Melanie Klein, and the application of this to the understanding of group relations following the work of W.R. Bion (1961) and others. The approach embraces the idea of a family as a system and attempts to understand the processes involved in such a system, but unlike other family therapy approaches it implies working with the group dynamics of the family, including unconscious processes, especially in terms of the way in which the family members perceive and engage the therapists. The aim is to create a space for the family to re-live and think about conflicts as they emerge in the therapeutic setting. Figure 8.4 compares the three main family therapy approaches, along with psychodynamic and behavioural approaches, according to five distinguishing features: the view taken of the family system, the view of the problem, the model of change, the role of the therapist, and the main skills and techniques employed by that approach. The most fundamental of these features is the view of the family system which informs all other features. The structural model takes its view of systems from organizational theory while the brief therapy and post-Milan/ Systemic approaches are based on a cybernetic model. The behavioural approach derives from learning theory and thus sees behaviour as being environmentally determined, whilst the psychodynamic approach sees intra-psychic factors as being most important (see Chapter 1). The differing views of systems have implications for the way in which change is seen to take place and therefore for the stance of the therapist. One possible way of integrating the approaches covered in this chapter is in terms of levels of psychotherapy.

Figure 8.4: Comparison of different models

	Structural	Brief Therapy Model	Post-Milan/Systemic	Behavioural	Psychodynamic
View of family System	• System is clearly structured • Hierarchically organized • Boundaries between subsystems	• System is structured on feedback • System maintains a steady state	• System is evolving • Constructed in language, co-ordinated through action	• Family is formed when sufficient potential for mutual reinforcement is perceived in spouse • Chains of behaviour are set up and maintained	• Family shares an internal world
View of Problem	• Structure inappropriate for life stage of family • Structure does not adapt freely to change • Inappropriate alliances between subsystems	• Too many repeating samenesses • Failed attempts at solution	• Brought forth in language • Stories become too limiting and restrictive	• Individual behavioural repertories no longer elicit appropriate reinforcement within family environment and may become punishing to other family members • Negative chains of interaction are set up and maintained	• Unconscious conflicts are acted out as recurring problems in the family
Model of change	• Force a change and system will reorganize • New relational realities become self-reinforcing	• Focus on solutions • Interruption of vicious circles of mishandled attempted solutions	• Dissolve problem determined system through co-evolution of new story in language	• Construct more appropriate behaviours	• Unconscious is made conscious, therefore allowing increased choice, growth and differentiation of family members
Role of Therapist	• Active intruder, joins, challenges and restructures family system	• Cheer-leader for solutions • Tracks sequences around exceptions to problems in order to construct solutions	• Co-creator of new stories • Triggers reflexivity between levels of meaning • Looks for 'fit': how historical and current pieces of puzzle 'fit' together	• Active and educative • Problem solver • Constructor of new sets of behaviours	• Facilitative • Containing • Providing space for exploration and under-standing
Skills and techniques	• Sculpting • Enactment • Goals set	• Reframing • Focusing on strengths • Goals set • Tasks	• Circular questioning • Circularity neutrality/curiosity • Hypothesising • Rituals and tasks	• Behavioural monitoring • Behavioural analysis • Communication skills training • Problem solving and training • Contingency contracting	• Containment • Making links through interpretation • Providing space for emergence of hidden attitudes and internal relationships • Working through these in therapeutic relationship

Figure 8.5: *Family therapy and levels of psychotherapy*

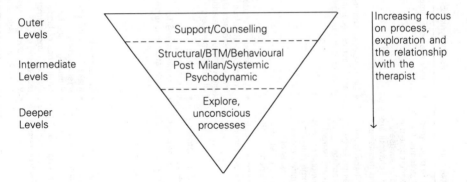

This idea is borrowed from Cawley (1977) and elaborated by Brown and Pedder (1979) but will be used in a modified form by the present author. Psychotherapy can be seen as operating at the three different levels as illustrated in Figure 8.5. Outer levels include support and counselling, intermediate levels include more focused therapeutic approaches which begin to use the relationship with the therapist while deeper levels include exploratory work addressing unconscious processes. This involves working through the relationship with the therapist as in psychoanalytic psychotherapy and psychoanalysis. The triangle is presented standing on its apex so that the areas within the triangle bear an approximate relationship to the comparative size of the population of people who may best be helped by each approach. According to severity of problems, individuals may require deeper levels of psychotherapy. For example, many people who present asking for help have less severe problems and may be best helped by outer levels of support and counselling. This might include people who have experienced life events such as bereavement, illness, redundancy, etc. A smaller proportion of people will require further help in terms of intermediate levels of therapy. A smaller proportion of people have more severe difficulties or may wish to explore further. They will need a deeper level of psychotherapy.

The approaches described here can be best placed at the intermediate level and could be described as comparable in level to other short to medium term focused therapeutic approaches, for example, to brief psychotherapy, cognitive analytical therapy, short to medium term group work, etc. Out of the five approaches presented here the structural, brief therapy model and behavioural family therapy approach could be described as being located towards the outer levels. With the exception of the psychodynamic approach all other models take an active stance. The structural, brief therapy model and behavioural approaches are all directive, in terms of setting explicit goals for therapy and in determining the direction and nature of change to occur. The post-Milan and psychodynamic approaches focus more explicitly on process and directly address the relationship between the clients and the therapist. The psychodynamic approach is the only approach outlined which views the working through of conflicts as a part of the therapeutic process. The other approaches see the aim of therapy as bringing about a change, which is then explored and implemented by the clients after therapy has ended. This means that these approaches tend to be more focused and short term in nature than the psychodynamic approach. So the psychodynamic approach is represented as spanning the boundary between intermediate and deeper levels of therapy.

The value of this integrating model is that it clearly illustrates that rather than one approach being better or preferable to another each approach has something different to offer in terms of its aims and appropriateness for a particular portion of the population. The behavioural, structural and brief therapy models could be seen as focusing directly on the production of explicit agreed changes and are more supportive in nature, whilst the post/Milan systemic and, to an even greater extent, the psychodynamic models focus more on exploration. This would imply, as the research evidence confirms, that the former may be most valuable in treating more frequently occurring, less complex problems which are already well defined, while the latter may most usefully address more complex and potentially chronic difficulties. Unfortunately, such an integration is at present lacking in the field of family therapy, and perhaps, as one might expect in such a relatively young field, proponents of the different models tend to have a combative and competitive relationship. One hopes that as the field matures greater communication will lead to creative and challenging new developments.

Recommended Reading

BENTOVIM, A., BARNES, G.G. and COOKLIN, A. (1982) *Family Therapy: Complementary Frameworks of Theory and Practice*, **1**, London, UK: Grune and Stratton Ltd.

A broad introduction to the family as a system and to family work.

BENTOVIM, A., BARNES, G.G. and COOKLIN, A. (1982) *Family Therapy: Complementary Frameworks of Theory and Practice*, **2**, London, UK: Grune and Stratton Ltd.

An outline of the family life cycle and family therapy.

BURNHAM, J. (1986) *Family Therapy* London, UK: Tavistock Publications Ltd.

A concise and thorough practioners handbook.

CAMPBELL, D. and DRAPER, R. (1985) 'Applications of systemic family therapy: The Milan approach', *Complementary Frameworks of Theory and Practice*, **3**, New York, NY: Grune and Stratton, Ltd.

An excellent collection of theoretical ideas and practical applications of the Milan Systemic approach.

HOFFMAN, L. (1981) *Foundations of Family Therapy: A Conceptual Framework for Systems Change*, New York, NY: Basic Books.

A comprehensive book which masters the current state of the field — an essential textbook.

References

ANDERSON, H., GOOLISHIAN, H.A. and WINDERMAND, L. (1986) 'Problem determined systems: towards transformation in family therapy', *Journal of Strategic and Systemic Therapy*, **5**, pp. 1–13.

ANDERSON, T. (1987) 'The reflecting team: dialogue and metadialogue in clinical work', *Family Process*, **4**, pp. 415–28.

BATESON, G. (1972) *Steps to an Ecology of Mind*, San Francisco, CA: Chandler.

BION, W.R. (1961) *Experiences in Groups*, London, UK: Tavistock Publications.

BOX, S., COPLEY, B., MAGAGNA, J. and MOUSTAKI, E. (1981) *Psychotherapy with Families: An Analytic Approach*, London, UK: Routledge and Kegan Paul.

BROWN, D. and PEDDER, J. (1979) *Introduction to Psychotherapy*, London, UK: Tavistock Publications.

CAWLEY, R.H. (1977) *The Teaching of Psychotherapy*, Association of University Teachers of Psychiatry Newsletter, Jan. pp. 19–36.

ERICKSON, M. (1963) *Advanced Techniques of Hypnosis and Therapy*, in HALEY, J. (Ed.) *Strategies of Pyschotherapy*, New York, NY: Grune and Stratton pp. 395–97.

FALLOON, I.R.H. (1988) *Handbook of Behavioural Family Therapy*, London, UK: Hutchinson.

FALLOON, I.R.H. and LIBERMAN, R.P. (1983) 'Behavioural therapy for families with child management problems', in TEXOR, M.R. (Ed.) *Helping Families with Special Problems*, New York, NY: Jason Aronson, pp. 127–47.

GURMAN, A.S. (1983) 'The old hatters and the new wavers', *Family Therapy Networker*, **7**, p. 37.

GURMAN, A.S. and KNISKERN, D.P. (1979) 'Research on marital and family therapy: progress, perspective and prospect, in GARFIELD, S.L. and BERGIN, A.S. (Eds) *Handbook of Psychotherapy and Behavioural Change*, 2nd. ed., New York, NY: Wiley.

HALEY, J. (1963) *Strategies of Psychotherapy*, New York, NY: Grune and Stratton.

HOFFMAN, L. (1981) *Foundations of Family Therapy: A Conceptual Framework for Systems Change*, New York, NY: Basic Books.

HOFFMAN, L. (1988) 'A constructivist position for family therapy', *The Irish Journal of Psychology*, **9**, 1, pp. 110–29.

KUHN, T. (1962) *The Structure of Scientific Revolutions*, Chicago, IL: University of Chicago.

LAING, R.D. and ESTERSON, D. (1964) *Sanity, Madness and the Family*, London, UK: Tavistock Publications.

LIBERMAN, R. (1970) 'Behavioural approaches to family and couple therapy, *American Journal of Orthopsychiatry*, **40**, 106–18.

MADANES, C., and HALEY, J. (1979) 'Dimensions of family therapy', *Journal of Nervous and Mental Disease*, **165**, pp. 88–98.

MACKINNON, L.K. (1987) 'The new epistemology and the Milan approach: feminist and sociopolitical considerations', *Journal of Marital and Family Therapy*, **13**, pp. 139–55.

MASTERS, W.H. and JOHNSON, V.E. (1970) *Human Sexual Inadequacy*, London, UK: Churchill.

MATURANA, H.R. and VARELA, F.J. (1980) 'Autopoiesis and cognition: the organization of the living', in MATURANA, H.R. and VARELA F.J., *Autopiesis: The Realization of the Living*, Boston, MA: Reidel Press.

MINUCHIN, S. (1974) *Families and Family Therapy*, Cambridge, MA: Harvard University Press.

MINUCHIN, S., ROSMAN, B. and BAKER, L. (1978) *Psychosomatic Families*, Cambridge, MA: Harvard University Press.

PALAZZOLI, M.S. 'Interview: Mara Selvini Palazzoli discusses the invariable prescription', *Australia and New Zealand Journal of Family Therapy*, **6**, pp. 211–14.

PALAZZOLI, S.M., BOSCOLO, L., CECCHIN, G. and PRATA, G. (1978) *Paradox and Counterparadox*, New York, NY: Jason Aronson.

PALAZZOLI, S.M., BOSCOLO, L., CECCHIN, G. and PRATA, G. (1980) 'Hypothesizing, circularity, neutrality: three guidelines for the conductor of the session', *Family Process*, **19**, pp. 3–12.

PALAZZOLI, S.M., BOSCOLO, L., CECCHIN, G. and PRATA, G. (1978) 'A ritualised prescription in family therapy: Odd days and even days', *Journal of Marriage and Family Counselling*, **4**, pp. 3–9.

PATTERSON, G.R., MCNEAL, S., HAWKSIN, N., and PHELPS, R. (1967) 'Reprogramming the social environment', *Journal of Child Psychology and Psychiatry*, **8**, p. 181–95.

PENN, P. (1984) 'Feed forward, future questions, future maps', *Family Process*, **24**, p. 3.

DE SHAZER, S., BERG, I.K., LIPCHIK, E., NUNNALLY, E., MULNAR, A., GINGERICH, W. and WEINER-DAVIES, M. (1986) 'Brief therapy: Focused solution development, *Family Process*, **25**, pp. 207–22.

STUART, R.B. (1969) 'Operant-interpersonal treatment for marital discord', *Journal of Consulting and Clinical Psychology*, **33**, pp. 675–82.

TOMM, K., (1984) 'One perspective on the Milan systemic approach: Part I overview of development, theory and practice', *Journal of Marital and Family Therapy*, **10**, 2, pp. 113–25.

VON BERTALANFFY, L. (1968) 'General Systems Theory—a critical review', in BUCKLEY, W. (Ed.) *Modern Systems research for the behavioural Scientist*, Chicago, IL: Aldine, pp. 11–30.

VON FOERSTER, H. (1981) *Observing Systems*, Seaside, CA: Intersystems.

VON GLASERFELD, E. (1984) 'An introduction to radical constructivism', in WATZLAWICK, P. (Ed.). *The Invented Reality*, New York, NY: WW Norton.

WATZLAWICK, P., BEAVIN, J.H. and JACKSON, D.D. (1967) *Pragmatics of Human Communication*, New York, NY: Norton.

WATZLAWICK, P., WEAKLAND, J. and FISCH, R. (1974) *Change*, New York, NY: W.W. Norton.

Chapter 9

Schizophrenia

Tony Lavender

Introduction

This chapter provides an overview of the major issues and approaches that are currently of importance in schizophrenia. It is perhaps most useful to begin with a brief description of what life can be like for an individual suffering from what have come to be regarded as the symptoms of schizophrenia:

John is a 26-year-old man who lives at home with his mother and two sisters. He was diagnosed as schizophrenic when he was 24. His initial contact with psychiatric services came three months after he had left home to take up a place at a further education college. During the period at college he found he was unable to cope with the academic work or living in a student house with five new people. When he began to experience difficulties he withdrew to his room for long periods, which led to him becoming something of an outcast in the house. During these periods alone he began to think and feel that people were against him — continually talking about him and plotting to get him moved out of the house. As he became more isolated, so his anxieties about the others grew to the point that he thought the people within the house, and indeed the college lecturers, were planning to get him out of the country. These thoughts gradually developed to the point that John was concerned that MI5 had become involved and had placed microphones in the wall. John did, however, have one friend in the house, a young woman who had always been friendly, whom he tried to tell about the plot. She actually became quite frightened by his story, especially when he described people outside his door talking to each other about him and shouting abuse at him, something she knew was not the case. She eventually decided to talk to the college counsellor, who contacted John's GP; he was persuaded to see a psychiatrist. The psychiatrist prescribed a small dose of a major tranquillizer and John returned to his family home. Since that time John has remained very dependent on his mother, is unemployed, has made two unsuccessful attempts to start evening classes and appears rather frightened about contact with people outside the home. He remains convinced that the students plotted against him. He now describes himself as having little energy and a lack of interest in anything.

Any overview of schizophrenia that attempts to describe the efforts that have been made to explain the occurrence of such problems can only provide a brief summary, and the reader will need to refer to the references to gain a fuller understanding. This is perhaps particularly important with schizophrenia because of the vast amount of research and associated literature available about the subject. The present chapter begins with the historical background and in this context presents the major problems involved in establishing 'schizophrenia' as a reliable and valid concept. This is followed by a discussion of what is known about the genetic and biological basis of the condition. The remaining two sections are devoted to a presentation of the main psychological and family approaches that have been applied to schizophrenia.

Historical Background: Defining the Condition

In 1898 Emil Kraepelin first presented the term dementia praecox to classify those severe mental disturbances which were not clearly organic in origin. Kraepelin (1905) originally thought that dementia praecox occurred in young people and was associated with a progressive emotional and intellectual deterioration, although he recognised that occasionally it occurred in later life and/or was associated with complete recovery. The common symptoms included auditory hallucinations (hearing voices when there is nobody there), delusions (a set of beliefs obviously discordant with reality), thought disorder (obvious lack of logical thinking), stereotypes (repetitive movements or actions), and flattened affect (lack of clear emotional response). Kraepelin separated this condition from *paraphrenia* in which there was less marked intellectual deterioration but pronounced delusions and hallucinations and paranoia (feeling persecuted without any objective evidence of persecution) in which the major feature was non-hallucinatory delusions.

Eugen Bleuler in 1908 proposed the term 'schizophrenia' to cover dementia praecox, paraphrenia and paranoia. Bleuler (1950) was much influenced by the newly developing psychoanalytic theory and attempted to define the core underlying psychological process which accounted for the disorder. He described this key process as the breaking or loosening of the associative threads which linked thoughts together. The effect of this breaking or loosening of associations led to severe difficulties in communication, an inability to respond appropriately to the surroundings and finally to withdrawal. Bleuler considered this loosening of associations not as a categorical distinction between abnormality and normality but as a dimension along which people varied and to which different physicians would apply different cut-off points. This conceptual change allowed Bleuler to classify all the types of disorder identified by Kraepelin under the one diagnostic label, 'schizophrenia'.

Kraepelin and Bleuler disagree over the progressive nature of the disorder, with Kraepelin emphasizing the progressive deterioration of the condition, whilst Bleuler remained optimistic about the chances of recovery. Warner (1985) has pointed out that this difference may have been due to differences in the management approaches adopted by the two clinicians. Kraepelin's work was largely undertaken in the large asylums where the conditions and practices advocated, it has since been acknowledged, have a deteriorating effect on patients. Bleuler on the other hand may have seen less disabled people because of his broader definition and his progressive management approach which attempted to remove people from hospital conditions as soon as possible and emphasized the importance of regulated work.

The original phenomena identified by Kraepelin and Bleuler have remained at the heart of what clinicians have referred to when using the label schizophrenia. During the rest of the first half of the century there was a tendency to expand the definitions of the condition. Langfeldt (1937) distinguished between a core group of *process* or *nuclear schizophrenics* who showed an insidious onset and a deteriorating course and *reactive schizophrenics* who showed more acute onset, better premorbid social functioning and a better prognosis. This expanding of the definition of schizophrenia was more pronounced in certain countries. For example, Kuriansky, Deming and Gurland (1974) point out that in the United States twenty per cent of patients at the New York State Psychiatric Institute were diagnosed as schizophrenics in the 1930s, but this had risen to eighty per cent in the 1950s. In contrast, only twenty per cent of patients were diagnosed as schizophrenic at the Maudsley Hospital, London, throughout this period.

From the late 1950s until the present day the most rigorous approach to developing a sound philosophical and empirical base for the classification of psychiatric conditions in general, and schizophrenia in particular, has been the phenomenological approach of Karl Jaspers (1963). Phenomenology is essentially concerned with the description and classification of observable phenomena. Jasper's approach involved going beyond a simple description of the phenomena, that is, the signs and symptoms, to produce a system of describing the phenomena which built on the clinicians ability (empathy) to understand the meaningful connections between the patients' experiences in the world and their current behaviour, thoughts and emotions. In Jaspers' system of classification what marked the schizophrenic experiences from others was the difficulty for the clinician to understand empathically those experiences. The case of John, described earlier, being convinced that there were microphones in the wall illustrates this point.

Schneider (1959) in his description of the so called first rank symptoms appears greatly influenced by Jaspers' thinking. Schneider identified a number of phenomena which he regarded as essential to the diagnosis of schizophrenia and these included:

- Hearing one's thoughts spoken aloud;
- Voices talking to each other;
- Voices that comment on one's behaviour;
- A conviction that external forces are interfering with bodily functions or interfering with or removing or broadcasting thoughts;
- The experience that emotions or behaviour or volition are under the control of an external agency.

The essence of this definition was a description of the phenomena which, in a Jasperian sense, were not understandable. This definition, unlike those of Kraepelin, Bleuler and others, was not based on notions of age of onset, prognosis and cause, but on both a description of the phenomena and the extent to which they were understandable to the psychiatrist.

In current practise the philosophical roots of Jaspers' system has been somewhat lost in the attempt to establish reliable diagnostic criteria (Farmer, McGuffin and Bebbington, 1988). Schneider's clarity, however, has proved useful and in many ways forms the basis for the current definitions of schizophrenic phenomena. A number of large-scale studies, in particular Cooper, *et al.* (1972) and the World Health Organization (1974) helped to establish standard criteria throughout the world. These studies used a standard interviewing technique known as the Present State Examination (PSE) and categorized people according to a set of rules which formed part of the CATEGO computer programme, which, in the main, defines the central syndrome of schizophrenia using Schneider's first rank symptoms (Wing, 1978).

Since these studies attempts have been made to establish international definitions of schizophrenia. Currently the most widely adopted system is the Revised Third Edition of the American Psychiatric Association Diagnostic and Statistical Manual (DSM 111 Revised). This system does not provide definitions of the constituent symptoms and historically has been relatively narrow, requiring that patients have been exhibiting schizophrenic-like symptoms for more than six months and should show a deterioration in functioning. Overall the evidence indicates that the well developed systems do improve inter-diagnostic reliability (Farmer, *et al.*, 1988). However, the problem remains that although a number of different but reliable diagnostic systems exist, the level of agreement between these systems is relatively poor (Brockington, Kendell, and Leff, 1978). Reliability, however, does not guarantee validity, because the fact that two or more people agree that specific symptoms are present does not mean that it is valid to call a number of such symptoms schizophrenia. It is the doubts about validity that remain most potent (Bentall, Jackson and Pilgrim, 1988), a problem that will be considered next.

Validity of Schizophrenia

During the 1960s a number of radical workers involved in mental health services began to question the validity of conceptualising mental health problems generally, and schizophrenia in particular, as diseases caused by organic malfunctioning (Laing, 1965). The roots of their disquiet can be traced to the research and their clinical experience concerned with the effects of family relations on identified patients. What emerged from this work was that the identified patients' difficulties appeared to be expressions of severe problems in their relationships with parents. Further, it was the difference between how these problems were expressed, rather than the similarities, which were crucial to understanding patients' difficulties. Consequently, the need for a concept, schizophrenia, to link or group these people was thought of not only as invalid but also harmful.

Given this historical background recent researchers have attempted to take a more traditional scientific approach to the problem of validity. Bentall, *et al.* (1988) suggest that there are three ways of assessing the validity of schizophrenia. First, the symptoms included in the syndrome should go together, that is, people suffering with one symptom should have a high probability of suffering with other symptoms included in the syndrome. Second, from the diagnosis it should be possible to predict onset, outcome and response to treatment. Third, diagnosis should be related to aetiology. It is helpful to summarise the major arguments which they put forward.

The first validity problem is that the symptoms thought to be crucial to the diagnosis of schizophrenia are found in patients with other psychiatric conditions. For example, thought disorder is common amongst people suffering with mania (Andreasen, 1979; Warner, 1985), delusions are found in people with affective disorders, and hallucinations are found in numerous conditions including depressive disorders and abnormal grief reactions. Further studies utilising the statistical techniques of factor analysis (Trouton and Maxwell, 1956) and cluster analysis (Everitt, Gourlay and Kendell, 1971) to identify common groups of symptoms have proved flawed on methodological grounds, in that they have used hospitalized samples and as such are unlikely to include patients with few psychotic symptoms (Slade and Cooper, 1979).

The second problem concerns predictive validity, that is, the onset and outcome for patients diagnosed as schizophrenic is extremely variable. Kraepelin's original theory of insidious onset and deteriorating course has been largely disproved. Ciompi (1980) in his study of 228 schizophrenics over a period of thirty-five years found the onset was either acute or, conversely, insidious in approximately half the cases. With regard to the course of the condition equal numbers had an episodic and continuous course whilst with outcome (that is, symptomatology) only half were left with a moderate or severe disability and more than a quarter showed full recovery. Other studies attempting to predict outcome have proved equally inconclusive (Kendell, Brockington and Leff, 1976). In addition, Strauss and Carpenter (1977) found that social factors, including work performance and social contacts, were better predictors of outcome than symptomatology. Similarly, Vaughn and Leff (1976) have found family variables (see later discussion) to be good predictors of relapse. Indeed Bentall, *et al.* (1988) argue that it is possible that these factors are sufficient to account for the marginal differences in outcome. Finally, the extent to which a diagnosis of schizophrenia enables prediction about response to treatment has proved problematic and will be discussed later in the chapter.

The third validity problem concerns the lack of a clear relationship between diagnosis and aetiology (cause of schizophrenia). Thus far it has proved impossible to discover a clear genetic, biochemical, neurological, cognitive, familial or psychodynamic cause or causes of schizophrenia. This is perhaps not surprising given the difficulties of identifying clearly the symptoms of schizophrenia and its variability in terms of onset, course and outcome. The factors implicated in the aetiology need to be examined in order to understand what is currently known about schizophrenia and to evaluate whether it remains a valid concept.

The Genetic Evidence

The vast majority of psychiatric and psychological texts concerned with schizophrenia (e.g., Gottesman and Shields, 1982) accept that there exists a convincing body of evidence that a predisposition for schizophrenia is transmitted genetically. This evidence falls into three categories: family, twin and adoptee studies, with the work with twins and adoptees providing the most powerful support for the genetic case.

Family Studies

The prevalence of schizophrenia in the general population is less than one percent (Jablensky, 1986) although there is some variation according to which diagnostic criteria are used. Relatives of schizophrenics have a higher chance of developing the condition than others. Zerbin-Rudin (1972) in summarising the evidence claims that the children of two schizophrenic parents have a 40 to 68 per cent chance, children of a single schizophrenic parent a 9 to 16 per cent chance, siblings an 8 to 14 per cent chance, and grandchildren a 2 to 8 per cent chance of developing the condition. With regard to whether this supports a genetic or environmental hypothesis about the aetiology of schizophrenia, the data is ambiguous in that it supports both views. The risk of developing the condition increases with the closeness of the genetic relationship, but also the relative will have shared similar familial and social experiences.

Twin Studies

The earliest and most widely quoted twin study is that of Kallmann (1946). Kallmann sought to test the genetic hypothesis by demonstrating that monozygotic (MZ) twins who had the same genetic material were more likely to develop schizophrenia than dizygotic (DZ) twins who have different genetic material. His sample was larger than any study before or since in that he located 174 MZ twins, at least one of whom was schizophrenic and 517 DZ twins. Kallmann (1946) reported an MZ concordance rate of 86.2 per cent and for DZ twins of 26.3 per cent. As Marshall (1984) points out, it is useful to analyse this study in some detail as it illustrates many of the methodological problems that beset all twin studies.

The first problem involves the definition of the phenotype, that is, the observable characteristics of the disorder and how reliably this was applied. There has been considerable variability in the definitions of schizophrenia and, as McGuffin (1988) points out, the different definitions produce different concordance rates. The general point emerges from reviews (Gottesman and Shields, 1972; McGuffin, 1988; Marshall, 1990) that the stricter the definition the lower the concordance rates. McGuffin, *et al.* (1984) in a study reanalysing case abstracts and comparing concordance rates when using different definitions found, when Schneider's first rank symptoms were used, the estimate of heritability was zero, whereas DSM III definitions give higher heritability estimates. Kallmann (1946) provided little evidence about how schizophrenia was defined or how reliable his diagnosis proved (Boyle, 1990).

The second problem concerns the difficulty of defining zygosity, that is, Kallmann never presented information about how this was diagnosed and at that time this was problematic technically (Jackson, 1960). Advances in genetic research have made this less of a problem for more recent studies although the reliability of the diagnosis of zygosity should be checked and raters of zygosity should always remain blind to information concerned with concordance. This has not always been the case (Marshall, 1984).

The third problem concerns the variability in terms of how concordance is calculated. The simplest method is pairwise concordance, where if out of a sample of 100 schizophrenics who are also twins, 40 pairs are diagnosed as schizophrenic, this will give a concordance of 40 per cent. However, the most commonly quoted way of calculating concordance is *probandwise* and this, it can be argued, inflates the concordance rates. The argument for using this is that if the twin pair who are diagnosed as schizophrenic are identified independently they are added to the number of concordant pairs. Using the figures in the example above this would give a concordance of 45 per cent. Finally, the casewise method involves counting both members of the affected pair. Thus the forty pairs identified above could be represented as eighty individuals with an affected partner. Using this method this would give a concordance rate of 57.1 per cent. Thus, when presenting concordance data, as well as making clear which definitions of schizophrenia have been used, it has also become customary to quote the method employed to calculate concordance (McGuffin, 1988).

Kallmann was never particularly explicit about how concordance was calculated and used a number of other methods to inflate his concordance rates that have been acknowledged by both his defendants (Shields, Gottesman and Slater, 1967) and his critics (Jackson, 1960; Marshall, 1984). The criticisms of Kallmann's work are so profound that it is somewhat surprising that his results are still frequently quoted in standard texts; such uncritical acceptance gives credence to Rose, Kamin and Lewontin's (1984) arguments that the 'existence of a genetic factor in the aetiology of schizophrenia has been treated as an axiom rather than a hypothesis.'

Other twin studies have been carried out since Kallmann's (1946) study (Slater, 1953; Kringlen, 1967; Gottesman and Shields, 1972; Fischer, 1973). Davison and Neale (1986), in reviewing this evidence, quote concordance rates for MZ twins of between 6 and 74.7 per cent and for DZ twins between 4 and 14.4 per cent. As Marshall (1990) points out the size of the concordance rate appears to be related to the scientific rigour of the studies. Quite simply the more controlled the studies the lower the concordance rates. Many reviews summarising the evidence are often quoted (Rosenthal, 1970; Zerbin-Rudin, 1972), but when the original evidence is subject to rigorous investigation (Schiff, Cassou and Stewart, 1980), the support for a genetic effect is less than convincing.

Adoptee Studies

There have been two major adoptee studies. Heston (1966) traced forty-seven people who had been born to schizophrenic mothers whilst they were in hospital and who had been brought up, since shortly after their birth, either by relatives or in children's homes. Fifty control children brought up in similar homes were then identified. Five of the forty-seven children (10.6 per cent) were diagnosed as schizophrenic and none of the control children. This study still provides the strongest adoptee evidence for the genetic hypothesis.

Kety *et al.* (1968) in the US-Danish adoption studies located all the children who had been adopted at an early age in Denmark between 1927 and 1947. All adoptees who were admitted to a psychiatric hospital were located and the biological parents, siblings and half-siblings were then traced. A control group without a psychiatric history was identified. A group of 150 biological relatives and 156 controls were selected. Kety, *et al.* (1968) claim that there was a 10 per cent prevalence rate for schizophrenia in the families of the naturally reared schizophrenics, but this depended on a broad definition of schizophrenia. Lidz and Blatt (1983) point out, that in fact only one 'chronic schizophrenic' was found in both groups, which clearly provides little support for a genetic aetiology. Kety, *et al.* (1975) interviewed the families of 33 schizophrenic adoptees and found 12.6 per cent of biological parents were schizophrenic or latent schizophrenics. This study has been critically reviewed by Rose, *et al.* (1984) who found problems similar to earlier studies with shifting diagnostic boundaries, a selective adoptive placement effect and cases where pseudo interviews were compiled from hospital records for a number of interviews where the relatives were dead.

In summary, the evidence that genetic factors are involved in the aetiology of schizophrenia is a good deal more problematic than is usually presented in standard psychiatric and psychological texts. Marshall (1990) interestingly points out that throughout the history of investigations into a genetic basis for schizophrenia researchers have perhaps been influenced by the desire to establish the link rather than adhere to the more conservative rules of scientific method. This position is not surprising given the reliability and validity problems associated with the condition.

Biological Models

There remains a fundamental problem involved in examining the work concerned with establishing a biological basis for schizophrenia. These issues are discussed fully by Bentall (1990a). If schizophrenia is not a clearly identifiable syndrome, but an umbrella term covering a range of symptoms with unclear onset, course and outcome, then it is obvious that much of the work investigating a specific biological basis will inevitably be inconclusive. This is, in fact, the case, which is not to imply that biological factors are unimportant. Obviously psychological changes have biochemical affects just as biological changes have psychological effects. The history of the search for a biological cause of schizophrenia has been overly based on the pursuit of a single abnormality leading to the variety of phenomena characteristic of schizophrenia. Such investigations have suggested either structural-neurological or biochemical abnormalities.

Structural-Neurological Abnormalities

Any structural abnormalities are only significant in terms of their effect on complex brain functioning and as such may help identify the processes which lead to 'schizophrenic symptomatology'. A number of global cortical abnormalities have been implicated. Cortical atrophy, that is the degeneration of brain cells, has been found by a number of researchers (Weinberger, Torrey and Wyatt, 1979), as have enlarged ventricles, that is, spaces in the cortex (Storey, 1966; Andreason, *et al.*, 1982) in people diagnosed as schizophrenic. Murray, *et al.* (1988) proposed a developmental model which suggested that neurological abnormalities characterised by increased cortical atrophy and ventricular size and disordered hippocampal areas arise with the development of the brain in the foetus and during the neonatal period. Other researchers have been unable to discover either cortical atrophy or ventricular enlargement (Jernigan, *et al.*, 1982) nor has the hypothesis that these structural abnormalities are progressive been confirmed (Nasrallah, *et al.*, 1986). Seidman's (1984) review of the literature estimates that only 20–30 per cent of schizophenics suffer from gross organic impairment and others have suggested that these structural changes may be the result of diet, institutionalisation, neuroleptic drugs and convulsion therapy (Trimble and Kingsley, 1978; Reveley, 1985).

Murray, *et al.*'s (1988) model implicates subcortical abnormalities and a number of researchers have found abnormalities in the hippocampal region and its connections with the cortex (Bogerts, Meertz and Schonefeldt-Bausch, 1985). The hippocampal formation (part of the limbic system) plays an important role in discriminating relevant and irrelevant stimuli and could provide the physical base for the abnormalities in information processing which have been used to explain the symptoms of schizophrenia (see Psychological Models pp. 182–6). As Lewis (1989) points out, these hypotheses are still speculative but seem more fruitful than the attempts to identify specific cortical abnormalities associated with particular lobes of the brain (Jackson, 1990).

Biochemical Abnormalities

Since Kraepelin's first attempts to define schizophrenia there has been a search for the biochemical 'cause'. It has been the feature of these investigations that, shortly after a possible chemical cause is identified, a series of disconfirming studies are reported. One example of this is the transmethylation hypothesis (Osmond and Smythies, 1952) based on the fact that the chemical structure of mescaline (an hallucinogen) is similar to naturally occurring neurotransmitters known as catecholamines (e.g., dopamine and noradrenalin). These neuro-transmitters are the chemicals responsible for the transmission of impulses between neurones at the synapse. The hypothesis was that schizophrenia was the result of overactivity in one of the processes of transmethylation of these amines which lead to the production of hallucinogenic toxic by-products. This hypothesis has since been abandoned due to the lack of correspondence between the experiences induced by mescaline, LSD and schizophrenia and the failure to replicate experiments where increasing the levels of amines led to 'schizophrenic-like' symptoms (Iversen, 1982). Many other neurochemicals have been implicated, these include serotonin, prostaglandin, GABA and neuro-peptides, but none have proved to be specifically associated with schizophrenia.

The dopamine hypothesis has been the most recent to receive widespread acceptance. The hypothesis is that there is a relative overactivity of certain tracts of neurones in which the chemical neurotransmitter is dopamine (Meltzer and Stahl, 1976). The evidence supporting this hypothesis has come from two sources. First, amphetamines stimulate the release of dopamine and other catecholamines and produces an acute psychosis similar to schizophrenia and can produce an exacerbation of psychotic symptoms in people diagnosed as suffering with schizophrenia (Angrist, Lee and Gershon, 1974). Second, antipsychotic drugs (for example, chlorpromazine) which are known to reduce the symptoms of at least some schizophrenics (Haracz, 1982) also inhibit the ability of the dopamine receptors at the synapse to respond to dopamine and thus reduce the activity in the dopaminergic tracts. The parts of the dopaminergic tracts particularly at risk are the mesolimbic and limbic systems which, as described earlier, appear particularly important in filtering environ-mental stimuli.

There are, however, a number of studies which have produced evidence against this hypothesis. Jackson (1986) in his review points out that no consist-ent differences in dopamine levels have been found between drug free schizophrenics and normals. Also, no increase in the levels of other dopamine metabolites, which would indicate greater dopamine activity, have been found in schizophrenia. Jackson (1990) concludes that problems with dopamine production and receptivity are unlikely to prove to be the basic biochemical abnormalities underlying all forms of schizophrenia, although it may play a fundamental role in some forms.

In this brief overview the possible roles of a number of other neuro-chemicals, for example serotonin, noradrenaline and prostaglandin have been omitted from the discussion. In general the evidence that they may play a part in the aetiology of schizophrenia is such that it does not lead to any easily stated general conclusions. This may, in fact, prove to be because schizo-phrenia includes such a wide range of symptoms that attempting to find a specific neurochemical cause will prove impossible. As Bentall (1990a) points out, perhaps the time has come to turn to investigations concerned with specific symptoms before attempting to find the biochemical cause of schizophrenia which could be regarded as a concept of dubious validity.

Psychological Models

It is important to state at the outset that there is no agreed psychological model to explain the behaviour and experiences that are found in people diagnosed as schizophrenic (Hemsley, 1988). There are a number of perceptual and cognitive abnormalities that have been investigated and a number of interesting lines of enquiry that have recently been suggested. The research investigating psychological variables has been beset by a number of methodological problems. These include both the use of 'schizophrenics' who have been diagnosed on the basis of case-note information and who are taking antipsychotic medication. The problem in such cases is that the reliability of the diagnosis and the effects of the medication on psychological functioning are often unknown, which limits the generalisability of the findings. In addition, studies often compare schizophrenics with 'normal' control subjects, which means that any difference found may not be specific to schizophrenia but may be common to many psychiatric disorders. Bearing in mind these difficulties, there are, however, a number of psychological variables which have been suggested as being of particular importance in schizophrenia.

Selective Attention

McGhie and Chapman (1961) suggested that the primary disorder in schizophrenia was a decrease in the selective and inhibitory functions of attention. This proposal used Broadbent's (1958) notion of a cognitive filter which screened irrelevant stimuli (see Chapter 1). In schizophrenia a deficit in the filter meant that the individual was flooded with stimuli and therefore in a state of information overload.

Broadbent (1971) elaborated his model by proposing a second mechanism involved in selective attention, which he termed 'pigeon holing' and which was more concerned with individuals' responses. When stimuli are received, decisions need to be made about which responses to make from an infinite number of possibilities. 'Pigeon holing' allows the stimuli to be keyed in to certain categories of response without having to process all possible responses. In schizophrenia it has been argued that this function is impaired so that the individual has considerable difficulty selecting the correct response from a large range of possible responses. This deficit frequently leads to the schizophrenic producing inappropriate responses.

Thus with selective attention two important processes have been suggested to be impaired in schizophrenia. Hemsley (1988) points out that the evidence for a defective filter mechanism is somewhat inconsistent. In experiments designed to test for a defective filter, schizophrenics have made more errors than normal subjects, but when compared with psychiatric control groups, the findings are less clear. The evidence for impairment in 'pigeon holing' which is largely dependent on semantic cues is scarce, although some evidence has begun to accumulate (Schwartz, 1982; Hemsley, 1988).

Slowness of Information Processing

The most well established finding is that schizophrenics have shown a generalised slowness of processing over a variety of tasks. The studies investigating this variable have usually involved some form of choice reaction time experiment where the speed of response to a particular stimulus is timed. In these experiments the uncertainty about the stimulus or response is varied. Hemsley's (1976) review indicates that although the evidence appears contradictory, it is clear that when the stimulus response link is not an obvious or natural one, then the greater the response uncertainty, and the worse schizophrenics perform. These findings are compatible with the possible deficit in response selection or 'pigeon holing' described earlier.

Controlled and Automatic Processing

Schneider and Shiffrin (1977) distinguished between automatic and controlled cognitive processes. Automatic processing occurs outside conscious awareness and involves a fixed sequence of mental operations in response to a particular stimulus set. Such processes can be trained but when learned they become relatively fixed. Controlled processing is relatively slow, under conscious control and involves temporary sequences of mental operations. Callaway and Naghoi (1982) suggest that schizophrenics have a deficit in controlled but not automatic processing. A number of authors (for example, Venables, 1984) have concluded that the deficit is most likely to be in the area of automatic processing, which means that all tasks have to be subject to controlled processing. This suggestion is consistent with the findings showing slowed information processing and with Frith's cognitive model described next.

Frith's Model — A Failure to Control Consciousness

Frith (1979) proposed that a deficit in the mechanism that controls and limits the contents of consciousness causes the three principal positive symptoms of schizophrenia, that is, hallucinations, delusions and thought disorder. Frith's model is a modification of the defective filter theory which he argues is unable to explain delusions and hallucinations and also why, if it is such a global deficit, schizophrenics function relatively well for large proportions of their lives. Within his model a distinction is made between conscious and preconscious processes. Preconscious processes occur below the level of consciousness. They include motor outputs and cognitive operations concerned with the selection of appropriate interpretations of and responses to stimuli. Frith argues that for schizophrenics these preconscious processes are frequently conscious. Thus auditory hallucinations are viewed as an awareness of the preconscious incorrect interpretations of auditory stimuli and therefore tend to increase in situations where there is ambiguous sensory input. Thus with John, described in the Introduction, p. 172, sounds outside the door are misinterpreted as people talking about him and to him. For most people such a preconscious interpretation would be discounted before reaching conscious awareness, but not for John. Similarly, delusions are attempts to explain and understand using normal principles of reasoning, misinterpretations which would normally not reach consciousness. Thought disorder arises out of the schizophrenic's awareness of the numerous possible meanings of words which again normally remain unconscious. This inability to inhibit alternative responses leads to the rapid production of neologisms and inappropriate words.

Maher (1983) put forward a similar model involving a deficit in the ability to exclude intrusions into consciousness. Thus material from either external stimulation or internally stored associations which would normally be excluded as irrelevancies reaches consciousness. The difficulty with such models is that so far they only provide explanations of some of the symptoms of schizophrenia, and it remains unclear why, if the deficit is fixed, that schizophrenics at times function without these symptoms and also are able to perform some tasks well (Pilling, 1988). In addition, questions about why particular misinterpretations occur and remain fixed (as with John) and why they should occur at particular times and not others are not addressed by these models.

Psychological Approaches to Symptoms

A major difficulty in investigating psychological factors involved in schizophrenia is the problem that the diagnostic label refers to a range of clinical experiences or symptoms. These experiences include hallucinations, delusions, thought disorder, poverty of speech, apathy and attentional impairments. Amongst others Bannister (1968), Slade and Cooper (1979) and Bentall, *et al.* (1988) have suggested abandoning investigations into the syndrome of schizophrenia and propose instead the investigation of the experiences and symptoms. Using such an approach some progress has been made in the work with positive symptoms (hallucinations, delusions and thought disorder) but less with negative symptoms (such as poverty of speech and apathy). It is perhaps helpful to briefly describe some of this work.

Hallucinations

In the last two decades a number of factors have been found to increase the likelihood of experiencing hallucinations (Slade, 1976); these include the experience of stress, sensory deprivation and unpatterned stimulation (for example, white noise). Other factors, including a reduction in arousal, have been linked with a decrease in hallucinations. Several models have been put forward to account for hallucinations, including Frith's, although with his model it is difficult to account for the finding that hallucinations decrease when subjects prone to hallucinations attend to what others say (Slade, 1974).

Collicutt and Hemsley (1985) suggest that hallucinations are caused when unexpected internally generated experiences are attributed to external events and further attempt to relate this process to a deficit in the 'pigeon holing' mechanism described by Broadbent (1971). Hoffman (1986), following a some-what similar theme, proposed that a deficit in speech production led to certain thoughts arising in an unintended fashion which were then interpreted as alien. Some of Hoffman's work has been criticised on methodological grounds but still forms an important part of the emerging body of literature.

Bentall and Slade (1985) and more recently Bentall (1990b) have put forward the idea that a deficit in the metacognition of reality testing, that is, the inferential skill of being able to discriminate between what is real and imaginary, results in the experience of hallucinations; thus hallucinations result from individuals wrongly inferring that internal cognitive events are external real stimuli. There is some experimental evidence to support this hypothesis (Bentall, 1990b) although the reasons why people develop this difficulty with reality testing is not clear. If some of Laing's ideas prove correct, it may be that certain patterns of interaction within the family, particularly when the child is very young, mean the child fails to acquire this ability. Similarly, it may be that in order to avoid painful experiences the developing child increasingly escapes into 'imaginary worlds' to such an extent that in times of crisis, the child re-experiences those 'imaginary experiences' as 'real'.

Delusions

In general there has been little work which has investigated the formation of abnormal belief systems. There have been a number of suggestions about pos-sible psychological mechanisms underlying delusions. Some investigators have suggested that they may arise out of rational descriptions of bizarre or entangled sets of events and that the delusion is a metaphorical understanding of those events (Laing, 1965; Bannister, 1968). Others have considered that delusions are rational interpretations of abnormal perceptual experiences (Maher, 1974). Indeed, the finding that people with delusions neither experi-ence more unusual events nor perform abnormally on tasks involving formal reasoning (Williams, 1964) lends support to such theories.

Hemsley and Garety (1986) suggest that delusions are the result of a deficit in information-processing, in that people with delusional beliefs are unable to weigh up new evidence and modify their beliefs. This suggestion is similar to the proposal that hallucinations result from a deficit in the metacog-nition of 'reality testing'. Kaney and Bentall (1989) have also investigated information-processing deficits through assessment of the attributional style of people with delusions. Their findings indicate that paranoid patients who tend to hold the delusional belief that others are against them attribute bad events to causes which would affect their entire lives, which were beyond their control and which were caused by factors external to themselves; thus, they showed external, global and stable attributions for negative events. It is evident that the investigation of delusions from a uniquely psychological perspective is still its infancy. The early work has, however, already indicated some possible treatment strategies (Watts, Powell and Austin, 1973; Chadwick and Lowe, 1990) and is worthy of further investigation.

Psychoanalytic Ideas

Any discussion of psychoanalytic ideas and how they relate to the experiences associated with schizophrenia needs to be prefaced with a reminder of the methods employed to gather information. Psychoanalysts have gathered data concerned with a knowledge of unconscious processes through intense contact with patients, up to five fifty-minute sessions per week. Freud developed this method and the associated theoretical ideas in order to understand the psyche of his patients (see Chapter 1). The strength of this method is the intensity and depth of understanding of the individual that can be achieved, but its weakness is the extent to which discoveries about individuals are applicable to others, that is, the generalisability of the findings. Many psychoanalysts including Freud (1940) have stated that the psychotic's problems are such that it is impossible to establish an appropriate therapeutic alliance to work using analytic methods. Although others (Fromm-Reichmann, 1950) have disagreed with this view, Klerman (1984) and Mueser and Berenbaum (1990) in reviewing the evidence support Freud's view; namely, that intensive individual psychotherapy has proved to be a failure with schizophrenia. Tarrier (1990) has commented that there is some evidence that the overstimulation provoked by such therapeutic encounters can promote relapse. Frosch (1983) provides an impressive historical review of the development of psychoanalytic ideas about psychosis, although he too, makes the point that whilst psychoanalysis has played a role in understanding the psychotic process, the extent to which this has been translated into meaningful therapy may be challenged.

In this brief chapter it is impossible to provide an overview of psychoanalytic theory as it relates to psychosis, but is perhaps useful to mention one of the theoretical ideas. Frosch (1983) considers that the presence of psychosis hinges on the loss of the capacity to test reality. Exploration of this capacity has a long tradition in psychoanalytic writings (Freud, 1911; Ferenczi, 1913; Glover, 1932; Weiss, 1950) and has interesting parallels with recent developments in cognitive theory which Bentall (1990a) has used to understand hallucinations (that is, the metacognition of reality testing). Frosch (1983) describes how reality testing is the ability to draw logical conclusions from a series of observable phenomena, the loss of which is psychosis. Freud (1925) states that one function of reality testing is to be able to distinguish between an idea and a perception, and between what is internal to the person and what is external. The question has then been asked, what processes interfere with this capacity?

A number of processes have been identified which distort the perception of reality. In relation to the development of psychosis and in particular paranoid delusions, the process of projection has been implicated. In simple terms this process involves splitting off bad, negative emotions and projecting them out into the external world, so that a person, group, society or even an inanimate object is regarded as the source of the badness. In psychoanalytic theory the two parts that have commonly considered to be split off are associated with an individual's aggressive/hateful impulses and unconscious homosexuality (Frosch, 1983); thus, these feelings are impossible for the individual to acknowledge and so are projected onto others. For example, as with John (see p. 172) the paranoid person sees his own projected aggression in the actions of others and consequently misinterprets their intentions. Reality is distorted.

The most significant contribution psychoanalytic theory has made to psychosis has been the attempts made to understand the meaning of symptoms in terms of both the current circumstances and how those circumstances relate to very early childhood experiences. It was Melanie Klein's view that the inability to tolerate negative emotional states could be traced to constitutional factors and inadequate mothering. Specifically the mother, or major caregiver, needed to be able to contain the negative emotions (e.g., anger) of the baby in a way that made those emotions bearable and therefore allowed them to be integrated into the developing self. If these emotions were not made bearable the child would split them off and project them into objects in the world. Klein clearly regarded projection as a primitive (occurring very early in the child's development) defence mechanism (Segal, 1979). Such a defence mechanism is likely to reoccur in situations which provoke that emotional response.

It is perhaps something of a tragedy that there has not been more cross-fertilisation between the ideas of psychoanalysis, where attempts have been made to understand the meaning of the symptoms, and more empirically-based developments in psychology. It would appear that there is a good deal to be gained from such cross-fertilisation for both our theoretical understanding and the development of psychological interventions to alleviate the disturbing experiences associated with schizophrenia.

Family Models

Even amongst strong proponents of the genetic hypothesis there is a recognition of the importance of environmental factors. In terms of the environmental variables that have been linked to the aetiology and maintenance of schizophrenic symptomatology, family factors are particularly prominent (Bateson, Jackson, Haley and Weakland, 1956; Wynne and Singer, 1963; Laing, 1965). The development of early theories rested mainly on clinical observations, and insights and the quality of the empirical work designed to test these theories has been somewhat inadequate. A brief review of this early work is, however, still useful.

Bateson, *et al.* (1956), developed the 'double-bind theory' to explain the emergence of what they regarded as the schizophrenic's key problem, namely a severe difficulty in the pattern of communication. Families of schizophrenics were considered to show a particular pattern of ambiguous communication in which the parent denied the contradictory nature of his/her command and did not allow the child to point out this contradiction. For example, 'You must love your parents and must be free to choose what you want to do, but if you go to that party it shows you can't love your father. Don't expect us to be able to love you if you do go.' Such double binds could either contain contradictions in the parent's speech, as with the above example, or in a contradiction between the oral message and the tone of voice or gesture. For example, 'No, of course, I'm not angry', said whilst ripping up the newspaper. There have, in fact, been few empirical investigations of this theory, although the evidence suggests that, first, it is difficult to identify double-bind messages, and, secondly, such messages are likely to occur in all families. It may be the case that it is not just whether such communication patterns occur, but the extent to which the child is subject to such communication from birth, that is important in producing the symptoms of schizophrenia in adulthood.

Wynne and Singer (1963) use the concept of 'pseudomutuality' to characterise the pattern of communication in schizophrenic families. This term described how interactions despite superficial appearances showed a fragmented and disjointed pattern with irrational changes in focus which prevented any continuity. Underlying this disordered communication were feelings of emptiness and meaninglessness, which were taken on by the children. As the children reach adolescence and begin to enter the world beyond the family, the disordered pattern of communication prevents them fitting in to this new world. Singer and Wynne (1966) produced an impressive study which showed that it was possible to discriminate between the communication pattern of families of schizophrenics, neurotics and adults with no psychiatric disorder on the basis of a Deviance Score. This Deviance Score was obtained by counting the number of communication defects or deviances recorded during a session in which the family were completing a projective test. Hirsch and Leff (1975) in part replicated the study and found parents of schizophrenics had significantly higher Deviance Scores than neurotic individuals. They explored these results in more detail and found that the differences in scores could have been accounted for by the increased verbosity observed in the schizophrenic families. Thus Hirsch and Leff concluded that the differences in Deviance Scores could have been no more than an artefact of the differences in verbosity between schizophrenic and neurotic families.

Laing (1965) developed a considerably more sophisticated theory to explain the origins of schizophrenia within the family. He regarded the content of the hallucinations, delusions and thought disorder as containing an 'existential truth'. Thus the symptoms developed as a way of coping with and communicating to others the impossibility of the familial environment. Laing published a number of thought-provoking accounts of the development of schizophrenia which produced clear testable hypotheses. It is something of a puzzle why nobody has developed research studies to investigate these essentially clinical and theoretical writings. Perhaps the answer lies in the lack of a traditional scientific mode of investigation within the model in which Laing's ideas were embedded and the published failure of Anna to work through her psychotic experience in the way advocated by Laing (Reed, 1978). On this latter point, Alice Miller's (1978) work may also be of relevance in that she eloquently describes the lengths to which individuals will go to avoid facing the unpalatable 'truth' about the harm that certain parental child-rearing methods have on an individual's development.

In recent years investigations prompted by the early work of Brown, Carstairs and Topping (1958) and Brown, Bone, Dalison and Wing (1966) have focused on the concept of Expressed Emotion (EE) within the family. The level of Expressed Emotion within a family is determined by the frequency of critical comments and positive remarks and ratings of hostility, emotional over-involvement and warmth in an audio-taped interview with a relative of the patient. The relative is rated as demonstrating high EE, if he or she makes six or more critical comments, and/or scores a rank of one or more on hostility, and/or three or more on emotional over-involvement. The research investigating this phenomenon has revealed a consistent finding that there is a strong relationship between relapse and living with a high EE relative. This has been found in Britain (Vaughn and Leff, 1976; Tarrier, *et al.*, 1988) the United States (Moline, Singh, Morris and Meltzer, 1985), Denmark and India (Wig, *et al.*, 1987).

Vaughn and Leff's (1976) study, although not without its methodological problems, is perhaps of most interest, because they attempted to look at the effect of medication, Expressed Emotion and the amount of contact with the high EE relative. They found that in the group of patients who lived with high EE relatives with whom they had high levels of contact (more than thirty-five hours a week), and who were not on medication, 92 per cent relapsed within nine months. Patients in a similar family, but who were on medication, had a 53 per cent relapse rate. This indicated that medication provided some protection from relapse in these high EE families. However, patients who lived with a low EE relative had a 12 per cent relapse rate if they were on medication and a 15 per cent rate if not on medication. This indicated that in low EE families there was little change in relapse rate when medication was taken.

This work is extremely valuable in that it is possible to specify factors within the family associated with relapse in a way that leads directly to therapeutic interventions designed to reduce those factors. A number of researchers have pointed to some problems with the work. Tarrier's (1990) criticisms concern the definition of relapse in the studies. For example, relapse is often equated with an increase in positive symptoms and to a large extent ignores exacerbation of negative symptoms or a deterioration in social functioning. In addition, questions have been raised about the extent to which ratings of EE obtained in a sixty to ninety minute audio-taped session are representative of interactions in the home environment (MacCarthy, *et al.*, 1986). These criticisms do not invalidate the previous studies, but point to the need for further work in the area.

The research into EE has led to the development of some extremely effective family interventions (Strachan, 1986). Falloon, *et al.* (1982) compared the effects on relapse of eighteen high EE families treated with individual supportive psychotherapy with eighteen similar families treated with a behavioural family intervention. This latter intervention consisted of three components. First, the education of patient and family about schizophrenia; second, communication training; and, third, problem-solving training. They found that after nine months, the relapse rate was 6 per cent in the family intervention group compared with 44 per cent in the supportive psychotherapy group. After two years the percentage relapse was 17 in the family group and 83 in the supportive therapy group. Similar findings have been reported by other research groups (e.g., Leff, *et al.*, 1982). It remains something of a mystery and tragedy that in spite of the strong evidence supporting the widespread use of these family interventions they are still rarely offered in most services for people with long term mental health problems (Lavender and Holloway, 1988). Perhaps Bentall (1990a) is right when he suggests that it is a consequence of the dominant role of biological psychiatry in the treatment of schizophrenia.

Concluding Remarks

In conclusion, it is important to say that frequently when a review such as this is written it is usual to propose some model for schizophrenia which includes all possible relevant factors. This would include some original constitutional vulnerability (genetic) related to an organic or biochemical abnormality that interacts with particular social and familial factors to produce schizophrenia (Warner, 1985). It is tempting to repeat such an enterprise, but the evidence so far indicates that it is perhaps too soon to propose such an all encompassing model to account for a disease which can reasonably be regarded as of dubious validity.

Researchers from all theoretical orientations (genetic/biological, cognitive, psychoanalytic and familial) until very recently, have investigated schizophrenia as a whole and paid little attention to the particular experiences which have traditionally been described as the symptoms of schizophrenia. The fact that these distressing experiences exist, as was evident with John on the first page of this chapter, is not in doubt. However, whether it is useful to group these disparate experiences together and act as if they were part of a single disease is questionable. The investigation of these separate symptoms, which has most recently been suggested by Bentall (1990a), would seem to offer an important and potentially fruitful source of information.

Perhaps a key to this integration lies in an exploration of the concept of reality testing which has long been regarded as crucial by psychoanalysts and has recently been highlighted by researchers following a more cognitive model. Difficulties in being able to reality test occur at a perceptual and response level and probably involve different processes for each symptom. It is clearly important to investigate the nature of these difficulties in a way which allows a psychological understanding of their meaning. Investigations about how these difficulties or distortions develop in the growing child and emerge in full force in adulthood are extremely important to undertake. Studies which attempt to bring together the knowledge that has accumulated from psychoanalytic, familial and cognitive work are likely to prove most productive. Of particular importance in this integration is the linking of psychoanalytic work which has sought to understand the processes which lead to distortions in the child's ability to reality test with the familial investigations which sought to identify factors in both the past and present associated with the development of psychotic symptoms. The newly emerging cognitive models could provide the framework within which such integration can take place.

Recommended Reading

BEBBINGTON, P. and McGUFFIN, P. (1988) *Schizophrenia: The Major Issues*, London, UK: Heinemann.

BENTALL, R.P. (1990) *Reconstructing Schizophrenia*, London, UK: Routledge.

LAING, R.D. (1965) *The Divided Self*, London, UK: Pelican.

LAVENDER, A. and HOLLOWAY, F. (1988) *Community Care in Practice: Services for the Continuing Care Client*, Chichester, UK: John Wiley & Sons.

MILLER, A. (1987) *For Your Own Good: The Roots of Violence in Child-Rearing*, London, UK: Virago Press.

WARNER, R. (1985) *Recovery from Schizophrenia*, London, UK: Routledge & Kegan Paul.

WING, J.K. (1978) 'Clinical concepts of schizophrenia', in WING, J.K. (Ed.) *Schizophrenia: Towards a New Synthesis*, London, UK: Academic Press.

References

ANDREASEN, N.C. (1979) 'Thought, language and communication disorders: II Diagnostic significance', *Archives of General Psychiatry*, **36**, pp. 1325–30.

ANDREASEN, N.C., SMITH, M.R., JACOBY, C.G., DENNERT, J.W. and OLSEN, S.A. (1982) 'Ventricular enlargement in schizophrenia: Definition and prevalence', *American Journal of Psychiatry*, **139**, pp. 297–301.

ANGRIST, B., LEE, H.K. and GERSHON, S. (1974) 'The antagonism of amphetamine induced symptomatology by a neuroleptic', *American Journal of Psychiatry*, **131**, pp. 817–19.

BANNISTER, D. (1968) 'The logical requirements of research into schizophrenia', *British Journal of Psychiatry*, **114**, pp. 181–88.

BATESON, G., JACKSON, D., HALEY, J. and WEAKLAND, J. (1956) 'Towards a theory of schizophrenia', *Behavioural Science*, **1**, pp. 251–64.

BENTALL, R.P. (1990a) (Ed.) *Reconstructing schizophrenia*, London, UK: Routledge.

BENTALL, R.P. (1990b) 'The Illusion of reality: A review and integration of psychological research on hallucination', *Psychological Bulletin*, **107**, pp. 82–95.

BENTALL, R.P., JACKSON, H.F. and PILGRIM, D. (1988) 'Abandoning the concept of "Schizophrenia": Some implications of validity arguments for psychological research into psychotic phenomena', *British Journal of Clinical Psychology*, **27**, pp. 303–24.

BENTALL, R.P. and SLADE, P.D. (1985) 'Reality testing and auditory hallucination: a signal detection analysis', *British Journal of Clinical Psychology*, **24**, pp. 159–69.

BLEULER, E. (1950) *Dementia Praecox or the Group of Schizophrenias*, New York, NY: International University Press (Translated from the German edition, 1911).

BOGERTS, B., MEERTZ, E. and SCHONEFELDT-BAUSCH, R. (1985) 'Basal ganglia and limbic system pathology in schizophrenia', *Archives of General Psychiatry*, **42**, pp. 784–91.

BOYLE, M. (1990) *Schizophrenia: A Scientific Delusion?* London, UK: Routledge.

BROADBENT, D.E. (1958) *Perception and Communication*, London, UK: Pergamon.

BROADBENT, D.E. (1971) *Decision and Stress*, London, UK: Academic Press.

BROCKINGTON, J.F., KENDELL, R.E. and LEFF, J.P. (1978) 'Definitions of schizophrenia: Concordance and prediction of outcome', *Psychological Medicine*, **8**, pp. 387–98.

BROWN, G.W., CARSTAIRS, G. and TOPPING, G. (1958) 'Post hospital adjustment of chronic mental patients', *Lancet*, **ii**, pp. 685–89.

BROWN, G.W., BONE, M., DALISON, B. and WING, J.K. (1966) *Schizophrenia and Social Care*, London, UK: Oxford University Press.

CALLAWAY, E. and NAGHDI, S. (1982) 'An information processing model for schizophrenia', *Archives of General Psychiatry*, **39**, pp. 339–47.

CHADWICK, P. and LOWE, C.F. (1990) 'The measurement and modification of delusional beliefs', *Journal of Consulting and Clinical Psychology*, **58**, pp. 225–32.

CIOMPI, L. (1980) 'The natural history of schizophrenia in the long term', *British Journal of Psychiatry*, **136**, pp. 413–20.

COLLICUTT, J.R. and HEMSLEY, D.R. (1985) 'Schizophrenia: The Description of a stream of thought' Unpublished manuscript.

COOPER, J.E., KENDELL, R.E., GURLAND, B.J., SHARP, L., COPELAND, J.R.M. and SIMON, R. (1972) *Psychiatric Diagnosis in New York and London*, Maudsley Monograph. London, UK: Oxford University Press.

DAVISON, G.C. and NEALE, J.M. (1986) *Abnormal Psychology (Fourth edition)*. New York, NY: John Wiley & Sons.

EVERITT, B.S., GOURLAY, A.J. and KENDELL, R.E. (1971) 'An attempt at validation of traditional psychiatric syndromes by cluster analysis', *British Journal of Psychiatry*, **119**, pp. 399–412.

FALLOON, I.R.H., BOYD, J.L., McGILL, C.W., RANZINI, J., MOSS, H.D. and GILDERMAN, A.M. (1982) 'Family management in the prevention of exacerbation of schizophrenia', *New England Journal of Medicine*, **306**, pp. 1437–40.

FARMER, A.E., McGUFFIN, P. and BEBBINGTON, P. (1988) 'The phenomena of schizophrenia', in BEBBINGTON, P. and McGUFFIN, P. (Eds) *Schizophrenia: the Major Issues*, Oxford, UK: Heinemann.

FERENCZI, S. (1913) 'Stages in the Development of a Sense of Reality', in FERENCZI, S., *Sex in Psychoanalysis*, Boston, MA: Badger.

FISCHER, M. (1973) 'Genetic and environmental factors in schizophrenia: A study of schizophrenic twins and their families', *Acta Psychiatrica Scandinavica Supp*, p. 223.

FREUD, S. (1911) 'Psycho-analytic notes on an autobiographical account of a case of paranoia', (Dementia paranoides) *Standard Edition* (1958), **12**, pp. 3–82. London, UK: Hogarth Press.

FREUD, S. (1925) 'Negation', *Standard Edition* (1961), **19**, pp. 235–39. London, UK: Hogarth Press.

FREUD, S. (1940) 'An outline of psychoanalysis', *Standard Edition* (1964), **23**, pp. 141–208. London, UK: Hogarth Press.

FRITH, C.D. (1979) 'Consciousness, information processing and schizophrenia', *British Journal of Psychiatry*, **134**, pp. 225–35.

FROMM-REICHMANN, F. (1950) *Principles of Intensive Psychotherapy*, Chicago, IL: University of Chicago Press.

FROSCH, J. (1983) *The Psychotic Process*, New York, NY: International University Press.

GLOVER, E. (1932) 'The relation of perversion formation to the development of reality sense', in GLOVER, E. *On the Early Development of Mind*, New York, NY: International University Press.

GOTTESMAN, I.I. and SHIELDS, J. (1972) *Schizophrenia and Genetics*, London, UK: Academic Press.

GOTTESMAN, I.I. and SHIELDS, J. (1982) *Schizophrenia: The Epigenetic Puzzle*, Cambridge, UK: Cambridge University Press.

HARACZ, J.L. (1982) 'The Dopamine hypothesis: An overview of studies with schizophrenic patients. *Schizophrenia Bulletin*, **8**, pp. 438–69.

HEMSLEY, D.R. (1976) 'Stimulus uncertainty: Response uncertainty and stimulus response compatability as determinants of schizophrenics reaction time performance', *Bulletin of the Psychonomic Society*, **8**, pp. 425–27.

HEMSLEY, D.R. (1988) 'Psychological models of schizophrenia', in MILLER, E. and COOPER, A. (Eds) *Adult Abnormal Psychology*, London, UK: Churchill Livingstone.

HEMSLEY, D.R. and GARETY, P.A. (1986) 'The formation and maintenance of delusion: A Bayesian analysis', *British Journal of Psychiatry*, **149**, pp. 51–6.

HESTON, L.L. (1966) 'Psychiatric disorders in foster home reared children of schizophrenic mothers', *British Journal of Psychiatry*, **112**, pp. 819–25.

HIRSCH, S.R. and LEFF, J.P. (1975) *Abnormalities in the Parents of Schizophrenics*, Maudsley Monograph No. 22 Oxford, UK: Oxford University Press.

HOFFMAN, R.E. (1986) 'Verbal hallucination and language production in schizophrenia', *The Behavioural and Brain Sciences*, **9**, pp. 503–48.

IVERSEN, L.L. (1982) 'Biochemical and pharmacological studies: The dopamine hypothesis', in WING, J.K. (Ed.) *Schizophrenia: Towards a New Synthesis*, London, UK: Academic Press.

JABLENSKY, A. (1986) 'Epidemiology of schizophrenia: A European perspective', *Schizophrenia Bulletin*, **12**, pp. 52–73.

JACKSON, D.D. (1960) 'A critique of the literature on the genetics of schizophrenia', in JACKSON, D.D. (Ed.) *The Aetiology of Schizophrenia*, New York, NY: Basic Books.

JACKSON, H.F. (1986) 'Is there a schizotoxin? A critique of the evidence of the major contender — Dopamine', in EISENBERG, N. and GLASGOW, D. (Eds) *Current Issues in Clinical Psychology*, **5**, Aldershot, UK: Gower.

JACKSON, H.F. (1990) 'Biological markers in schizophrenia', in BENTALL, R.P. (Ed.) *Reconstructing Schizophrenia*, London, UK: Routledge.

JASPERS, K. (1963) *General Psychopathology*, Manchester, UK: Manchester University Press.

JERNIGAN, T.L., ZATZ, L.M., MOSES, J.A. and BERGER, P.A. (1982) 'Computed tomography in schizophrenia and normal volunteers: I. Fluid volume', *Archives of General Psychiatry*, **39**, pp. 765–70.

KALLMANN, F.J. (1946) 'The genetic theory of schizophrenia', *American Journal of Psychiatry*, **103**, pp. 309–22.

KANEY, S. and BENTALL, R.P. (1989) 'Persecutory delusion and attributional style', *British Journal of Medical Psychology*, **62**, pp. 192–8.

KENDELL, R.E., BROCKINGTON, I.F. and LEFF, J.S. (1976) 'Prognostic implications of six alternative definitions of schizophrenia', *Archives of General Psychiatry*, **36**, pp. 25–31.

KETY, S.S., ROSENTHAL, D. WENDER, P.H. and SCHULSINGER, F. (1968) 'The types and prevalence of mental illness in biological and adoptive families of adopted schizophrenics', in ROSENTHAL, D. and KETY, S.S. (Eds) *The Transmission of Schizophrenia*, Oxford, UK: Pergamon.

KETY, S.S., ROSENTHAL, D., WENDER, P.H., SCHULSINGER, F. and JACOBSEN, B. (1975) 'Mental illness in the biological and adoptive families of adopted individuals who have become schizophrenic: A preliminary report based on psychiatric interviews', in FIEVE, R., ROSENTHAL, D. and BRILL, H. (Eds) *Genetic Research in Psychiatry*, Baltimore, MD: John Hopkins University Press.

KLERMAN, G. (1984) 'Ideology and science in the individual psychotherapy with schizophrenia', *Schizophrenia Bulletin*, **10**, pp. 608–12.

KRAEPELIN, E. (1905) *Lectures on Clinical Psychiatry*, London, UK: Balliere Tindall.

KRINGLEN, E. (1967) *Heredity and Environment in the Functional Psychoses*, London, UK: Heinemann.

KURIANSKY, J.B., DEMING, W.E. and GURLAND, B.J. (1974) 'On trends in the diagnosis of schizophrenia', *American Journal of Psychiatry*, **131**, pp. 402–7.

LAING, R.D. (1965) *The Divided Self*, London, UK: Pelican.

LANGFELDT, G. (1937) *The Prognosis in Schizophrenia and the Factors Influencing the Course of the Disease*, Copenhagen, Denmark: Levin and Munksgaard.

LAVENDER, A. and HOLLOWAY, F. (Eds) (1988) *Community Care in Practice: Services for the Continuing Care Client*, Chichester, UK: John Wiley & Sons.

LEFF, J., KUIPERS, L., BERKOWITZ, R., EBERLEIN-FRIES, R. and STURGEON, D. (1982) 'A controlled trial of social intervention in families of schizophrenic patients', *British Journal of Psychiatry*, **148**, pp. 727–31.

LEWIS, S.W. (1989) 'Congenital risk factors in schizophrenia', *Psychological Medicine*, **19**, pp. 5–13.

LIDZ, T. and BLATT, S. (1983) 'Critique of the Danish-American studies of the biological and adoptive relatives of adoptives who become schizophrenic', *American Journal of Psychiatry*, **140**, pp. 426–31.

MACCARTHY, B., HEMSLEY, D.R., SHRANK-FERNANDEZ, C., KUIPERS, L. and KATZ, R. (1986) 'Unpredictability as a correlate of expressed emotion in the relatives of schizophrenics', *British Journal of Psychiatry*, **148**, pp. 727–31.

MAHER, B.A. (1974) 'Delusional thinking and perceptual disorder', *Journal of Individual Psychology*, **30**, pp. 98–113.

MAHER, B.A. (1983) 'A tentative theory of schizophrenic utterance', in MAHER, B.A. and MAHER, W.B. (Eds) *Progress in Experimental Personality Research, Vol. 12. Psychopathology*, New York, NY: Academic Press.

MARSHALL, J.R. (1984) 'The genetics of schizophrenia revisited', *Bulletin of the British Psychological Society*, **37**, pp. 177–81.

MARSHALL, J.R. (1990) 'The genetics of schizophrenia', in BENTALL, R. (Ed.) *Reconstructing Schizophrenia*, London, UK: Routledge.

McGHIE, A. and CHAPMAN, J. (1961) 'Disorders of attention and perception in early schizophrenia', *British Journal of Medical Psychology*, **34**, pp. 103–16.

McGUFFIN, P. (1988) 'Genetics of schizophrenia', in BEBBINGTON, P. and McGUFFIN, P. (Eds) *Schizophrenia: The Major Issues*, London, UK: Heinemann.

McGUFFIN, P., FARMER, A.E., GOTTESMAN, I.I., MURRAY, R.M. and REVELEY, A. (1984) 'Twin concordance for operationally defined schizophrenia: Confirmation, familiarity and heritability', *Archives of General Psychiatry*, **41**, pp. 541–5.

MELTZER, H.Y. and STAHL, S.M. (1976) 'The dopamine hypothesis of schizophrenia: A review', *Schizophrenia Bulletin*, **2**, pp. 19–76.

MILLER, A. (1987) *For Your Own Good: The Roots of Violence in Child-Rearing*. London, UK: Virago Press.

MOLINE, R.E., SINGH, S., MORRIS, A. and MELTZER, H.Y. (1985) 'Family expressed emotion and relapse in schizophrenia in 24 urban American patients', *American Journal of Psychiatry*, **142**, pp. 1078–81.

MUESER, K.T. and BERENBAUM, H. (1990) 'Psychodynamic treatment of schizophrenia', *Psychological Medicine*, **20**, pp. 253–62.

MURRAY, R.M., LEWIS, S.W., OWEN, M.J. and FOERSTER, A. (1988) 'The neurodevelopmental origins of Dementia Praecox', in BEBBINGTON, P. and MCGUFFIN, P. (Eds) *Schizophrenia: The Major Issues*, London, UK: Heinemann.

NASRALLAH, H.A., OLSEN, S.C., MCCALLEY-WHITTERS, M., CHAPMAN, S. and JACOBY, E.C. (1986) 'Cerebral ventricular enlargement in schizophrenia: A preliminary follow-up study', *Archives of General Psychiatry*, **43**, pp. 157–9.

OSMOND, H. and SMYTHES, J. (1952) 'Schizophrenia: A new approach', *Journal of Mental Science*, **98**, pp. 309–15.

PILLING, S. (1988) 'Work', in LAVENDER, A. and HOLLOWAY, F. (Eds) *Community Care in Practice*, Chichester, UK: John Wiley & Sons.

REED, D. (1978) *Anna*, London, UK: Penguin.

REVELEY, D.A. (1985) 'CT scans and schizophrenia', *British Journal of Psychiatry*, **146**, pp. 367–71.

ROSE, S., KAMIN, L.T. and LEWONTIN, R.C. (1984) *Not in Our Genes*, London, UK: Penguin.

ROSENTHAL, D. (1970) *Genetic Theory and Abnormal Behaviour*, New York, UK: McGraw-Hill.

SCHIFF, M., CASSOU, B. and STEWART, J. (1980) *Genetics and schizophrenia: The recommendation of a consensus.* Unpublished English version of the 1980 French monograph by CASSOU, B., SCHIFF, M. and STEWART, J. (1980).

SCHNEIDER, K. (1959) *Clinical Psychopathology* (Translated by HAMILTON, M.W.). London, UK: Grune & Stratton.

SCHNEIDER, W. and SHIFFRIN, R.M. (1977) 'Controlled and automatic human information processing: I. Detection, search and attention'. *Psychological Review*, **84**, pp. 1–66.

SCHWARTZ, S. (1982) 'Is there a schizophrenic language?', *Behavioural and Brain Sciences*, **5**, pp. 175–9.

SEGAL, H. (1979) *Klein*, Glasgow, UK: Fontana/Collins.

SEIDMAN, L.J. (1984) 'Schizophrenia and brain dysfunction: An integration of recent neurodiagnostic findings', *Psychological Bulletin*, **94**, pp. 195–238.

SHIELDS, J., GOTTESMAN, I. and SLATER (1967) 'Kallmann's 1946 schizophrenic twin study in the light of new information', *Acta Psychiatrica Scandinavica*, **43**, pp. 385–6.

SINGER, M.T. and WYNNE, L.C. (1966) 'Principles for scoring communication defects and deviances in parents of schizophrenics: Rorschach and TAT scoring manuals', *Psychiatry*, **29**, pp. 260–88.

SLADE, P.D. (1974) 'The external control of auditory hallucinations: An information theory analysis', *British Journal of Social and Clinical Psychology*, **15**, pp. 415–23.

SLADE, P.D. (1976) 'Toward a theory of auditory hallucinations: Outline of a hypothetical and factor model', *British Journal of Social and Clinical Psychology*, **15**, pp. 415–23.

SLADE, P.D. and COOPER, K. (1979) 'Some conceptual difficulties with the term 'Schizophrenia': An alternative model', *British Journal of Social and Clinical Psychology*, **18**, pp. 309–17.

SLATER, E. (1953) *Psychotic and Neurotic Illnesses in Twins*, London, UK: HMSO.

STOREY, P.B. (1966) 'Lumbar air encephalography in chronic schizophrenia: A controlled experiment', *British Journal of Psychiatry*, **112**, pp. 135–44.

STRACHAN, A.M. (1986) 'Family intervention for the rehabilitation of schizophrenia', *Schizophrenia Bulletin*, **12**, pp. 678–98.

STRAUSS, J.S. and CARPENTER, W.T. (1977) 'Prediction of outcome in schizophrenia: III. Five year outcome and its predictions', *Archives of General Psychiatry*, **34**, pp. 154–63.

TARRIER, N. (1990) 'Family management of schizophrenia', in BENTALL, R.P. (Ed.) *Reconstructing Schizophrenia*, London, UK: Routledge.

TARRIER, N., BARROWCLOUGH, C., VAUGHN, C., BAMRAH, J.S., PORCEDDV, K. WATTS, S. and FREEMAN, H.L. (1988) 'The community management of schizophrenia. A controlled trial of family intervention with families to reduce relapse', *British Journal of Psychiatry*, **153**, pp. 532–42.

TRIMBLE, M. and KINGSLEY, D. (1978) 'Cerebral ventricular size in chronic schizophrenia', *Lancet*, **i**, pp. 278–79.

TROUTON, D.S. and MAXWELL, A.E. (1956) 'The relation between neurosis and psychosis: An analysis of symptoms and past history of 819 psychotics and neurotics', *Journal of Mental Science*, **102**, pp. 1–21.

VAUGHN, C.E. and LEFF, J.P. (1976) 'The influence of family and social factors on the course of psychiatric illness: A comparison of schizophrenic and depressed neurotic patients', *British Journal of Psychiatry*, **129**, pp. 125–37.

VENABLES, P.H. (1984) 'Cerebral mechanism, autonomic responsiveness and attention in schizophrenia', in SPALDING, W.D. and COLE, J.K., *Theories of Schizophrenia and Psychosis*, Lincoln, NB: University of Nebraska Press.

WARNER, R. (1985) *Recovery from Schizophrenia*, London, UK: Routledge & Kegan Paul.

WATTS, F.N., POWELL, G.E. and AUSTIN, S.V. (1973) 'The modification of abnormal beliefs', *British Journal of Medical Psychology*, **46**, pp. 359–63.

WEINBERGER, F.N., POWELL, E.G. and AUSTIN, S.V. (1979) 'Cerebellar atrophy in chronic schizophrenia', *Lancet*, **ii**, pp. 718–19.

WEISS, E. (1950) 'Sense of reality and reality testing', *Samiska*, **4**, pp. 171–80.

WIG, N., MENON, D., BEDI, J., LEFF, J., KUIPERS, L., GHOSH, A., DAY, R., KORTEN, A., ERNBERG, G., SARTORIUS, N. and JABLENSKY, A. (1987) 'Distribution of expressed emotion components among relatives of schizophrenic patients in Aarhus and Chandigarh', *British Journal of Psychiatry*, **151**, pp. 160–65.

WILLIAMS, E.B. (1964) 'Deductive reasoning in schizophrenia', *Journal of Abnormal and Social Psychology*, **69**, pp. 47–61.

WING, J.K. (1978) 'Clinical concepts of schizophrenia', in WING, J.K. (Ed.) *Schizophrenia: Towards a New Synthesis*, London, UK: Academic Press.

WORLD HEALTH ORGANISATION (1974) *Glossary of Mental Disorders and Guide to Their Classification*. Geneva, Switzerland: WHO.

WYNNE, L.C. and SINGER, M.T. (1963) 'Thought Disorder and Family Relations', *Archives of General Psychiatry*, **9**, pp. 199–206.

ZERBIN-RUDIN, E. (1972) 'Genetic research and the theory of schizophrenia', *International Journal of Mental Health*, **1**, pp. 42–62.

Notes on the Contributors

Margie Callanan is currently employed half-time as Research Organiser on South East Thames Regional Clinical Psychology Training Scheme where part of the duties include being the Academic Tutor for Models of Adult Dysfunction. Clinical work takes place in a half-time post as an employee of the Bethlem and Maudsley Special Health Authority, providing a primary care clinical psychology service to adults with a wide range of presenting disorders (funded by the local GPs).

Lorna Champion obtained her first degree in psychology from the University of Sussex. She then trained as a clinical psychologist and obtained a PhD from the University of Birmingham. She has worked as a clinical psychologist in the NHS in the West Midlands and in London specialising in adult mental health. She is currently employed by the Medical Research Council conducting a long-term follow-up of high risk children. She is also honorary clinical psychologist with the Bethlem and Maudsley Special Health Authority and Honorary Lecturer at the Institute of Psychiatry, University of London.

Padmal de Silva is Senior Lecturer in Psychology at the Institute of Psychiatry, University of London, and Top Grade Clinical Psychologist for the Bethlem and Maudsley Special Health Authority. He has had a clinical and research interest in obsessive-compulsive disorder for many years and is the author of several publications in this area. His other interests are sex and food.

Greg Dring is a chartered clinical psychologist and a freelance family and marital therapist trainer. He currently works in Bristol and is a member of the Institute of Family Therapy.

Helen Fensome is a Senior Clinical Psychologist with Greenwich Health Authority. Her interest in eating disorders began with research for her doctoral thesis, which was on anorexia nervosa and family systems theory. At present half of her clinical work is with adult outpatients with a range of psychological problems and half is with people who have long term mental health problems in Greenwich's rehabilitation service.

Breda Kingston is a chartered clinical psychologist working with the Bath District Health Authority in the specialism of women's mental health. She also has extensive experience of work with couples with sexual problems.

Tony Lavender is a clinical psychologist who has worked in services for people with long term psychiatric problems since qualifying. He has taken part in providing and developing services in Rehabilitation in Bexley and in Maidstone Health Authority. He currently is the Director of the South East Thames Regional Health Authority Clinical Psychology Training Scheme and continues clinical work in Rehabilitation in Medway Health Authority.

Jean Mitchell has worked clinically for the past eight years with women who have eating disorders. She has also carried out research on anorexia nervosa and bulimia nervosa for her doctoral thesis which included an examination of the phenomenon of body image disturbance. She currently works as a Senior Clinical Psychologist with Greenwich Health Authority in the specialties of adult mental health and acute psychiatry.

Karen Partridge completed her clinical psychology training at Birmingham University in 1981. She became interested in systems through her research into organisational change and trained as a systemic therapist at the Kensington Consultation Centre. She now works as a clinical psychologist for Newham Health Authority and is a member of the teaching staff at the Kensington Consultation Centre.

Jane Powell graduated in Experimental Psychology from Oxford University in 1983. She did her clinical psychology training at the Institute of Psychiatry where she subsequently completed her doctoral research on the role of classical conditioning and cognitive factors in drug dependence. She is currently working clinically with drug addicts and is writing up research on the outcome of controlled clinical trials carried out together with her colleagues.

Mick Power obtained psychology degrees from the Universities of London, Sussex, and Birmingham. He has worked as a clinical psychologist at Guy's Hospital and at the Bethlem and Maudsley Special Health Authority. He was also a director of the South East Thames Clinical Psychology Training Scheme. He is currently a Senior Lecturer in Clinical Psychology at Royal Holloway and Bedford New College, University of London, where he is hoping to establish a new clinical psychology training course. He is an attached worker with the Medical Research Council.

Index